Islamic
Fundamentalism
in the West Bank
and Gaza

Indiana Series in Arab and Islamic Studies
Salih J. Altoma, Iliya Harik, and Mark Tessler, general editors

Islamic Fundamentalism in the West Bank and Gaza

Muslim Brotherhood and Islamic Jihad

■

Ziad Abu-Amr

Indiana University Press
Bloomington and Indianapolis

The paper used in this publication meets the minimum requirements of American National Standard for Information Sciences—Permanence of Paper for Printed Library Materials, ANSI Z39.48-1984.

Manufactured in the United States of America

Library of Congress Cataloging-in-Publication Data
Abū 'Amr, Ziyād.
    [Ḥarakah al-Islāmīyah fī al-Ḍiffah al-Gharbīyah wa-Qiṭā' Ghazzah. English]
    Islamic fundamentalism in the West Bank and Gaza : Muslim Brotherhood and Islamic Jihad / Ziad Abu-Amr.
        p.   cm — (Indiana series in Arab and Islamic studies)
    Includes bibliographical references (p.   ) and index.
    ISBN 0-253-30121-1 (alk. paper). — ISBN 0-253-20866-1 (pbk. : alk. paper)
    1. Islam and politics—West Bank. 2. Islam and politics—Gaza Strip. 3. West Bank—Politics and government. 4. Gaza Strip—Politics and government.   I. Title.   II. Series.
BP63.P32W47413   1994
322.4'2'0956953—dc20   93-28504

1   2   3   4   5   00   99   98   97   96   95   94

For
Bashir, Nadia, and Hind

Contents

∎

PREFACE

■ With the emergence of Islamic fundamentalist groups in the Occupied Territories, the authority of the secular nationalist movement led by the Palestine Liberation Organization (PLO) has been challenged for the first time in many years. While Israel and the Israeli occupation have been the apparent target, and the rallying point for both trends, an underlying struggle between the two focuses on defining the orientation of the Palestinian society and its leadership.

This book studies the two major groups of the Islamic movement in the West Bank and the Gaza Strip, the Muslim Brotherhood Society and the Islamic Jihad movement. The book deals with the origins of these two groups, their development, the basic points of departure for each, and the relationship between them. It also deals with the position of each group toward the Palestinian question, the relationship with the PLO, and the role of each group in the Palestinian *intifada* [popular uprising] of December 1987. The book tries to assess the current influence of the Muslim fundamentalists vis-à-vis that of the PLO, as well as the future prospects for fundamentalists and nationalists.

While the study of the Islamic movement in the West Bank and Gaza is significant in its own right, a number of internal and regional developments and factors make the study of this movement even more pressing. These include: (1) the eruption of the Palestinian *intifada* of 1987 and the subsequent rise of the Islamic movement in the Occupied Territories; (2) the rise of the Islamic movements in other Arab countries such as Jordan, Algeria, Tunisia, and Sudan; (3) the presence in both Egypt and Syria, the two major Arab countries surrounding Israel, of powerful Islamic movements (though the movement in Syria is currently suppressed or dormant); (4) the potential radicalization or rise to power of one or more of these movements in their respective countries and the consequences of such an eventuality; (5) the presence of an Islamic government in Iran and the regional ramifications of such a government being in place; and (6) the future configuration of the Middle East region in the context of an Islamic revival and the relationship of this region to the West.

In preparing this study, I have relied on a variety of sources and references. These included pamphlets, statements, and documents issued by the Islamic groups and the factions of the PLO, personal interviews, and secondary Arab and foreign sources that deal with the subject of the Islamic groups in Palestine. The Muslim Brotherhood Society in the Occupied Territories relies for advice and guidance on the societies in both Egypt and Jordan. Therefore, I have drawn on sources relevant to the Muslim Brotherhood Society in both countries. I have also relied on materials and literature published outside the Occupied Territories reflecting the views of the Islamic Jihad movement in Palestine. Access to sources and data has not been easy because the Islamic groups in the West Bank and the Gaza Strip tend to cloak themselves and their activities in secrecy.

Within the context of this study, certain expressions are used to signify specific meanings. The term "fundamentalism" describes the Islamists' attempts to go back to the fundamentals of Islam in all spheres of life. In this sense they are identified as fundamentalists. The terms "nationalist", "nationalist trend", and "nationalist movement" refer to the PLO factions and their followers or supporters. The expression "Islamic movement" refers to the two Islamic groups under discussion, despite the fact that the Muslim Brotherhood Society, alternately referred to as Hamas, comprises the bulk of the Islamic movement in the West Bank and the Gaza Strip.

Finally, I would like to thank those who have read this manuscript for their many important observations. I wish to emphasize that the responsibility for this study and for any errors or deficiencies rests solely on the shoulders of the author.

ACKNOWLEDGMENTS

■ Many people read this manuscript before it went to the publisher. I would like to thank them all. I would like in particular to thank the Center for Contemporary Arab Studies at Georgetown University for hosting me as a research fellow while writing the manuscript. I also would like to thank Ann Lesch for her useful comments on the manuscript and Edward Myers for his support and assistance in the initial editing. But my deep appreciation goes to Rebekah Lynn, who worked very hard on the final editing and revision of the manuscript.

This study was partially funded by a grant from the Friedrich Ebert Foundation of Germany. For this grant I am grateful. And to Birzeit University, which gave me the time and encouragement to carry out my research and writing, goes my deep gratitude and appreciation.

INTRODUCTION

■ The contemporary Islamic movements in the Arab world have so far failed to achieve their stated fundamental goal of establishing the Islamic state. The contemporary Islamic revival has also failed, in more than one way, in bringing that goal closer to realization. This revival has been unable to "guide the political construction of the contemporary Arab countries, to unify these countries, and to create the will in them to confront Israel, or to firmly respond to the violation of the Islamic holy places in Palestine. This revival has failed to enrich the idea of national unity, and failed in its dialogue with other political doctrines and ideologies, and in containing the spread of these doctrines and ideologies, or in minimizing their impact on the vanguard groups in the Arab society."[1]

The Arab Islamic movements reject the validity of such an argument: "We must not imagine that the ends are attained in the presence of the means . . . . The goal of the Muslim Brotherhood is to rule by God's book and to live by His laws in all walks of life. No man can make the judgement that we have not achieved this goal at a given point in time . . . because this goal is a long-range objective that is renewed with the renewal of days. The range of this goal does not end on any given day in order for us to say that we have reached our goal."[2]

While some Islamic intellectuals acknowledge that the Islamic movements have so far been unable "to establish the Islamic state and resume Islamic life" in their respective societies, these intellectuals argue that the movements have, nevertheless, "left behind, as a legacy, a great wealth of experience in the realm of work and preparation for the achievement of this goal, and have also left a vast intellectual heritage that paves the way for the birth of one international Islamic movement which will combat the ignorance of the twentieth century."[3]

The Islamic movement in the Occupied Territories is an integral part of the world Islamic movement, affecting it and affected by it, both positively and negatively. The Muslim Brotherhood Society is considered one of the oldest political groups in Palestine, enjoying a historical, organizational, and objective presence that cannot be ignored. However, the society did not become a major contender for the leadership of the Palestinian people in the Occupied Territories until after the eruption of the popular uprising (*intifada*) of December 1987. The *intifada* has transformed the Islamic movement in the Occupied Territories into a major force that has become able to shake up the existing balance of political power in the Palestinian society. However, it is premature to make a final assessment of the extent of success or failure of the Islamic movement in the West Bank and Gaza. It is true that in the last few years the Palestinian Islamic movement has risen to prominence, but it has not yet achieved any of its major goals as stated by the movement itself.

Since the mid-seventies, the Islamic movement has steadily grown until it has become one of the strongest political forces in the West Bank and the Gaza Strip. The political Islamic groups in the Occupied Territories include the Muslim Brotherhood Society, the Islamic Jihad movement, and the Islamic Liberation party. The Muslim Brotherhood is the largest of the Islamic groups, both in numbers and in influence. The Islamic Jihad movement, which was established in the early 1980s, is an offshoot of the Muslim Brotherhood. The Islamic Liberation party enjoys little influence and little is known about it today. There are a few other Islamic groups whose focus is more theological than political. These groups include *al-Tabligh wal-Daʿwa* [Conveyance and Call], *al-Takfir wal-Hijra* [Atonement and Holy Flight], *al-Sufiyyia* [the Sufis], and *al-Salafiyya* [the Salafis].

Despite their different methods, the goal of the Islamic groups is to transform society into an Islamic one, modeled after the first Islamic society, established by the prophet Muhammad and his companions. These groups also believe in the need to establish an Islamic state; they argue that the cause of all political, economic, and social conflicts engulfing the world today lies in the absence of this state. These groups make no distinction between religion and state and consider the Koran and the *sunna* as the basis for all aspects of life. They also note that nationalist, socialist, and Communist political parties have failed to solve the world's problems and that the time has come to apply the Islamic *shariʿa* laws in society.

Followers of the Islamic groups in the West Bank and the Gaza Strip derive their ideas from leaders of Islamic thought and Islamic movements in many countries: Hasan al-Banna and Sayyid Qutb (Egypt), Sa'id Hawwa (Syria), Fathi Yakin (Lebanon), Taqi-al-Din al-Nabhani (Palestine), Abu-al-A'la al-Mawdudi (Pakistan), Abu-al-Hasan al-Nadawi (India), and Ayatollah Khomeini (Iran). In addition, they seek guidance today from the views, positions, intellectuals, and leaders of contemporary Islamic movements in other Arab countries.

A number of factors have contributed to the growth and rise of the influence of the Islamic movement in the West Bank and the Gaza Strip since the mid-1970s. While Islamic groups have had their own appeal, activities, and followings, setbacks of the Palestine Liberation Organization (PLO) have translated into additional influence for these Islamic groups. For example, the loss of PLO bases in Jordan and Lebanon weakened the influence of the PLO and increased the visibility of the Islamic movement in the Occupied Territories. The balance of power between the Islamic movement and the nationalist movement began to change. The Islamic movement attributes its gains to an evolving clear and correct vision, on the part of the masses, of what ought to be done, and the failure of the secular materialist trend to define clearly how to deal effectively with existing problems, especially the national and the social.

The rise of the Islamic movement in the Occupied Territories was also aided by the support this movement has received from influential Palestinian social segments in Palestine and in the diaspora, from some Arab governments, and from Islamic movements in other countries. In this regard, the role of Islamic groups in Jordan and the Gulf States is emphasized.[4]

In addition, the Islamic movement has enjoyed the support of leaders in the Fatah movement. Some Fatah leaders had begun their political lives in Islamic organizations, the Muslim Brotherhood and the Islamic Liberation party, and have continued to be sympathetic to Islamic groups. Other Fatah leaders supported the Islamic groups because they wished to control the Islamic movement or at least to co-opt it or neutralize its challenge to the PLO. Some of those leaders believed that an alliance with the Islamic groups might be useful in order to counterbalance competing alliances, if the need arose.

There is no doubt that the increased influence of Islamic groups

in some Arab countries and the emergence of the increased phenomenon of Islamic revival or fundamentalism have contributed to
the strengthening of the Islamic groups in the West Bank and the
Gaza Strip. The Iranian Islamic revolution, in particular, has been
significant in mobilizing Islamic groups and offering them a model
to emulate. The current rise of Islamic influence in Sudan, Tunisia,
and Algeria is providing the Palestinian Islamists with moral, psychological, and political support.

The rise of Islamic resistance in southern Lebanon and Islamic
militant groups in the aftermath of Israel's invasion of that country
in 1982 has been another catalyst for the consolidation of Islamic
influence in the West Bank and Gaza. Lebanese Islamic militants
waged a number of spectacular attacks against American and Israeli
targets causing the death of hundreds of American and Israeli soldiers. Such spectacular acts inflamed Islamic feelings in the Occupied
Territories. The assassination of President Anwar Sadat by a militant
Egyptian Islamic group in 1980 created a similar effect.

The majority of the Palestinian people are Muslims, and Islam
plays a basic role in Palestinian society. Therefore, the Islamic movement has been able to rely on the support of broad segments of the
population. The continuing Israeli occupation, which is seen as a
foreign occupation posing a threat not only to the Arab identity of
Palestine but also to its Islamic character, has been an important
factor in the rise of the Islamic movement. Increased Israeli political
and religious intransigence (represented in the positions of the right-
wing Israeli political parties and Jewish fundamentalists) has attracted
many Palestinians to join the Islamic movement.

It is also argued that the Israeli occupation itself has helped to
expand the influence of the Islamic movement.[5] The Israeli reasoning
was "to grant permission for religious and Islamic movements to
expand the areas of their activities and their support within the ranks
of the Arab citizens, hoping to undermine the influence of, and
support for, the Palestinian nationalist forces, especially those loyal
to the PLO."[6]

Despite participation in opposing the Israeli occupation, the role
of the Islamic movement in this regard was, prior to the *intifada,*
relatively limited. But after the eruption of the *intifada,* Islamic
resistance to Israel began to take on a different dimension. As a
result, the Islamic movement in the West Bank and Gaza began to
enjoy broader support. Today, for the first time in the history of

the Palestinian problem, there exist in the Palestinian society two major trends, the Islamic and the nationalist, which are ideologically and politically opposed. Yet, both of these trends can count on the support and favorable response of the Palestinians in the Occupied Territories. No single political group can now have an exclusive claim to being the driving force among the Palestinian people.

An argument can be made about a resurgence of Islamic fundamentalism in the West Bank and Gaza. While this fundamentalism is uniform with regard to the achievement of the ultimate goal of establishing an Islamic state and society in Palestine, it does vary in degree in reference to specific issues, tactics, or approach. Both the Muslim Brotherhood Society and the Islamic Jihad movement are viewed as fundamentalist. But due to their different styles, the Muslim Brotherhood's brand of fundamentalism is described as less militant than that of the Islamic Jihad. For this reason, the Brotherhood is often considered reformist and even conformist.[7] By contrast, the Islamic Jihad movement, which is an offshoot of the Muslim Brotherhood Society, split from the mother organization because of the latter's lack of revolutionary spirit and style.

Discrepancy in militancy between the two groups is also evident in their respective approaches toward Israel. While Ahmad Yasin, the leader of the Muslim Brotherhood in Gaza and the founder of Hamas, occasionally resorts, for political or tactical reasons, to ambiguous articulations, his counterparts in the Islamic Jihad are categorical in their rejection of Israel and its right to exist. Sheikh As'ad Bayoud al-Tamimi, the leader of a faction in the Islamic Jihad, argues that the destruction of Israel is a Koranic imperative and that the Muslims, through the exercise of *jihad,* can only hasten this inevitable conclusion.[8]

On a different plane, while the Muslim Brotherhood has coexisted with and even participated in a non-Islamic rule during the Jordanian control over the West Bank, the Islamic Jihad is avowedly committed to changing the existing order in the Arab and Muslim worlds. Fathi al-Shaqaqi, the key leader in the Islamic Jihad, provides in his book, *Al-Khomeini: al-Hall al-'Islami wal-Badil [Khomeini: The Islamic Solution and Alternative],* an exposition of the significance of the Islamic revolution in Iran as a model for changing a corrupt order and establishing an Islamic order in its place.[9]

Islamic
Fundamentalism
in the West Bank
and Gaza

1

The Emergence and Evolution of the Muslim Brotherhood Society

The Muslim
Brotherhood
before 1967

■ The mother organization of the Muslim Brotherhood Society was founded in March 1928 in Isma'iliyya, Egypt, by Hasan al-Banna and a small group of his compatriots. The goal of this organization, which later became one of the largest political parties in Egypt and the Arab East, was to build an Islamic society by applying Islamic law (*shari'a*). Since its establishment, the Muslim Brotherhood has called and worked for achieving that goal.

The relationship of the Muslim Brotherhood Society with Palestine began in 1935, when 'Abd-al-Rahman al-Banna, Hasan al-Banna's brother, visited Palestine and met with Hajj Amin al-Huseini, who was the Mufti of Jerusalem and head of the Higher Islamic Council at that time. During the Palestinian revolt of 1936, the Egyptian Muslim Brotherhood carried out propaganda activities on behalf of the Palestinians. They formed a committee (the General Central Committee to Aid Palestine), headed by Hasan al-Banna, the Muslim Brotherhood's general guide, to protest against Britain and to defend the Palestinian cause. The society established a students' committee to explain the Palestinian issue to Egyptian students. In addition, a small group of Muslim Brotherhood members took part in armed attacks on Jewish installations in Palestine during the 1936 revolt.[1]

In the aftermath of World War II, the Muslim Brotherhood sent representatives to Palestine, not only to spread the *da'wa* [call to Islam] and invite opposition to Zionism, but also to assist in the training of Palestinian scouts. The most prominent of these representatives was a retired officer named Mahmud Labib, who supervised the Brotherhood's volunteer movement and led its military units. Labib, who later became deputy general guide for military affairs, was sent to Palestine to assist in the military training of civilian groups and to help Palestinian paramilitary organizations, such as al-Najjada and al-Futuwa, unify ranks.[2]

The Brotherhood's position on Palestine increased the society's popularity, especially after its active participation in the Palestine war of 1948, in which many Muslim Brotherhood volunteers joined.[3] In April 1948, before the end of the British mandate over Palestine and some weeks before the start of the war, the Muslim Brotherhood in Egypt sent three battalions of volunteers. The majority of the volunteers were members of the Muslim Brotherhood. The three battalions were led by Lieutenant Colonel Ahmad 'Abd-al-'Aziz, Lieutenant Colonel 'Abd-al-Jawwad Tabbala, and Captain Mahmud 'Abdu.[4] Moreover, the Muslim Brotherhood in Jordan sent a force led by 'Abd-al-Latif Abu-Qura, head of the Muslim Brotherhood in Amman. A force was also sent from Syria, under Mustafa al-Siba'i, the Muslim Brotherhood leader in Damascus.[5] The total number of Muslim Brotherhood volunteers from Egypt, Syria, Jordan, Palestine and other countries was 471.[6] Ahmad 'Abd-al-'Aziz, the leader of one of the volunteer battalions, stated that he had 804 volunteers under his command, including 344 Egyptians. The remainder were members of the regular Egyptian army with some volunteers from other Arab countries.[7] In March 1948, Hasan al-Banna noted that he had 1,500 volunteers inside Palestine.[8]

Despite its limited scope, the role of the Muslim Brotherhood in the war was highly publicized. No other political group had engaged in such an activity. The size of Muslim Brotherhood participation in the volunteer efforts in Palestine was not commensurate with the size of the society's membership, which at that time was in the hundreds of thousands and perhaps surpassed a million.[9] One of the reasons for this discrepancy could have been the Egyptian government's reluctance to assist the Muslim Brotherhood. The government feared that the group would exploit the situation, obtain arms and ammunition and training, and then try to overthrow the ruling regime in Egypt. Nevertheless, the Muslim Brotherhood continued to smuggle in volunteers on a smaller scale. The society disguised this endeavor by forming "scientific missions" whose declared task was to conduct explorations in the Sinai desert. Other volunteers went to Syria, on their way to Palestine, by sea.[10]

The Egyptian government later changed its position. In March 1948 it announced its willingness to train volunteers and to arm them for the *jihad* in Palestine. In fact, it opened two military training camps, the first in Hakstab, near the Suez Canal, and the second in the Marsa Matruh area, near the Libyan border. Officers of the Egyptian army were asked to supervise the camps and the training. The Muslim Brotherhood's officer in charge of military affairs, Mahmud Labib, assisted in this effort. Despite the fact that Brotherhood members were unable to continue their *jihad* in Palestine, according to one source they were successful in dragging Egypt into taking part in the Palestine War.[11]

With the assistance of the Muslim Brotherhood Society in Egypt, another Brotherhood branch was opened in Palestine. Sa'id Ramadan, a Muslim Brotherhood leader, opened the society's first branch in Jerusalem on October 26, 1945. In 1947, there were about twenty-five Brotherhood branches in the country with a membership that ranged from twelve thousand to twenty thousand active members. These branches were under the supervision of Muslim Brotherhood leaders in Cairo. Hajj Amin al-Huseini was designated a local Brotherhood leader in Palestine. The use of the Mufti's name helped the society to spread its influence in Palestine.[12]

The physical presence of the Muslim Brotherhood volunteers in Palestine and along the border with Egypt, in the areas of Rafah and al-'Arish, and the presence of Muslim Brotherhood officers and troops in the ranks of the regular Egyptian forces stationed in those areas, increased opportunities for contact between the Muslim Brotherhood and Palestinians, especially in the Gaza area. At the end of 1949, Brotherhood members who had fought with Egyptian troops in Palestine went to the Hebron area to establish branches in several towns and villages, such as Jenin, Qalqiliya, 'Anabta, Dura, Surif, Sur Bahir, Tubas, Kafr Burqa, Jericho, and a number of refugee camps, including 'Aqabat Jabr near Jericho, and al-'Arrub in Bethlehem.[13]

The West Bank

The situation of the Muslim Brothers in the West Bank prior to 1967 was different from their situation in the Gaza Strip. After the West Bank was annexed to Jordan in 1950, its inhabitants became Jordanian citizens. The West Bank Muslim Brothers were not subjected to the same harsh treatment their counterparts received in Gaza under the Egyptian administration. The Muslim Brotherhood in the West Bank was permitted to pursue its activities openly, after the Jordanian government had recognized them as a legal, nonpolitical organization. The society had established branches in different areas of the West Bank. The government's relative tolerance of the Muslim Brotherhood was attributed to the nature of the society's activities, which were basically confined to the publication and distribution of Islamic literature, as well as to the conduct of social activities. It was also due to the nonantagonistic relationship that existed between the government and the society. The Jordanian government hoped to use the Muslim Brotherhood to counter the influence of other political parties in the country that were forbidden by law. Despite the fact that the regime granted the society some encouragement and support, the Muslim Brotherhood was not given absolute freedom to pursue its objectives.

For its part, the Muslim Brotherhood did not hesitate to criticize the regime and even to occasionally clash with it over certain issues. The society opposed the regime's strong ties with the West, especially Britain. In 1954, the Brotherhood staged demonstrations against the presence of British officers in the Jordanian army and demanded their ouster. Sources state that the Muslim Brotherhood Society in Jordan was anti-West from its inception and had publicly and vehemently attacked colonialism. Moreover, the society opposed certain domestic Jordanian policies, such as permissiveness toward the use of alcoholic beverages, the visible disregard of Islamic *shari'a* principles, and the nonobservance of the moral values that Islam proclaims. This opposition led to the arrest of the society's general guide several times in the early 1950s. The Brotherhood supported Jamal 'Abd-al-Nasir in his anti-Western positions. Such attitudes provoked the resentment of the Jordanian government and created a climate of mutual suspicion between the regime and the Brotherhood.[14]

As a result of its stands, the Brotherhood was placed under surveillance and restrictions, and some of its leaders were arrested. However, these measures were not as rigid as those imposed on other political parties in the country. Because the Muslim Brotherhood Society was a legal organization, its activites and the regime's reaction to them differed from the experience of other political parties. The Brotherhood's meetings were held openly, and at times government officials, army officers, and prominent religious leaders attended them.[15]

The relationship between the Muslim Brotherhood and the Jordanian regime changed over time. It was characterized by tension and frequent disputes, although interests coincided on some occasions. The Brotherhood gave its support to King Hussein in the confrontations that occurred between him and other local political forces, such as the Communists, the Arab nationalists, and the pro-Nasir elements. In 1957, during a showdown between the king and his prime minister, Suleiman al-Nabulsi, who had enjoyed the support of nationalist forces, the Brotherhood held several mass rallies in suport of the king, praising his role as a "supporter of Islam."[16]

Some Muslim Brotherhood Society leaders attribute their non-confrontational position toward the Jordanian regime in the 1950s to King Hussein's tolerance of them and to the fact that he did not treat them harshly, as Nasir treated the Brotherhood in Egypt. Yusuf al-'Azm, one of the Muslim Brotherhood leaders in Jordan, states: "The Muslim Brotherhood did not provoke the king. We had a truce with him, because we were unable to open fronts with all sides at one time . . . . We agreed with the king because Nasir was irrational in his attacks against him. We were skeptical about Nasir's relations with America . . . We stood with the king in order to protect ourselves, because if Nasir's followers had risen to power, or a pro-Nasir government had been established in Jordan, the Muslim Brotherhood would have been liquidated, as they were liquidated in Egypt."[17]

The Muslim Brotherhood Society in Jordan entered all parliamentary elections, even those boycotted by nationalist political parties. The society, in both the West and East banks of the river Jordan, was able to obtain four seats in one of these elections. Of the thirty seats allocated to the West Bank, the Brotherhood won one seat. However, during several election sessions, the number of Muslim Brotherhood members in parliament fluctuated between two and four.[18] Muslim Brotherhood candidates ran for elections, though as individuals, when other political parties were banned from participation. The Muslim Brotherhood's relationship with the Jordanian regime during the period before 1967 could be described as "loyal opposition."[19]

It is difficult to determine the exact size of Muslim Brotherhood membership in the West Bank just before 1967, but this membership is estimated at between seven hundred and one thousand. Obviously such an estimate reflects a sharp decline from the society's membership in 1947. The loss of Palestine and the annexation of the West Bank to Jordan, together with some other intervening circumstances, may account for the weakening of the Brotherhood Society and this decline in its membership. Members came from all social and economic strata. About 25 percent of the members were merchants and property owners of different kinds, while 13 percent were from the intelligentsia, 13 percent were workers, and an equal percentage were farmers.[20]

In contrast to the post-1967 situation, the Muslim Brotherhood did not, prior to this date, gain widespread support among students. They had not achieved any tangible success in terms of recruitment among this segment of the population. In the 1957 elections of a student committee, which represented the student body in the West Bank, the Communists won five seats, the Ba'thists won four, while the Muslim Brotherhood did not win a single seat.[21] However, the branches that the society had opened in the main refugee camps did have some following. In the 'Aqabat Jabr refugee camp in Jericho the society competed with the Islamic Liberation party to win the allegiance of teachers and students.

The Gaza Strip

In the Gaza Strip the Muslim Brotherhood Society was popular because of its participation in the 1948 Palestine war. As a result, many Palestinian youths in the Strip joined the society's volunteer battalions. A number of Gazans who worked in Egyptian army camps in the neighboring areas of Rafah and al-'Arish were exposed to the influence of Egyptian officers and troops who were members of the society. The Egyptian officers were led by 'Abd-al-Mun'im 'Abd-al-Ra'uf, a member of the Muslim Brotherhood leadership. These officers and troops tried to organize Brotherhood cells among the Palestinian workers. The circumstances were propitious for such an endeavor, considering the sympathy and admiration the Muslim Brothers enjoyed. The first Brotherhood recruits in Gaza included Muhammad Abu-Seidu, 'Uthman Abu-Seidu, Musa Subeita, Faheem Saqr, and 'Ayish 'Amira.[22]

With the spread of the Muslim Brotherhood's ideas and the growth of its membership among the various segments of the population, the Brotherhood's presence in the Gaza Strip began to take on a defined organizational shape, and the society's first branch was formed in Gaza by 'Ayish 'Amira. This branch was similar to the Brotherhood branches in Haifa and Jerusalem, which were established in the 1930s. When the Brotherhood was banned by the Egyptian government in 1949, the society in Gaza turned its branch into a religious educational center. The *Jam'iyat al-Tawhid* [Unification Society] was founded as a front organization for the Muslim Brotherhood.

The revolution of July 23, 1952, in Egypt marked a turning point in Muslim Brotherhood relations with the masses. Relations between Brotherhood leaders and the Free Officers who deposed King Faruq and ended monarchical rule in Egypt were good. These relations increasingly improved to a point where the Muslim Brotherhood was perceived as the "party of the government."

In the aftermath of the revolution, an official religious mission, *Ba'that al-Wa'dh wal-Irshad* [the Mission of Admonition and Guidance], was sent from Cairo to the Gaza Strip. Leading members in the society were part of this mission. The first group included Sheikh Muhammad al-Ghazali and Sheikh Muhammad al-Abasiri. In addition to their work as religious advocates, members of this mission acted as liaison officers between the Muslim Brotherhood Societies in Egypt and the Gaza Strip.[23]

The relationship between the Muslim Brotherhood leadership in Egypt and the revolutionary government of Nasir deteriorated in 1954 following the government's endorsement of the Evacuation Treaty between Britain and Egypt.[24] The Brotherhood opposed the treaty because it believed that its terms were unjust to the Egyptians. An attempt was then made on the life of Nasir, and the Muslim

Brothers were accused of being accomplices. The Brotherhood organization was consequently banned in Egypt as well as in Gaza. As a result of the ban, the activities of the Brotherhood became secretive or discrete. This change in circumstances largely affected the position of the Muslim Brotherhood in the Gaza Strip. After being a party that enjoyed the sympathy of the government as well as freedom of movement and organization, the Muslim Brothers were chased down and the development of their organization was impeded due to the restrictions imposed on them.

Before the ban, the Muslin Brotherhood in the Gaza Strip was one of the largest organizations. In 1954, membership totaled more than one thousand in eleven society branches.[25] Most of the members were school students in the refugee camps because the Muslim Brotherhood was active in the schools for Palestinian refugees operated by the United Nations Relief and Works Agency (UNRWA). Students who were studying in Egyptian universities also joined. The League of Palestinian Students was formed in Cairo and was controlled by students who belonged to or sympathized with the Muslim Brotherhood. One of the most prominent of these sympathizers was Yasir Arafat (who was even thought of as a member of the society). A few members of the society later became founders of the Fatah movement. Those included Salim al-Za'nun, Salah Khalaf, and 'Abd-al-Fattah al-Hmoud. Most of the leaders of the society's administrative center in Gaza, *al-Markaz al-Idari al-'Am,* were civil servants and included Sheikh 'Umar Suwwaan, Zaki al-Susi, Kamal Thabit, Hasan al-Nakhal, Zuhdi Abu-Sha'ban, and 'Ali Hashim Rashid.[26]

Compared to other groups, the Muslim Brotherhood had more financial resources. Because of the poor economic conditions in the Gaza Strip, the Muslim Brothers received support from the mother organization in Egypt. Support also came from certain Brotherhood members and sympathizers working in Saudi Arabia and the Gulf region and from donations by certain wealthy people in those countries. The Brotherhood always had good relations with individuals of the Saudi royal family who gave material support to the Muslim Brotherhood Society in Egypt and the Gaza Strip. Muslim Brotherhood contacts in the Gaza Strip were confined to Saudi Arabia and to the mother organization in Egypt.[27]

The most visible political activities of the Brotherhood in Gaza started in 1955. In that year, the Brotherhood participated with other political groups in mass demonstrations protesting a proposed plan to resettle Palestinian refugees from the Gaza Strip in the Sinai desert in Egypt. The Egyptian government, which endorsed the plan, had to abandon it under popular pressure.[28] In 1956 the Brotherhood participated in the opposition to the Israeli occupation of the Gaza Strip. And in 1957 the Muslim Brothers took part in nationalist demonstrations rejecting a plan to internationalize the Gaza Strip.[29]

The Egyptian administration in the Gaza Strip and the Muslim Brotherhood continued to have poor relations up to the 1967 war. Every time the mother organization in Egypt was persecuted, members of the Gaza organization would also suffer. After an attempt by the Brotherhood to seize power in Egypt in 1965, members of the society in Gaza were subjected to widespread arrests, which resulted in the detention of several of the society's known leaders such as Sadiq al-Muzeini, 'Abd-al-Rahman Barud, Riyad al-Za'nun, and Shakir Shubair.[30] Among the members who were arrested then was Ahmad Yasin, who later became the leader of the Islamic Resistance Movement (Hamas).

Despite sympathy for the Muslim Brotherhood, adverse conditions and difficulties of underground work reduced the society's following and membership. When the cadres in the group found themselves chased and under siege, they began to search for a refuge. Some of these cadres emigrated to Saudi Arabia and the Gulf region. Consequently, since the late 1950s until 1967, the Muslim Brotherhood organization was weakened and reduced to a small number of senior members, who had been part of the society from the beginning, in addition to a small number of high-school students. The structural foundation of the Brotherhood had disintegrated and only ideological loyalty remained. However, some traditional dignitaries continued to represent the Muslim Brotherhood Society, including Sheikh Hashim al-Khuzundar, Sadiq al-Muzeini, and As'ad Hasaniyya.[31]

Between 1948 and 1967 a number of new political organizations had emerged in the Gaza Strip. In addition to the Gaza Communist and Brotherhood organizations, two pan-Arab nationalist organizations, the Ba'th party and the Arab Nationalist Movement, were founded in 1953 and 1958 respectively. These two organizations enjoyed at varying times the support of the Nasir regime in Cairo and the Egyptian administration in Gaza. In the second half of the

1950s, the Fatah movement also began to emerge. With the rise of these political organizations, popular support was no longer limited to the Brotherhood or the Communists. Availability of alternative choices had eroded some of the support that could have been accorded to the Brotherhood.

Between 1958 and 1967, the Brotherhood in the West Bank and in the Gaza Strip was weakened by a high tide of Arab nationalism. It was a time when anti-imperialist ideas and slogans predominated, and when the Arab people tried to consolidate national independence and achieve progress and social justice. During that period the issues of nationalism, Arab unity, socialism, and the liberation of Palestine dominated the attention of both the governments and the peoples of the Arab world. Such issues, with the exception of Palestine, did not greatly concern the Muslim Brotherhood, which focused on Islam as a frame of reference and as an identity.

The Muslim Brotherhood after 1967

After the Israeli occupation of the West Bank and Gaza in 1967, the Muslim Brotherhood Society remained weak. The beginning of Palestinian armed resistance immediately after the occupation and the Brotherhood's reluctance to participate in this resistance impeded the emergence of the society as an active political power. Unlike the Palestinian resistance movement, the Muslim Brotherhood in the Occupied Territories was not willing or prepared politically, ideologically, or militarily to undertake direct and organized military action against the Israeli occupation. Some Brotherhood elements, however, joined the Fatah movement in Jordan until the resistance movement was expelled from there in 1970/1971.[32] Nevertheless, the society remained a dormant political power which was to emerge a few years later in the late 1970s.

In the mid-1970s, the leadership of the Muslim Brotherhood was reorganized. The Muslim Brotherhood Societies of the Gaza Strip, the West Bank, and Jordan formed one organization called "The Muslim Brotherhood Society in Jordan and Palestine."[33] The Gaza Muslim Brotherhood became part of the society in Jordan and no longer belonged to the society in Egypt. The new relationship affected the positions and policies of the Muslim Brothers in the West Bank and the Gaza Strip, who began to receive guidance from the society's leadership in Jordan and from the International Organization of the Muslim Brotherhood, represented by the General Guidance Bureau. Reliance on external Brotherhood guidance did not, however, mean complete compliance or coincidence of views. The Muslim Brotherhood believed that each Islamic movement must enjoy some freedom in its own country in order to meet its own needs and to address its peculiar circumstances.

From the very beginning, the rise of the Muslim Brotherhood's influence and the emergence of the Palestinian Islamic groups in general were linked to a number of outside domestic factors. One of the most important external factors was the Arab defeat of 1967, which the Islamic movement regarded as a defeat for secular, nationalist, and socialist thinking in the Arab world. This defeat also led to an increase in the influence of the conservative Arab camp, which had an Islamic orientation, in contrast to the nationalist camp, which tended to be socialist, especially in the case of Nasir's Egypt and the Ba'thist regime in Syria.

The wars of 1967 and 1973 were used by Islamic groups to raise Islamic consciousness in the region. The Muslim Brothers in Egypt, for example, considered the 1967 defeat a "divine revenge" against the regime for what had befallen them and the torture they were subjected to in government prisons. The society tried to use the defeat for its own purposes. It argued that the state's lack of religious faith and its failure to follow divine laws were the primary causes of the disaster.[34]

The 1973 war, on the other hand, served to strengthen the religious climate in Egypt. The Egyptian "victory" in the war was attributed to the faith of the troops and the power of doctrine. It was reported that Egyptian troops shouted *allahu akbar* [God is great] while crossing the Suez Canal, proving that religious sentiment was an effective motivation for liberation and resistance.[35] Furthermore, Islam and the 1973 war were linked in other ways. The war occurred in the holy month of Ramadan, during which Muslims fast. In addition, the code name given to the war was "Badr", which is a reference to the battle of Badr in which the Muslims, led by Prophet Muhammad, fought against idolaters in the Islamic year of 623 and in which they achieved victory.[36]

Another factor contributing to the rise of the Islamic movement was the oil revolution. The oil wealth enhanced the influence of the oil-producing states in the Arab world, especially Saudi Arabia and the Gulf states. These states had a strong Islamic orientation, which other Arab countries could not ignore. Islamic movements within and outside the oil states benefited from the new wealth and power.

The emergence of fundamentalist Islamic groups in Egypt such as the Saleh Sirriyya Group, the Atonement and Holy Flight, and the Jihad Organization, and the acts of violence these organizations undertook, were not only a challenge to the ruling regime in Egypt, but also to the Muslim Brotherhood, both in Egypt and in neighboring countries. The formation of these militant Islamic groups had increased public awareness of Islamic issues and organizations. A few years later, these groups became relevant to the Palestinian context since they provided a source of inspiration for a splinter group, the Islamic Jihad, to break away from the Muslim Brotherhood Society in Gaza.

The Islamic revolution in Iran had a great impact on Islamic groups in other countries, including the Islamic movement in the Occupied Territories. This revolution offered proof that an Islamic state could be established, and it offered hope that the Islamic movement could triumph over tyranny and repression. The Islamic revolution in Iran gave other Islamic movements a model to emulate.

Finally, one can look at the rise of the Islamic movement in the West Bank and the Gaza Strip as a part of the phenomenon of Islamic revival in the region and the world in reaction to what is perceived as Western challenge and hegemony. This Islamic revival sought to rid the Islamic societies of subjugation, to confront westernization, to halt decline in traditional Islamic values, and to restore Islamic character to these societies.

Palestinians were motivated to join Islamic groups by the continuing Israeli occupation. This occupation threatened Palestinian Arab and Islamic identity. It was perceived as having distortive and foreign values. The rise of fanatical rightist and Zionist tendencies within Israel itself was a catalyst for the expansion of Islamic influence. The Islamic groups also grew because supporters of these groups spread the argument that Israel's victory was a result of the adherence of the Jews to their religion, and that the Arabs' defeat was caused by their failure to adhere to Islam.[37]

The Israeli occupation of the West Bank and the Gaza Strip

provided both access and opportunity for communication and co-operation among Islamic groups in Palestine. Under the occupation, these Islamic groups acquired a new demographic and geographic depth, which made it possible for the groups in the West Bank, Gaza, and Israel itself to exchange visits, ideas, and publications.

Although the influence of the Islamic groups grew as the influence of the PLO declined, neither the growth nor the decline was directly caused by the relationships between the two sides. The change in the balance of power was the result of local and regional political factors. One such factor was the ouster of the Palestinian resistance movement from Jordan in 1970–1971, which resulted in the weakening of the movement and of its relationship to the Occupied Territories. The expulsion of the PLO forces from Lebanon in 1982, in the aftermath of the Israeli invasion of that country, further weakened the movement and brought into question its conduct, its efficacy, the quality of its leadership, and the soundness of its strategy, tactics, and political program as a whole.

Another factor was the October 1973 war which refocused attention on the importance of Arab armies and opened the doors for a political settlement with Israel. In the aftermath of that war, the PLO entertained political and diplomatic solutions instead of armed struggle. The organization began to consider the concept of establishing a national authority on any piece of land freed from Israeli occupation. This is the concept that later evolved into the idea of the Palestinian state in part of Palestine, instead of slogans of complete liberation of Palestinian soil or the establishment of a secular democratic state in Palestine. The Islamic groups in the West Bank and Gaza depicted such evolution of PLO stands as concessions that were not reciprocated by Israel.

The failure of the PLO to deliver on its declared objectives, the problems that the organization faced in Jordan and Lebanon, the frequent changes of its political positions, and the corruption and inefficiency attributed to its institutions and leaders affected the image of the PLO in the minds of the masses in a negative way. The PLO's problems and changing positions created a state of anxiety, uncertainty, and sometimes despair. After more than twenty-five years since its establishment, the PLO seemed to be going nowhere. As a result, trying an alternative to the PLO was no longer unthinkable. Islam, which is an intergral part of Palestinian society, was to provide that alternative.

The Islamic movement managed to capitalize on the differences and divisions within the PLO and its following. These differences and divisions decreased public trust in the PLO and in the soundness of its policies and turned attention to the Islamic alternative. The Palestinian Muslim Brotherhood raised political slogans and offered theoretical alternative answers to critical issues without having to put them to the test. The fact that the Muslim Brotherhood did capitalize on the weakness of the PLO was recognized by the pro-PLO nationalists themselves. One such nationalist writer attributed the rise in the Islamic movement's influence to the problems the PLO was facing inside and outside the Occupied Territories:

> It is evident that the organizational and political problems inside and outside the Occupied Territories have been one of the main factors for the growth of the irrational religious trends which now threaten to divide the people in these territories. The growth of these trends began after the mid-seventies, exactly when the bureaucratic apparatus of the PLO was formed and completed.[38]

The PLO factions that engaged in direct confrontation with the Israeli occupation (either through armed resistance or nationalist and political work) suffered from Israeli repression. The Muslim Brotherhood was not subjected to the same treatment because it was not involved in armed resistance. Therefore, the Brotherhood was able to build an organizational structure, to reach the masses, and subsequently to organize them with less Israeli intervention.

The PLO supporters claim that Jordan played a role in strengthening the influence of the Islamic groups. When the influence of its supporters in the West Bank was weakened, Jordan began to rally support and to seek new allies, the motive being to counterbalance the influence of the PLO, whose followers seized a number of local institutions. Jordan offered political support and money to certain Islamic groups, including the clergy and the Islamic Waqf Office, which supervised the mosques and endowment property. Aid was also given to Islamic colleges. Saudi Arabia, for its part, gave assistance to Islamic institutions in the West Bank and the Gaza Strip.[39]

Beginning in 1967, the Muslim Brotherhood began to establish mechanisms to spread its ideas and increase its influence. The society founded Islamic charity associations, which supervised religious schools. It also managed nursery schools and kindergartens, which were usually attached to mosques. The Brotherhood also established neighborhood libraries and sports clubs. In subsequent years, the Muslim Brotherhood and other Islamic elements formed several Islamic societies and organizations in Hebron, Nablus, Jenin, Jerusalem, the Gaza Strip, and other Palestinian towns.

These organizations helped to spread religious ideas and rally support for the Islamic movement. The Muslim Brotherhood used alms money *zakat* to help thousands of needy families. And thousands of students and children were enrolled in schools and kindergartens run by the Islamic movement. Loans were also extended to students in Palestinian and Arab universities. The Islamic movement also benefited from traditional Islamic institutions. The Muslim Brotherhood was able to stay in touch with the masses and to influence them through charitable, social, and religious activities and celebrations. *Waqf* (religious endowments) and mosques provided useful mechanisms for the spread of Islamic influence.

The religious institution of *waqf* controls an extensive network of property that it leases to the local inhabitants. In the Gaza Strip, for instance, the *waqf* constitutes "10 percent of all real estate. . . . hundreds of shops, apartments, garages, public buildings, and about 2,000 acres of agricultural land belonged to its trusts, and the *waqf* employed scores of people, from preachers and other clerics to grave diggers."[40] Since Muslim Brothers or sympathizers are among these employees, the Brotherhood achieves significant access to the population and thereby gains an unofficial influence, because the people will credit the Brotherhood for the variety of services rendered.

The mosque has been one of the most effective means of expanding Islamic influence. Unlike other institutions, the mosque remains open all the time. Being a sanctuary, the mosque could be used as a place for political work and organization, away from the eyes or interference of the Israeli authorities. Religious functions and activities are not subject to the same restrictions to which the nationalist or political activities are subjected. The Muslim Brotherhood has used mosques to recruit followers.

The increase in the number of mosques in the West Bank and Gaza is also an indication of the rise in Islamic influence. In the period between 1967 and 1987, this number nearly doubled in the West Bank, rising from 400 to 750. During the same period of time, the number of mosques in the Gaza Strip had tripled, rising from 200 to 600.[41] This increase, which helped raise Islamic political influence and consciousness, was the result of political, religious and charitable considerations. The Islamists have been aware of the significance of the mosque as a mechanism for spreading and consolidating political influence vis-à-vis secular and nationalist forces. For this reason, they turned to building more mosques. Mosques are also needed for their religious significance as places of worship. As the population of worshippers increased, more mosques would be needed. Charity directed at building new mosques is most appealing to wealthy believers who wish to be remembered on earth and later rewarded by God in heaven.

In 1973, *al-Mujamma' al-Islami* [the Islamic Center], a front organization for the Muslim Brotherhood Society in Gaza, was established. The center provided an umbrella for Muslim Brotherhood activities in the Gaza Strip. The Brotherhood pursued most of its activities through this center. From a practical standpoint, all religious organizations and institutions belonging to the Brotherhood, including the Islamic University in Gaza, were subject to the authority of the center and its leadership.[42]

The center was primarily established as a mosque, but attached to it were a medical clinic, a youth sports club, a nursing school, an Islamic festival hall, a *zakat* committee, and a center for women's activities and for training young girls. The founders of the center included Sheikh Ahmad Yasin (the leader of the Muslim Brotherhood in the Gaza Strip), Salim Shurrab, Ahmad Ibrahim Dalloul, Isma'il Abu-al-'Awf, As'ad Hasaniyya, Mustafa 'Abd-al-'Al, 'Umar 'Abd-al-'Al, 'Abd-al-Hai 'Abd-al-'Al, Lutfi Shubair, Ya'qub Abu-Kuwayk, and Ahmad Abu-al-Kas.[43] The most prominent leaders of the center, in addition to Yasin, include pharmacist Ibrahim al-Yazuri, the center's executive director, Dr. 'Abd-al-'Aziz al-Rantisi and Dr. Mahmud al-Zahhar.

The center extended its influence over a large number of the mosques in the Gaza Strip. Currently the center controls about 40 percent of these mosques.[44] The center has also opened branches in other parts of the Gaza Strip. Since its establishment its membership has grown to more than two thousand. In 1979, six years after it was founded, the Israeli authorities granted the center a legal license.[45] Ahmad Yasin is considered the leading figure in the Islamic Center.

Islamic influence has also found its way to educational institutions in the Occupied Territories. The Palestinian universities in the

West Bank and Gaza have been an important field for Muslim Brotherhood activity and a platform for the dissemination of ideas and for gaining influence. In the aftermath of the Iranian revolution of 1979, local Muslim leaders and activists visited these universities and urged the youth to pay attention to political questions. Such appeals were not common before the revolution. Islamic student bodies began to compete successfully with nationist student groups, and the influence of Islamic student groups steadily increased in subsequent years. In the 1979 elections of the student council of Najah University in the West Bank, for example, the Islamic Bloc won ten out of eleven seats. In 1980 this group had five seats, while the National Unity Bloc, representing PLO factions, had six. In the 1981 elections, the Islamic Bloc won all student council seats.[46] One of the important reasons for this victory was the failure of the nationalist rivals to unite in order to counter the Islamic Bloc. In the student council elections of 1986, the Islamic Bloc received 1,160 votes, compared to 1,480 votes for the Student Youth Movement, which supports the Fatah movement.[47]

The Muslim Brotherhood enjoys strong support in the universities of the West Bank and Gaza. The votes of the society's supporters fluctuate between 30 and 50 percent. Even in Birzeit University, which has been known for its strong nationalist, leftist, and liberal tendencies, the Islamists muster considerable support in the student body. Muslim students have always controlled the student council in the Islamic University in Gaza. Currently, they also control the student council in the University of Hebron.

The Islamic University in Gaza, founded in 1978, is considered the principal Muslim Brotherhood stronghold. The university's administration, most of the employees who work there, and the majority of students are Brotherhood supporters. Current student enrollment in the university is estimated at five thousand. This university, together with other Palestinian universities, supplies the mosques in the West Bank and Gaza with young preachers. More importantly, these universities graduate a new breed of educated Muslim leaders who can occupy key positions in society. But the Muslim Brotherhood's influence in the Palestinian universities, including the Islamic University in Gaza, especially on the student level, has not been unchallenged. In the student council elections of 1987, the Islamic Bloc received nearly 800 votes while the Fatah supporters won 650. The Islamic Jihad movement won 200 votes, while supporters of the Popular Front for the Liberation of Palestine (PFLP) won 150 votes. In a previous year, the Islamic Jihad was able to win 400 votes.[48] Islamic student groups control student councils in several high schools and community colleges across the West Bank and Gaza.

The society particularly targets youth in the villages and refugee camps, school students, teachers, civil servants, and low income people in general. To date, however, the Brotherhood has not actively sought to recruit workers or women in trade unions or professional organizations.

Availability of financial resources has helped the Muslim Brotherhood to spread its ideas and influence. Money comes from membership dues, from donations from abroad, and from within the Occupied Territories. As part of a regional and international Islamic movement, the Muslim Brotherhood could rely on its brotherly links with other Islamic groups to ensure not only moral and political support, but also financial and material assistance. Muslim institutions and individuals from all over the world could send *zakat* money to the "Muslim *mujahidin* [Islamic fighters] in Palestine." Members of the Muslim Brotherhood inside the Occupied Territories are known for their correct conduct, benevolence, and anticorruption stands. The religious orientation of the Islamic groups solicits sympathy from a society that is essentially Muslim. This sympathy can be expressed in financial donations that are given for the religious and moral purpose of helping the poor and the political purpose of strengthening Muslims vis-à-vis their enemies.

To spread their ideas and to expand their influence, the Muslim Brotherhood has distributed religious books published by well-known Islamic leaders. The shelves of Islamic libraries and associations are filled with hundreds of these books and other relevant writings. More than half of the publications found in West Bank libraries and bookstores are of a religious nature. Some of these publications have been imported from abroad. At home, several magazines are published, either regularly or intermittently, by Islamic institutions or student groups in Palestinian universities or community colleges.[49] The contents of these publications concentrate on individual behavior and suggest that the Islamic culture has been distorted by Western influence. Anti-Israeli rhetoric was tolerated because of the religious nature of these publications. But since the eruption of the *intifada*, these publications have contained

strong political messages. In addition to a constant call for a return
to Islam, strong criticism is directed at local nationalism and secularism. Israeli occupation is described as a curse or punishment from
God because the Palestinians have left the true path of Islam. Israel,
the United States, the West and Arab governments are also targets
for attacks. Together with published material, the Muslim Brotherhood circulates recorded sermons and speeches of famous Islamic
leaders and preachers. Tapes containing such sermons and speeches
are found in street stands or shops in all locations of the West Bank
and Gaza. The ultimate message being disseminated in Islamic literature, tapes, and other media is that the resolution of the Palestinian problem can only be attained through Islam.[50]

On several occasions supporters of the Islamic movement attacked shops that sold alcoholic beverages, and on a few other
occasions they attacked women who were not covering their heads
or wearing sufficiently modest clothing. They also attacked wedding
ceremonies that were not being conducted in traditional ways. Such
actions created negative feelings and caused anxiety and fear among
many people. The Islamists were criticized for using intimidation to
force conformity and obedience.

The overall conditions in the Occupied Territories seemed to
have been conducive to a rise in Islamic influence. While Islam has
been an integral part of Palestinian society, all the factors that have
been discussed above are contributing dynamics. A field study of a
group of entrepreneurs conducted between 1971 and 1973 indicated that 55 percent of those who responded preferred to have
religion incorporated into social life. The study also indicated that
Islam was the frame of reference for 76 percent of those who
responded.[51]

An opinion poll conducted on people randomly selected from
towns, villages, and refugee camps in the West Bank and the Gaza
Strip indicated that approximately 26.5 percent of the respondents
preferred a system of government based on the Islamic *shari'a* in
the event an independent Palestinian state was established; 29.6
percent said that they would choose an Islamic Arab Palestinian
state; 10.4 percent indicated that they would want a democratic
secular Palestinian state; and 12.2 percent said that they wanted a
democratic Palestinian state.[52]

Another opinion poll conducted in 1982 among 150 Muslim
college students who were mostly from villages and refugee camps

in the West Bank and the Gaza Strip, found that 54 percent of the respondents came from families all of whose members prayed regularly and fasted during the month of Ramadan, with the females dressed in traditional Islamic ways. Twelve percent of these students came from families in which only the father performed Islamic duties, 16 percent from families where the mother carried out these duties, 14 percent from families where brothers or sisters performed these duties, and only 4 percent from families where no one practiced these duties.[53] Fifty-four percent of the fathers were workers, 30 percent were farmers, and 16 percent worked in service occupations.[54]

Sixty-four percent of the 150 Muslim students who were polled said that they strongly supported the Muslim Brotherhood Society and 32 percent said that they moderately supported the society. Only 4 percent said that they strongly opposed the society and accused it of furthering the interests of Israel and the United States.[55] These polls indicate a strong leaning toward religion, especially in villages and refugee camps, where the largest number of Palestinians live. The Muslim Brotherhood is not the only beneficiary of the support of religious-oriented individuals. Nationalist organizations, such as the Fatah movement, are also supported by people who want an Islamic Palestinian state.

Although the Muslim Brotherhood Society, according to one Muslim leader on the West Bank, is still weaker than the PLO in terms of following,[56] the strength and influence of the Brotherhood cannot be underestimated. The society has an excellent organization and a potential to generate strong sympathetic feelings and loyalty in a community that is generally religiously inclined.

The Muslim Brotherhood seems to enjoy stronger influence in the Gaza Strip than on the West Bank. This is attributed to historic and socioeconomic reasons. The Muslim Brotherhood connection in the Gaza Strip dates back to the 1930s. Moreover, the proximity of the Gaza Strip to Egypt provided the Brotherhood with means of communication with the mother organization. Palestinian students studying in Egyptian universities were exposed to, and influenced by, Islamic ideas and trends. Society in the Gaza Strip is more socially conservative and less susceptible to outside influences than the Palestinian society in the West Bank. The West Bank Palestinians have been more mobile than the Gaza inhabitants. The dense population, poverty, and harsh economic conditions, together with tra-

ditional social relationships, have provided a propitious climate for
the followers of the Islamic movement to gain influence.

Although the period from 1975 to 1985 witnessed a steady
increase in the Muslim Brotherhood's influence, the PLO's gradual
recovery from the setback it suffered in Lebanon in 1982 restored a
political balance in favor of the PLO. Another intervening factor
mitigating the Brotherhood's influence has been the emergence of
the Islamic Jihad movement in the early 1980s which came to challenge the moderate nonmilitant line of the Muslim Brotherhood. A
decline of the Muslim Brotherhood's influence in the Gaza Strip was
reflected in the elections of the Arab Medical Association. In 1985
the Muslim Brotherhood won three seats, Fatah four, and the leftist
factions won the other four seats. In the association's elections of
1987, the PLO groups won nine seats, while the Muslim Brotherhood won only two. In the Engineers Association the Muslim
Brotherhood won only one seat in the 1987 elections, after having
won the majority of seats in 1981.[57] But in the elections of 1989,
the Brotherhood (Hamas) won five out of nine seats in the association, which reflected a decline in the PLO's influence.

Regarding the relative strength of the Brotherhood vis-à-vis the
PLO in Gaza, it was suggested that if elections had been held before
the *intifada,* the PLO supporters would have obtained the majority
of votes, and the Islamic trend would not have won more than 10
percent of the vote.[58] In the West Bank the number of committed
Muslim Brotherhood members in the early 1980s was estimated at
no more than a few thousand, although the number of supporters
was much higher than that. But the ability of the Muslim Brotherhood to mobilize the masses greatly surpassed its numerical size.[59]
The society has always enjoyed the sympathy of landowners, merchants, and shopkeepers. During the 1980s, the Brotherhood has
found its way into student bodies and elite circles, including intellectuals and university professors in Gaza, Nablus, and Hebron.

Geographically, the Muslim Brotherhood's following in the West
Bank traditionally been concentrated in the northern and southern towns, which are predominantly conservative. After 1948, the
northern towns had maintained some links with the Palestinian
Muslims in Israel. The southern towns were particularly influenced
by the Muslim Brotherhood volunteers in 1948.

In the Gaza Strip, the Brotherhood following was concentrated
in Gaza City and in the southern part of the Strip. But over the

years, the society expanded in all parts of Gaza, as well as among the refugee camp population.

In the central part of the West Bank, where the cities of Jerusalem, Ramallah and Bethlehem lie, there is a sizable Christian minority. These cities have also been centers of secular influence. Jerusalem and Bethlehem are sites for Christian holy places and are therefore exposed to foreign visitors and their influence. Ramallah has traditionally been a center for Arab nationalist and Communist political groups, and a large segment of the city's population live or work in North or South America but keep returning to Ramallah.

Open coordination between the Islamic groups of the West Bank and Gaza and their counterparts inside Israel is prohibited by Israeli law. Yet several Muslim leaders in Israel have received their training in the West Bank. For example, Sheikh 'Abdallah Darwish, one of the most prominent of these leaders, received his religious education at the Islamic Institute in Nablus. During his study, Darwish had the opportunity to establish relationships and communications between the Islamic groups in Israel and those in the Occupied Territories. Religious leaders in both communities exchange visits and participate in joint activities. Other forms of cooperation may be taking place, perhaps secretly. Islamic leaders in the West Bank and the Gaza Strip are usually reluctant to talk openly about their ties with the Islamic groups in Israel, but these leaders argue that Islam calls for cooperation with Muslims both inside and outside of Palestine.[60]

2

The Muslim Brotherhood and the Palestine Question

The Brotherhood Strategy toward Palestine

■ Since the establishment of the state of Israel in 1948, the ideological and theoretical attitude of the Muslim Brotherhood Society toward Palestine has not changed. The society considers all of Palestine to be Muslim land and holds that Israel has no right to exist. The society also believes that no one has the right to concede any part of Palestine and considers any political settlement that leaves Israel intact a matter of treason. The Brotherhood rejects the establishment of a Palestinian state in the West Bank and Gaza, or on any part of Palestine, if that entails conceding the rest of Palestine to Israel. Recognizing Israel, from the Muslim Brotherhood's point of view, is an acknowledgment of the legitimacy of conquering Muslim land.

According to the society, the *jihad* for Palestine will start after the completion of the Islamic transformation of Palestinian society, the completion of the process of Islamic revival, and the return to Islam in the region. Only then can the call for *jihad* be meaningful, because the Palestinians cannot alone liberate Palestine without the help of other Muslims. The Palestinians are only the spearhead in the battle for liberation, and the Muslims in Palestine are the vanguard of fighters.[1]

Unlike nationalist groups, the Muslim Brotherhood does not make its claim to Palestine, or define its attitude toward it on nationalist or geographic bases alone. The concept of nationalism, according to the society, has geographic boundaries. Commitment to land alone is a grave mistake, since one piece of land can be replaced by another. From an Islamic point of view, Palestine is a religious matter. But on the other hand, Palestinian Islamists cannot confine their message to Palestine only. In the words of one Brotherhood leader in the West Bank, Islam was not revealed to solve the Palestinian problem.[2]

In this regard, one Islamic writer goes as far as rejecting the notion of making Palestine the primary and central issue for Muslims. Muhammad 'Ali Qutb says: "It is a matter of obscured vision or shortsightedness or treason for Arabs and Muslims to be preoccupied with the Palestinian issue and to make it the pivotal point of the struggle between them and the Zionists, who are supported by Western imperialist capitalism, and to forget, or pretend to forget, that the toppling of the Ottoman State . . . with all its political, military and geographic, and even regional realities, was the major step toward the breaking down of the gateway to the East and the onslaught on the Islamic world. They also forget, or pretend to forget, the disputes that have occurred, and are occurring, in Kashmir, Cyprus, Afghanistan, Somalia, Eritrea, and the Moroccan (Spanish) Sahara."[3] But perhaps Qutb is trying to alert the Arabs and the Muslims to what he believes to be a foreign onslaught whose magnitude goes beyond Palestine.

The Muslim Brotherhood views Israel as a spearhead of Western influence and the tool that spreads Western corruption, with its plots against Islam.[4] Failure to make Palestine part of the broader Muslim concern amounts to treason, since that would exclude millions of Muslims from the struggle against Israel and its allies. The Muslim Brotherhood invokes history to prove the validity of such an argument. Palestine, they recall, was liberated from the crusaders under the banner of Islam. The society, therefore, calls for the abandonment of secular ideas and the adoption of Islam as a way to liberate Palestine.

The society rejects the secular nationalist program of the PLO and the programs of its various factions. It also rejects the notion of "liberation first, then ideological commitment," which was raised initially by the Fatah movement. Liberation, according to the Muslim Brotherhood, cannot be achieved without commitment to the Islamic religion, which provides the Palestinians with the necessary ideological, spiritual, and psychological preparedness they need.[5]

The Muslim Brotherhood traces the current adverse conditions of the Muslims in Palestine to the "coup" that was staged against the Muslim Ottoman empire during World War I. A Muslim Brotherhood advocate writes: "Who brought the English and the non-believers to the Muslim homeland? It was us. When Britain emerged victorious, it issued the Balfour Declaration which promised the Jews a homeland [in Palestine]. And we here ask: Was the Arab revolution against Turkey a necessity as they claim? The truth is that it was not a necessity or even a semi-necessity for us to participate in it. If the Turks had won the war, we would have gained. And if they had lost, we would not have lost the soldiers and endeavor that we lost. We would have remained safe and untouched by that defeat."[6]

The Muslim Brotherhood holds the Arab governments responsible for the loss of Palestine in 1948 because these governments "handed Palestine over to Israel in a theatrical battle which lacked planning, military training, and the amassing of arms."[7] The society believes that the way to Palestine and the holy struggle for it cannot be realized without "returning to Islamic principles and containing the existing non-Islamic reality," in order to "liberate all the land and return it to Islam and for the sake of Islam."[8]

The society considers any position that contradicts this understanding to be false and too concessionary. The Brotherhood argues that the Muslims' right in Palestine is a fixed historical and religious right that cannot be removed or deleted. This right is derived from belonging to Islam, the revealed religion which supersedes all preceding heavenly monotheistic religions. The society also argues that the Muslims' rights in Palestine are firmly embedded in history, in the recognized concepts of human rights, and in the modern concepts of international law.[9]

The Muslim Brotherhood argues that Muslims who are silent about the occupation of Palestine are committing a sin because Islam requires them to engage in a holy war. True Muslims, according to the society, are required to sacrifice their lives and money to liberate every inch of the holy land. Inaction is considered "fatal treason," and any philosophy that justifies submission and does not urge the sacrifice of souls and resources is "heretical."[10]

The Muslim Brotherhood tends to view the loss of Palestine to the Jews as both a curse and a blessing. It is a curse because the Jews, who are "the dirtiest and meanest of all races, are defiling the most sanctified and honored spot on earth, a spot to which Allah sent a herald angel, and where the Prophet Muhammad made his midnight journey." And it is a blessing because the Jewish conquerors provide strong motivation to the people to recommit themselves to Islam and "to remove the vagueness of humiliation and the veils of submission from Muslim souls, and to guide the people to the pleasure, beauty, glory, and reward inherent in the craft of death."[11] Unlike the nationalist factions of the PLO, the Muslim Brotherhood makes no distinction between Jews, Zionists, and Israelis. Insistence on using the term "Jews" reflects the underlying religious nature of the conflict as defined by the Brotherhood.

The Muslim Brotherhood perceives itself as the only party capable of "extracting the fate of the [Palestinian] cause from the hands of the negligent and the weak." It sees itself as the only party "capable of the steadfastness and *jihad,* and of sincere giving and persistence, that will enable future Islamic generations to build a bright future under the supreme word of God."[12] The society believes that the way to Palestine is an Islamic way: "The contemporary Islamic movement everywhere in the world has proven to the whole world that there is only one way to Palestine, and that is Islam, as a doctrine, movement, and holy war. The proof lies in the failure of other approaches which faltered in spite of big sacrifices."[13] The reference here is to the approaches embraced by the PLO factions and the secular and pan-Arab nationalist regimes. The Brotherhood attributes the defeats which the Arabs and the Palestinians have suffered to the fact that those who are in power did not raise the banner of Islam.[14]

The Muslim Brotherhood has an alternative strategy toward Palestine. The strategy of the society seeks the establishment of an Islamic state, society, and regime in one of the Arab countries neighboring Israel, such as Syria, Egypt, or Jordan. This Islamic entity will function as a base for the Islamic movement in Palestine, and as a basic prerequisite to realize the general goal embodied in the victory of the Islamic call. This state should be ruled by an Islamic elite that is committed to Islam as a constitution and a way of life. This elite should be elected by a people which is also committed to Islam. The ruler of this state will, during a period of a decade, unite and prepare the *umma* [the Muslim nation] for the "decisive battle with the Jews."[15]

One Islamic writer describes the Brotherhood's strategy in the following manner: "We must effect a broad popular change. If we manage to do that, we can establish an Islamic bloc or state which we can use as a springboard. Then we could invite battalions of *mujahidin* from all parts of the world."[16] It seems that this Islamic writer was alluding to Syria, where the Syrian Muslim Brotherhood was involved during the 1980s in a bloody and violent struggle with the regime of President Hafiz al-Asad: "The Muslims who are engaged in a holy war in our beloved Syria will provide the demographic and strategic depth for our fighting brothers in Palestine. If the Islamic revolution in Syria succeeds, this will provide the faithful of the Aqsa Mosque and the Palestinians everywhere with the best of news, that the time of their salvation is near. They will be inspired in their holy war against their enemy and will be relieved of all those forces which oppress them."[17]

During times of material weakness, the Muslim Brotherhood stresses the importance of upholding the will of doctrinal change through steadfastness and resisting attempts to kill this will "by those who are clearly and openly hostile to Islam, or by those who indirectly are trying to do the same by raising the slogan of Islam and Islamic revival, while taking a contradictory path to Islam, and stabbing Islamic revival in the chest and back."[18]

The steadfastness that the Brotherhood calls for "is not simply a negative rejection as has been practiced, but is rather a positive and active initiative which cannot be limited to the Palestinian issue or to the sons of Palestine and their Muslim brothers in other countries. It is an initiative that rejects everything that is in contradiction with the truth in the case of Palestine, and in the case of every other issue and aspect of our lives, our world, and our era."[19]

The Muslim Brotherhood and the PLO

Ideological and political differences between the Muslim Brotherhood Society and the PLO have resulted in suspicion, tension, and even confrontations. Suspicion has been nourished by past experience dating back to the 1950s when the Muslim Brotherhood in the West Bank sided with the regime in Jordan against the nationalist and secular political parties.

The Muslim Brotherhood criticizes the PLO for its position toward the Palestinian issue. The society is especially critical of leftist groups, which the Brotherhood fears might gain too much influence or even dominate within the PLO. The Muslim Brotherhood believes that leftist factions, such as the Popular Front for the Liberation of Palestine (PFLP) and the Democratic Front for the Liberation of Palestine (DFLP) have been trying to undermine the control of the Fatah movement over the PLO.

The Muslim Brotherhood has always been especially hostile toward the Communists. A local publication of the Brotherhood states: "Communism has caused setbacks for our society in the areas of doctrine and politics. It is a mercenary party working on behalf of great powers. Communism serves its own interests and the interests of Israel. This is in addition to the actual blasphemy that is contained in communist books, pamphlets, and festivities. Furthermore, communists lack all Islamic moral values and obligations . . . in their private lives, and in their relationship with our beloved society."[20]

Despite the fact that Fatah continued to be ideologically the closest of the PLO factions to the Brotherhood, disputes between the two sides continued. On specific occasions, confrontations between the two sides took place and were more violent than any confrontations between the Brotherhood and leftist groups. The relationship between the Muslim Brotherhood and Fatah could best be described as a love-hate relationship. In a way, the Muslim Brotherhood sees in Fatah a legitimate son, but it feels alarmed by Fatah's gradual abandonment of its Islamic leanings.[21] The Fatah movement is also perceived as the society's most serious rival in terms of popularity and influence. Several of the Fatah founders were former Brotherhood members who have maintained over the years friendly relations with the society.[22]

The Muslim Brotherhood believes that the Palestinian issue has gradually deteriorated because of the PLO's efforts to separate the religious beliefs of the Palestinian people from the rifle: "It is the Occupied Territories these days that are seeing an increase in the fruits of the *jihad* of the youths of the Islamic movement . . . on all levels, while the Palestinians locally and abroad are seeing a clear decline in the numbers of those who separate religious beliefs from the rifle."[23] With the gradual decline of nationalist influences, the Muslim Brotherhood has become more vocal in its challenge of the PLO: "From now on, monopoly of Palestinian action by those movements, which proved their failures for the past 20 years, will not be tolerated. Nor will the exclusion of Islam from the Palestinian struggle be tolerated, because Islam, with its impact on life, is the sole element that is able, if given the opportunity to fight, to upset the balance and change realities. Islam can liberate the land and restore the usurped rights."[24]

The Muslim Brotherhood criticizes the PLO because "it is an organization that does not serve God."[25] The society is opposed to the principles endorsed by the factions of the PLO. It sees the return of these groups to Islam as the beginning of the journey along the true path: "The Palestinian factions are founded on principles that are contradictory and controversial, and some of them are clearly based on leftist or rightist ideas that are inimical to Islam. Some factions declare that they want a secular state in Palestine. This inconsistency has caused woes, disasters and tribulations. Therefore, we see that the first step along the true path is to repudiate these destructive ideas, and bring these factions, leaders and ranks, back to God. . . . They must unify their ranks under the banner of Islam and adopt the Islamic solution for their cause. They must boycott all attempts to surrender to the Jews, and fight those attempts with all available means."[26]

The Muslim Brotherhood opposes the PLO because the society believes that the PLO is a product of the Arab regimes: "Each regime formed a group subservient to it ideologically, financially, and politically. Then, each regime tried to get that group into the PLO through summit conferences on the one hand, and through armed plots on the other. Therefore, the PLO's decisions have been derived from the policies of those regimes and are subordinate to them."[27] The Muslim Brotherhood hopes that "the PLO will recover its senses . . . and return once again to strike at the Jews inside occupied Palestine." But the society questions the ability of PLO leaders to do that: "Will it be possible for those who are used to the spotlight to return to the trenches of the *mujahidin?*"[28]

The Muslim Brotherhood opposes the PLO's once-held strategic goal of establishing a secular democratic state in Palestine. The society also opposes the goal of establishing an independent

Palestinian state on part of Palestine. Moreover, the Muslim Brotherhood opposes the PLO's attempts to reach a political or diplomatic solution to the Palestine question. The society considers this attempt tantamount to liquidating the Palestinian cause. Therefore, the Brotherhood opposes the idea of holding an international peace conference, conducting negotiations or concluding an accord with Israel, and any Palestinian-Israeli dialogue. From the Muslim Brotherhood's point of view, Palestine is, in its entirety, an Islamic country in which an Islamic state must be established.

The Muslim Brotherhood Society believes that the Palestinian issue is an Islamic issue, and not an issue of one people or one nation. This view is shared by other Islamic groups in the Arab world. Muhammad Hamid Abu-al-Nasr, the general guide of the Egyptian Muslim Brotherhood, stresses that no one group of people has the right to claim that they can "concede or abandon territory or a homeland or conclude deals."[29] Abu-al-Nasr adds that viewing the issue from an Islamic point of view means that the "abandonment or the conceding of one inch of territory would be treason. To allow an alien entity to share our land would be even more serious than treason. To search for banners other than the banner of Islam, under which we will march to confront an enemy who occupies our land, and who has shed and is shedding our blood; or to search for processes or paths, such as an international conference; or to wander aimlessly in the corridors of international organizations; or to sharpen the pencils that compose communiques of denunciation, condemnation, and protest is only tantamount to fleeing from the battles, avoiding the confrontation, and turning back without advancing."[30]

Because political activities under the Israeli occupation were legally banned, the various political trends, including the Muslim Brotherhood, have relied on student groups in the relatively autonomous Palestinian universities of the West Bank and the Gaza Strip as arenas for their political action. These groups have expressed the positions of the political trends they identified with through publications or statements or through other functions, whenever that was possible. In 1987, posters belonging to the Islamic Bloc of the Brotherhood in Birzeit University defined the society's position regarding the PLO as representative of the Palestinian people. These posters clearly indicated that in no case was it permissible to give allegiance to anyone who did not endorse the ideas and practices of Islam.

Another election statement gave the response of the Islamic Bloc to questions about the Muslim Brotherhood's lack of commitment to the PLO as the sole legitimate representative of the Palestinian people: "The Islamic Bloc supports all those who carry arms, who fight and become martyrs in order to liberate the land, help truth prevail, and triumph over the tyrants. However, the Islamic Bloc does not recognize as representatives (whoever they may be), those who attempt to reach an accord with the Jews at the expense of our usurped land, our displaced people, our plundered heritage, and our destroyed sacred places."[31]

The Brotherhood opposes Palestinian contacts with progressive Jews or democratic forces in Israel on religious grounds. This question has been a matter of dispute between the Brotherhood and PLO factions from the beginning. The Brotherhood also blamed PLO Chairman Yasir Arafat for his friendly and close relations with the now-defunct socialist regimes of Eastern Europe and the former USSR.

Ahmad Yasin, the head of the Islamic Center in the Gaza Strip, summarizes the Muslim Brotherhood's position toward the PLO as follows: "The PLO is secularist. It cannot be accepted as a representative unless it becomes Islamic."[32] However, in an interview during the *intifada,* Yasin said that the PLO did in fact represent the Palestinian people, but he expressed certain reservations regarding its political line, which called for the establishment of a secular state on any part of Palestine. Yasin insisted that Islam ought to be the state's religion and constitution.[33]

Regarding the differences with the PLO, Yasin argued that it was only natural to have differences: "We have an idea, and the PLO has an idea, and the sole arbiter is the people. What the people decide is acceptable to us."[34] The Brotherhood's support of Yasir Arafat is "proportional to Arafat's support for the Islamic idea."[35] The Muslim Brotherhood makes no explicit claims to being an alternative to the PLO. But when the society argues that Islam is the alternative to the failing nationalist and secular ideologies and programs, it logically follows that the Brotherhood projects itself as the alternative to the PLO, which refuses to become Islamic.

Because of the Israeli occupation, and because of the large support the PLO still enjoys among the Palestinians, the Muslim Brotherhood cannot openly express its real intentions. Therefore, its statements are ambiguous and sometimes appear contradictory. The concept of *taqiyya* in Islam justifies concealing the true beliefs

if expressing such beliefs would harm Muslims. The following ex-
cerpts from an interview given by Yasin reflect his mastery of political
ambiguity:

> *Question:* Do you want a Palestinian state from the river to the sea?
> *Answer:* I want a Palestinian state.
> *Question:* What are its boundaries?
> *Answer:* Palestine has well-known boundaries; these are the borders
> of the Palestinian state.
> *Question:* Where is Israel then?
> *Answer:* Israel is in Palestine.
> *Question:* Can you clarify your concept of the Palestinian state?
> *Answer:* The Palestinian state must be founded on every inch of
> Palestine that we liberate, but without conceding the rest of our
> rights.
> *Question:* Do you recognize Israel?
> *Answer:* If I recognized Israel, the problem would be finished, and
> we would have no rights left in Palestine.
> *Question:* But if Israel withdrew from the West Bank and the Gaza
> Strip, would you recognize it?
> *Answer:* When it withdraws, I will say.
> *Question:* But at that time, should it be recognized?
> *Answer:* I leave this matter to the representatives of the Palestinian
> people.
> *Question:* Who are they?
> *Answer:* Those whom the Palestinian people will elect.[36]

Yasin says that the caution lying behind this kind of answer was
intentional and should be understandable. He also says that deep
in his heart, he does not believe that there is a possibility of solving
the Palestinian problem by political means. But from the tactical
viewpoint, he should propose what the enemy rejects. When the
Israelis reject a proposal, their rejection gets him out of a critical
situation.[37]

There are other Islamic points of view that take essentially the
same position toward the PLO, but with more flexibility. Bassam
Jarrar, one of the prominent intellectuals of the Islamic movement
in the West Bank, says: "The Islamic movement does not base its
considerations on the assumption that the decline of the PLO's
influence means the rise of Islamic influence, or vice versa. On the
contrary, the Islamization of the PLO means the rise of Islam."
Jarrar also believes that the PLO will form an alliance with the

Islamic movement after it gives up its hopes for peaceful solutions. He adds that the Islamic movement cannot be an alternative to the PLO in negotiations with Israel. The role of the PLO is a political one and poses no danger to the ideological role of the Islamic movement. Jarrar says that there is no reason to reject alliances between the Islamic groups and the PLO if these alliances are established on clear and defined bases, and if they do not conflict with the principles of the Islamic movement.[38]

In the context of clarifying this view, Jarrar says that the Islamic movement is as comprehensive as Islam itself and is only partly political. Therefore, it cannot confine itself and its work to a narrow, nationalist framework, as does the PLO. If the Islamic movement has focused on political action at any particular state, it is because the nationalist movement has retreated. Jarrar says that when the PLO has restricted its activities to military actions only, the Islamic movement has not opposed it.[39] Other Muslim Brotherhood views are at variance with Jarrar's opinion. A Brotherhood alliance with a non-Islamic group or movement, according to these views, is incompatible with Islam. The Brotherhood can not authorize the PLO to speak on its behalf or on behalf of the Muslims.[40]

The Muslim Brotherhood has a specific concept regarding possible cooperation with the PLO. One Islamic publication in the Occupied Territories defined the terms for the kind of cooperation that is acceptable to the Muslim Brotherhood: "The Islamists extend their hands to every sincere national group that is working for the liberation of the country and for ridding it of Zionist and imperialist dangers, provided that group has not condemned Islam and is not known to be an enemy of Islam or the Islamists."[41] But, this publication adds: "The Islamists look at the issue of cooperation and integration with secularist and heretical groups with extreme caution, because secularism and heresy are at war with Islam and are incompatible with its precepts. . . . We call on all nationalist groups to undertake national action in accordance with the Islamic way."[42] According to an Egyptian Islamic writer, Islam does not permit a Muslim to give up his "Islam" in the name of "national unity," no matter what the reasons are.[43]

The PLO factions reject as pretexts the reasons that the Muslim Brotherhood offers to justify its unwillingness to form an alliance with the PLO. In September 1987, the Birzeit student group reflecting the views of the PFLP distributed a statement entitled, "Why doesn't the Muslim Brotherhood recognize the PLO?" The statement pointed out that it was inconsistent for the Muslim Brotherhood to demand the Islamization of the PLO as a precondition for cooperation, while the Brotherhood was already working with other organizations that did not have Islamic leadership. The statement said that Yusuf al-'Azm, who is a Muslim Brotherhood leader in Jordan, "stands behind the rostrum of the Jordanian Parliament to praise the king and his constitution and his royal hereditary regime."[44]

The statement added that the Muslim Brotherhood in Egypt was participating in a parliament that was ratifying a peace treaty with Israel, and that the society allied itself with political parties, such as the Wafd party and the Socialist Labor party, which are not Islamic. The statement asked whether the Muslim Brotherhood considered the regimes in Jordan and Egypt to be Islamic regimes and said it was odd that the Muslim Brotherhood refused to recognize the PLO, while some Brotherhood members from the West Bank, such as Hafiz 'Abd-al-Nabi al-Natsha, were accepting membership in the Jordanian Parliament. The statement accused the Muslim Brotherhood of treason: "Doesn't all this prove the depth of this group's capitulation to treacherous Arab regimes and this group's firm ties to the intelligence apparatus of those regimes and to imperialism?"[45]

The Muslim Brotherhood rejects such accusations and argues that "Islam, which is concerned with all facets of life, is more than just a homeland. The homeland is a part of Islam, one of its special characteristics, an object of its love and protection with whatever is dear to the heart and the soul. Because of this concern, we are in the vanguard of the nationalist ranks. We are not waiting for anyone to put us in, or to remove us from these ranks."[46]

In a booklet published by a pro-Fatah student group, the Brotherhood in the Occupied Territories was compared to the Muslim Brotherhood in Egypt under the regime of President Anwar al-Sadat. The booklet stated that Sadat had opened the door for the Brotherhood to operate freely, because they were the only group capable of undermining the Egyptian nationalists who threatened the Sadat regime. The booklet also stated that Sadat allowed the Brotherhood to dominate the universities to such a degree that the society's authority became stronger than the authority of the universities' presidents.[47] This view corresponds to opinions expressed by well-known Egyptian writers. Dr. Hasan Hanafi wrote: "The political leadership decided to use the religious groups, which began to appear in the universities after the 1973 war and after the release [from jail] of the Muslim Brothers in 1971, to counter the Nasirite influence which was dominant in these universities. The Islamic groups were indebted to the government at that time for the release of many Brotherhood members from jail."[48]

PLO groups believe, and openly argue, that the Israeli authorities opened the door for the Palestinian Muslim Brotherhood in the same way the Egyptian authorities did to the society in Egypt, so that they could compete with, oppose, and undermine the PLO. Certain nationalist circles go as far as to claim that Ahmad Yasin, the leader of the Islamic Center in the Gaza Strip, swore on the Koran, before the Israeli investigators, that weapons seized in his possession in 1984 were meant to be used against leftist forces. The Muslim Brotherhood rejects such an accusation, and asks: "Are the Israeli authorities so concerned about the life and security of nationalists that they would arrest those who wish to kill them?"[49]

The Israeli authorities believed that the rise of the Islamic groups and the spread of their influence in the West Bank and the Gaza Strip was bound to weaken the PLO in these two areas. In this context David Shipler, a former correspondent for the *New York Times* in Jerusalem, stated:

> Politically speaking, Islamic fundamentalists were sometimes regarded as useful to Israel because they had their conflicts with the secular supporters of the PLO. Violence between the groups erupted occasionally on West Bank university campuses, and the Israeli military governor of the Gaza Strip, Brigadier General Yitzhak Segev, once told me how he had financed the Islamic movement as a counterweight to the PLO and the Communists: "The Israeli Government gave me a budget and the military government gives to the mosques," he said. In 1980, when fundamentalist protesters set fire to the office of the Red Crescent Society in Gaza, headed by Dr. Haidar Abdel-Shafi, a Communist and PLO supporter, the Israeli army did nothing, intervening only when the mob marched to his home and seemed to threaten him personally.[50]

The PLO factions, for their part, accuse Israel of supporting the Islamic groups in order to weaken the PLO's influence and create rifts in the ranks of the Palestinian people. They usually point to deferential treatment and to the degree of tolerance the occupation authorities display toward Brotherhood activities. The PLO leaders abroad have urged their following in the Occupied Territories to avoid open conflict with the Brotherhood and to continue to make conciliatory statements, arguing that the Muslim Brotherhood's basic antagonism was with Israel. PLO leaders stress publicly their belief in pluralism.[51] But as the influence of the Brotherhood grew and its opposition to the PLO became more vocal, the PLO leadership began to feel troubled by the potential threat.

Israeli security sources deny reports that Israel is giving support to the Islamic movement, saying that the struggle between this movement and the PLO nationalists is an internal Palestinian affair in which Israel will not intervene, as long as Israeli security is not threatened. But while Israel hopes that the Islamic movement will undermine the strength of the PLO, Israel is also concerned that the rising Islamic influence may become a real problem that Israel will have to face in the longer term.

Failure of the Brotherhood to challenge the Israeli occupation, let alone cooperating with the occupation to weaken the PLO factions, would undermine the society's popular support. The Brotherhood would lose its following to other political groups if it becomes known that such cooperation does in fact exist. The fact of the matter is that the Israeli authorities deal with the various groups inside the Occupied Territories in ways that serve the interest of Israel. These authorities do not hesitate to strike at any individual or group. Events have shown, especially during the *intifada,* that Israeli measures against the Islamic groups are not less harsh than the measures taken against the PLO factions. Israel's attempts to manipulate the various competing groups do not mean that these groups cooperate consciously or deliberately with the occupation authorities to undermine each other.

Friction and mutual accusations between the PLO and the Muslim Brotherhood are embedded in political and ideological differences. The PLO supporters repeatedly refer to Brotherhood positions that are difficult to accept or to justify, at least from a nationalist perspective. The Muslim Brotherhood, the PLO nationalists argue, demands the liberation of all of Palestine from Jewish control and the establishment of an Islamic state in it, while the society practically refused to engage in armed resistance or in actual *jihad* against the Israeli occupation, at least until the eruption of the *intifada* in 1987. The Brotherhood, for its part, bases its objection to armed struggle on two counts: that the Brotherhood has been preoccupied with preparing a Muslim generation capable of combating the enemy, and that public endorsement of armed struggle would simply give the Israeli authorities pretexts to strike at the Brotherhood prematurely. Privately, Sheikh Ahmad Yasin says that the Muslim Brotherhood is resisting the Israeli occupation and that the society is for armed struggle. But Yasin would not declare that as a formal public position, unlike the Islamic Jihad movement, for example.[52]

Conscious of consistent criticism by the nationalists, the Brotherhood's position regarding resistance to the Israeli occupation began to reflect a gradual change even before the *intifada*. The Islamic student group in Birzeit University took part more than once in violent clashes between Israeli troops and students in the university. The Islamic Bloc of the Brotherhood claimed the two students, Sa'ib Dhahab and Jawad Abu-Silmiyya, who were killed in a confrontation with Israeli soldiers in the December 4, 1986, demonstration on the university campus.[53] Muslim Brotherhood students participated in subsequent demonstrations at the university. Supporters of the Islamic Bloc had in the past justified the Muslim Brotherhood's reluctance to participate in armed resistance on the grounds of the society's conviction that the intentions of the PLO nationalists were not sincere. Addressing its supporters, an Islamic Bloc pamphlet stated: "You should be the first to sacrifice if the goal was the liberation of your country and your people. But if their goal is to seize power, then there is no blame on you for not sacrificing yourselves."[54]

The gradual evolution of the Brotherhood's position toward a more militant role was reflected in the slogans the Islamic Bloc had raised during the student council elections at Birzeit University in January 1987. Only a few of these slogans contained the usual religious appeals and references. They also reflected less emphasis on issues of conduct, such as the separation between male and female students in the study halls and science laboratories, and the "mixed trips which are pregnant with corruption and shamelessness."[55] Instead, national themes and Palestinian symbols were stressed and projected. Perhaps this change reflected a new and more realistic orientation by the Muslim Brotherhood. In a liberal university, such as Birzeit, one could not find sympathy for the demand to segregate male and female students. Moreover, it would be difficult to ignore nationalist issues in a university considered to be a stronghold for the nationalists. Excessive focus on religion and the marginalization of nationalist issues and politics was not the best formula to attract the student body. A combination of religion and nationalism was more appealing. Hence the evolution in the position of the Brotherhood.

In the continuing debate between the supporters of the PLO and the Brotherhood, the nationalists take issue with the Brotherhood's exaggerated claims of resisting the Israeli occupation. For example, the Brotherhood credits the Islamists for the continuing Islamic resistance against Israel in Lebanon, the assassination of Sadat by Islamic elements in Egypt, and the actions of the Islamic Jihad movement in Palestine. The nationalists argue that the Islamic groups that carried out these actions were different from the Muslim Brotherhood and do not even agree with the Brotherhood's stands on the PLO and resistance to the Israeli occupation. The nationalists say that the Islamic resistance in Lebanon is carried out by the Hizbullah, which is loyal to Iran, which the Muslim Brotherhood views negatively for being a Shi'ite party.[56] Furthermore, those who assassinated Sadat belonged to the Jihad Organization in Egypt which split from the Muslim Brotherhood in protest.[57] Finally, the supporters of the Islamic Jihad movement in Palestine, who carry out daring attacks against Israeli targets in the Occupied Territories, also broke away from the Brotherhood in protest.

In the same vein, the nationalists accuse the Muslim Brotherhood of constantly bragging about its role in Palestine in 1948, and they question the Brotherhood's role in the long years that followed 1948. They ask why the Brotherhood in Syria boasts of armed action against the Syrian regime and at the same time does nothing of the sort against Israel. The PLO supporters also ask how the Syrian Muslim Brotherhood can attack Syrian President Hafiz al-Asad because of his position toward the PLO, and approve of an alliance between the Brotherhood and secularist parties in Syria to oppose him, while at the same time the Palestinian Brothers refuse to make an alliance with the PLO in the Occupied Territories to oppose Israel. Reference is also made to alliances forged in Lebanon in the past between Fatah and Islamic groups, such as the Islamic Unification movement, led by Sheikh Sa'id Sha'ban, and also between Fatah and Hizbullah, headed by Sheikh Muhammad Hussein Fadlallah.

The PLO nationalists accuse the Muslim Brotherhood of having abandoned the Palestinian resistance movement in Jordan in 1970 during the confrontation with King Hussein. But the Muslim Brotherhood argues that the Brotherhood could not work within the PLO framework "because the PLO had capitulated and conceded everything, and that the Society was then willing to coordinate with the PLO, but without having to accept it as a frame of reference."[58] The Brotherhood points out that the leftist inflammatory actions in 1970 caused King Hussein to strike at the Palestinian resistance movement in Jordan.[59] The Muslim Brotherhood's point of view is that it would have been better for the PLO leaders, and especially Yasir Arafat, to have avoided the trap that was set for them, saved their forces and weapons, spared the blood of their people, and gone to another place, where they could have saved their strength, weapons, and honor.[60]

The president of the Islamic University in Gaza offers an explanation for the Muslim Brotherhood's reluctance to forge an alliance with the PLO: "The Islamic movement was persecuted by the Arab regimes, and this persecution was one of the causes of the 1967 defeat of these regimes. The Islamic movement believes that the PLO is an offshoot of the regimes and, therefore, it will work in their service and will be used in the fights of these regimes against one another."[61]

The Brotherhood in the Occupied Territories sees itself as part of a world movement. It also sees itself as an organization that is the oldest historically, the richest in heritage, and the most comprehensive in program. The society cannot subject its world ideology to a narrow nationalist program championed by groups that endorse secular ideas. The Brotherhood believes that its ideas and strategy are the best for dealing with the various issues, including the Palestinian issue. Accordingly, the Muslim Brotherhood will not accept any alternative idea, strategy, or frame of reference.

Generally, the PLO nationalists express reservations with regard to the Muslim Brotherhood's statements, positions, and actions. For example, the nationalists do not accept the Brotherhood's position that they could not participate in the resistance against Israel because the society was educating and indoctrinating the Muslim generation. The nationalists cynically ask for a specific date for the completion of that stage, and about the time the Brotherhood would engage in *jihad* against Israel. The nationalists also reject the Brotherhood's explanation that it stayed out of armed resistance so that it would not be subjected to repression by Israel. After all, the nationalists argue, there is a price that must be paid in order to resist the occupation. The nationalists equally reject the Muslim Brotherhood's claims that the society was going through an ordeal and harsh circumstances which prevented it from carrying out its obligations toward Palestine.

Dr. Ahmad Nawfal, a prominent Islamic figure in Jordan, explains why Brotherhood members were absent and not engaged in the armed struggle: "Work for Palestine does not come just in one form, that is, bearing arms. It also includes the awakening of the youth in order to work for Palestine. Only the Muslims can undertake this duty, taking the youth out of their soft childhood to manhood, from nothingness to self realization, from fragmentation and diverse concerns to unity and cohesiveness. The Muslim Brotherhood does all of these things, and all such efforts are being made on the road to the liberation of Palestine, which is a part of the land of Islam." Dr. Nawfal adds: "When the Arab regimes plotted against the [PLO] factions, they were able to put them in a bottleneck; what if it were the Islamists alone who were in the field?"[62] Nawfal's implication is that it would have been risky for the Brotherhood to engage in armed struggle, when the PLO, which was stronger than the Brotherhood, could not bear the consequences.

But the Muslim Brotherhood is also questioned by writers known to be sympathetic to the society about the reasons that prevented the Brotherhood from engaging in the *jihad*. The well-known Egyptian Islamic writer Fahmi Huwaydi says: "Where was the Muslim Brotherhood throughout the 20 years that followed the 1967 defeat? Why did their *jihad* stop during those years? Why did not their cadres defend Palestine, which is considered a *waqf* land, in order to fulfill the individual duty (*jihad*), and embark on the armed struggle throughout that period?"[63]

Responding to Fahmi Huwaydi's questions, Ziad Abu-Ghanima, a Muslim Brotherhood spokesman in Jordan, says: "The Muslim Brotherhood was not absent from the field of *jihad* by choice, but by force and compulsion. If you want evidence, ask the gallows of the revolutionaries who brought about the crime and shame of our defeat in 1967, and you will find out that the bodies of the Muslim Brothers were hung by the revolutionary ropes. . . . Forget, if you wish, the prison cells of the revolutionary regimes in those lean years, but remember the thousands of youths and women of the Islamic movement who crouched in these cells unjustly, and the many thousands who still crouch in them until today . . ."[64] However, this reply did not satisfy Huwaydi, who states: "Abu-Ghanima did not address the question regarding the Muslim Brotherhood's position in the West Bank. The Palestinian Brothers were not hanging on the gallows, nor crammed together in prison cells! Therefore, the question I posed is still unanswered."[65]

It is hardly known that some Muslim Brotherhood members had participated in Palestinian armed resistance in Jordan before 1970, but under the Fatah umbrella. Dr. Nawfal says: "We were completely independent, except in name. No one interfered in our decisions, operations, planning, or training. Fatah for us was only an umbrella."[66] Muslim Brotherhood leaders cite in their writings the reasons why they were forced to work under Fatah. Yusuf al-'Azm notes that after the refusal of some PLO leaders to allow the Brotherhood to engage openly in armed action under the Brotherhood's name, the society agreed to operate under Fatah.[67] Al-'Azm says that the Muslim Brotherhood did not form a fighting organization of its own because the society did not get support from anyone due to its position which calls for the liberation of all of Palestine, while the other parties were looking for minimalist deals.[68] Dr. Ahmad Nawfal points out that 'Abd-al-Nasir was putting pressure on Yasir Arafat to prevent the Muslim Brotherhood from forming its own armed organization.[69]

However, these reasons do not sufficiently justify the Muslim Brotherhood's acquiescence in submitting to the wishes or the will of others and not engaging in armed resistance as an independent movement. The Brotherhood was then one of the oldest and largest parties and had the resources as well as the experience to engage in this kind of resistance. The society even claims that it was the party which had inspired the Palestinian *fedayeen* movement to adopt armed struggle: "Despite the circumstances of the ordeal that surrounded the Muslim Brotherhood on all sides, no one could deny that the Islamic spirit, which prevailed in the Palestinian *fedayeen* movement from the outset, was one of the fruits of Muslim Brotherhood thought."[70]

The nationalists find it difficult to accept Muslim Brotherhood condemnation of PLO supporters for meeting with foreign and Israeli

officials, when certain Brotherhood leaders in the Occupied Territories are themselves taking part in such meetings. In this context,
reference can be made to the participation of Dr. Muhammad Siyam,
the former acting president of the Islamic University in Gaza, in a
meeting held during the *intifada* between a group of Palestinians
and Mr. Wat Claverius, an assistant to American Secretary of State
George Shultz. Reference can also be made to another meeting,
held in May 1988 between Shimon Peres, the Israeli foreign minister
at the time, and Dr. Mahmud al-Zahhar, one of the society's leaders
in Gaza, and to another meeting on June 1, 1988, between al-
Zahhar and Ibrahim al-Yazuri, the executive director of the Islamic
Center, and Yitzhaq Rabin, the Israeli defense minister at that time.
Attending this last meeting, in addition to al-Zahhar and al-Yazuri,
were the pro-PLO Zuhair al-Rayyes and Dr. Riad al-Agha. All four
individuals came from the Gaza Strip.[71]

The PLO supporters say that the Muslim Brotherhood's rejec-
tionist and ambiguous position with respect to the PLO's right to
represent the Palestinian people and the Brotherhood's rejection of
the idea of an international conference and a Palestinian state co-
incide objectively, no matter what the motives or doctrinal justifi-
cations are, with the positions of Israel and the United States
regarding these issues.

Finally, the supporters of the PLO say that one cannot take
seriously the Brotherhood's claims of its commitment to regain all
of Palestine from the hands of the Jews while the Brotherhood is
closely linked to regimes that do not believe in this goal and do
nothing to achieve it, such as Jordan and Saudi Arabia. Jordan's
public position favors the land for peace formula, and the establishment of a confederation between a Palestinian state in the
West Bank and Gaza, and Jordan. As for Saudi Arabia, it was the
country which devised the "Fahd Plan" in August 1981, calling
for the establishment of a Palestinian state, the acceptance of the
existence of all states in the region, and the achievement of peace
among those states. The PLO nationalists argue that the mere
verbal calls of the Brotherhood for the liberation of Palestine and
the establishment of an Islamic state in it, without matching such
calls with deeds, is something that Israel can tolerate for hundreds
of years.

A Palestinian leftist publication depicted the Brotherhood during
the *intifada* as an active, and even violent, opponent of the PLO.
The publication indicated that the Brotherhood acts

with the direct support of reactionary Arab regimes, especially Saudi Arabia, Egypt, Jordan, and some of the Gulf states, in collusion with the Israeli occupation. This trend has carried out organized and methodical sabotage operations which climaxed in direct attacks against nationalist institutions, such as the Red Crescent office in Gaza, . . . and against nationalist strugglers who had been hit with clubs and chains (the attack on Dr. Rabah Mahanna in Gaza on July 26, 1986), as well as the clashes with nationalist student blocs in universities (Najah and Gaza). The Islamic groups have continued to perpetuate crimes, even during the *intifada,* especially the so-called *al-Mujamma' al-'Islami* in the Gaza Strip, which carried out reckless attempts at the beginning of the *intifada* to turn it to its advantage. The *Mujamma'* tried to put the religious stamp on the *intifada,* banning pro-PLO slogans, spreading false rumors, and calling on the people to destroy the homes of communists. The danger of this trend, and the reactionary and conspiratorial role it plays, reached its peak when certain demonstrations were organized against democratic, nationalist and communist strugglers in the al-Sabra quarter of Gaza. That was a serious attempt to serve the occupation authorities directly.[72]

One of the worst manifestations of the deteriorating relationship between the PLO and the Muslim Brotherhood was the violent confrontations and clashes that took place between the two sides. These clashes occurred in more than one place in the West Bank and the Gaza Strip, and especially in the Palestinian universities. At the Islamic University in Gaza, disputes occurred over control of the university, as well as over peripheral issues. The PLO supporters wanted the university in the Gaza Strip to be a secular nationalist educational institution for all social, political, and religious groups of the Palestinian people. The Brotherhood wanted to maintain the university as an Islamic university. On June 4, 1983, a violent clash took place between the Brotherhood and the nationalists on the campus of the university. More than two hundred students were injured in this clash.[73] This incident coincided with another similarly violent clash at Birzeit University in which a number of students were injured. Both the PLO nationalists and the Brotherhood supporters accused one another of triggering the clashes and held one another responsible for what happened.

In a statement issued by the nationalists in the Occupied Territories, the pro-PLO elements accused the Brotherhood of sending their followers to Birzeit University to fight the nationalists, who were making preparations to mark the first anniversary of the 1982 invasion of Lebanon. The statement described the Muslim Brotherhood as the "emergency reserve of Arab reactionaries in the midst of our masses," and of being a constant and "willing tool in the hands of these reactionaries, in order to achieve their aims and their capitulationist and liquidationist plots." The statement added: "The Muslim Brotherhood gang has insisted, as it always has since its foundation, on positions that are hostile to our people, their aspirations, and their representatives, the PLO."[74]

The pro-Brotherhood Islamic student bloc at Birzeit University issued a statement in which it clarified the circumstances surrounding the clash that had occurred on the university campus. The bloc accused the nationalists of blocking an activity the youth were undertaking "to express their anger at everything that reminded them of the tragedy of our nation, upon which befell the 1967 war and the tragedy that struck Lebanon on June 6, 1982."[75] The Brotherhood accused the Birzeit University administration and the residents of the town of Birzeit of acting in collusion with the nationalists in opposition to the Islamic trend:

> The Muslim youth asked for the assistance of those responsible in the university administration, and demanded that they put an end to what was happening. However, the administration showed hatred exceeding the hatred of the attackers, since they themselves closed the doors and blocked their ears to cries for assistance, allowing themselves, driven by their callous and Phalangist hatred, to give the attackers the opportunity to do what they wished to the Muslim youth. . . . In this context, and while we are talking about the mediation of some of the Birzeit residents, we wish to say a word of blame, taking into account that we were only guests in their town. Those residents, men, women and children, took part in hitting the Islamic youth. We do not know why, which makes us suspect that they were only motivated by their callousness and Phalangist tendencies. In any event, we thank that group of people which mediated to resolve the crisis, and supplied vehicles to transfer the students of both sides to their places of residence.[76]

Birzeit University was founded by a Christian Palestinian family.

In the aftermath of the Birzeit University incident, a committee was formed to investigate what had happened. In its report, the committee expressed regret that the university's administration had not intervened with the student council, which was dominated by the pro-PLO nationalists, to prevent the incident. The student council, on its part, issued a statement in response to the findings of the report. It said that those findings were nothing more than fabrications by Muslim Brotherhood elements "who are well known for their connections with reactionary Arab intelligence organizations and with world imperialist intelligence agencies, especially the American."[77]

Najah University in Nablus was the site for other confrontations and clashes. In the last part of 1981, the university was the scene of violent clashes between Muslim Brotherhood and pro-PLO students. The conflict erupted as a result of the nationalist students' demand to restore four lecturers to their positions after the university administration had dismissed them. On January 9, 1982, more than twenty-five persons were injured in a similar clash at the same university over the same issue. During this clash, Muhammad Hassan Sawalha, a lecturer at the university known for his sympathy for the nationalists, was thrown from the third floor of a university building and suffered serious injuries.[78] On January 14, 1982, similar clashes occurred at the Polytechnic Institute in Hebron. These clashes spread to the Gaza Strip where, on January 21, the Islamists attacked the headquarters of the Red Crescent Society in the city of Gaza and burned down its library. Similar incidents between the nationalists and Islamists took place at Birzeit University in 1984 and in the Gaza Strip in 1986.

It is worth mentioning that it was the Fatah supporters who in 1980–1981 stood up to the supporters of the Muslim Brotherhood despite the historic relationship and general rapprochement between Fatah and the Brotherhood. The clashes that took place between 1982 and 1986 at the Islamic University in Gaza were also basically between Fatah and the Brotherhood, except for a few cases in which confrontations took place between the Brotherhood and leftist groups, such as the PFLP or the Communists. Supporters of the Brotherhood believed that the only group capable of competing with them was the Fatah movement. It was easy for the Brotherhood, for example, to undermine the leftist factions, which were easily discarded as Communists. However, the case was different with regard to Fatah, because the latter represented a nationalist mainstream, enjoyed strong influence inside and outside the Occupied Territories, and could not be accused of Communism.

Later, the struggle between Fatah and the Muslim Brotherhood became more intense, when As'ad al-Saftawi, a Fatah leader in the Gaza Strip at that time, was attacked by the Muslim Brotherhood.

The Brotherhood, for its part, held Fatah responsible for the assassination of Dr. Isma'il al-Khatib, a Muslim Brotherhood lecturer in the Islamic University in Gaza. In January 1982, the Brotherhood expressed their displeasure at Fatah's alliance with other nationalist groups in the Occupied Territories and its signing of a political statement condemning the Muslim Brotherhood.

Clashes were not confined to Islamic and nationalist groups. Similar incidents occurred between the Islamic groups themselves, the Brotherhood, and the Islamic Jihad. Sheikh 'Abd-al-Majid Kallub, a Gaza cleric, wrote: "By God, tell us how you feel when you see Muslims using clubs, knives, and iron chains against other Muslims, under the roof of a holy place?... Everyone who is zealous of religion is embarrassed by these deeds."[79] The reference here is to clashes that took place in Gaza between supporters of the Muslim Brotherhood and the Islamic Jihad movement.

The Muslim Brotherhood leaders in the Occupied Territories complained about what they believed to be a deliberate media blackout campaign directed against them by the press which was dominated by the pro-PLO nationalists: "Every media outlet has been closed to us, especially in the Occupied Territories' newspapers and magazines, while they are wide open to communists to publish their lies and fabrications against the people. They agitate to strike blows at Islam and Muslims; but the communists are not content with that! On the contrary, they spread their insolent slogans everywhere, even on walls of houses. All of this is a well-conceived plot to destroy the facts, misguide the nation, and distort the reputation of sincere and respected people, who are prevented from responding to the lies, even if that was through a paid advertisement."[80]

Despite the differences and the clashes between the PLO and the Muslim Brotherhood, some Fatah leaders at home and abroad maintained a cordial relationship with the Brotherhood leadership. Ideological affinity between the founders of Fatah and the Muslim Brotherhood Society underlies this attitude. Moreover, an alliance was established between Fatah and the Islamic groups in Lebanon. Furthermore, the Fatah leaders needed the financial support of Saudi Arabia, also the Brotherhood's backer and supporter, and could not afford to alienate this valuable ally. In addition, the Fatah leaders were anxious to maintain friendly relations with the Muslim Brotherhood because the society could be a reserve ally for Fatah at home, if alliances shifted among the factions of the PLO. But a cordial relationship with the Brotherhood was not to be accepted by Fatah at any cost, as it became clear later, when the Fatah-dominated PLO leadership challenged the wishes and opposition of the Brotherhood and sanctioned Palestinian participation in peace negotiations with Israel in October 1991.

This Islamic orientation of certain Fatah leaders became more apparent after 1982 and after the secession that occurred inside Fatah. For example, religious references in the words and speeches of Yasir Arafat, the leader of Fatah and chairman of the PLO, had become more frequent. Despite the fact that a part of these references could be a reflection of sincere conviction and a religious background, it is not unlikely that some of these references have political aims and are intended to appease the leaders and followers of the Islamic movement, not only in the Occupied Territories, but also in other places, such as Lebanon, Syria, and Jordan. Moreover, these religious references were perhaps meant to allay the fears of conservative Arab states like Saudi Arabia and the gulf states with regard to leftist influence within the PLO ranks. The message that Yasir Arafat sent out to the Palestinian people in January 1987, on the 22nd anniversary of the establishment of the Fatah movement, contained six Koranic verses, while the message he sent on the same occasion in 1988 contained five, and similar messages sent in previous years contained about a similar number of verses.[81]

In an interview with Arafat, the answers of the Fatah leader contained some of these religious allusions:

> *Question:* Who is the person who fascinates you and whom do you admire in Islamic history?
> *Answer:* 'Umar Ibn-al-Khattab, may God bless him.
> *Question:* And in the world?
> *Answer:* Muhammad, may God's peace be upon him.
> *Question:* If you wanted to go to the moon, would you go on an American or on a Russian spacecraft?
> *Answer:* I have no need for this moon.[82]

The Fatah leaders were also keen to maintain good relations with the Muslim Brotherhood for practical purposes. Following one of the violent clashes that took place between Fatah and Brotherhood supporters in Najah University in the summer of 1981, Fatah leaders abroad asked their followers not to burn their bridges with the Muslim Brotherhood because Fatah needed the Brotherhood as a bargaining card in its relationship with Syria. The Syrian Brothers were at the time engaged in a bloody conflict with the regime of President Hafiz al-Asad. Furthermore, the Fatah leaders abroad undertook certain decisions that were more favorable to the Muslim Brotherhood than to Fatah in the Occupied Territories in order to maintain a good relationship with the society. When rivalry heightened between Dr. Riad al-Agha, a close supporter of Fatah, and Dr. Muhammad Saqr, a Muslim Brotherhood sympathizer, over the position of president of the Islamic University in Gaza, the Fatah leadership endorsed Saqr.[83] Saqr says that the decision to appoint him president came from the university's board of trustees and took place with the approval of Yasir Arafat and his deputy, Khalil al-Wazir.[84]

The Fatah leaders made persistent attempts to co-opt the Islamic movement in the Occupied Territories through coordination and offers of support. Fatah appointed a prominent Islamic figure, Sheikh 'Abd-al-Hamid al-Sa'ih, to the presidency of the Palestine National Council (PNC), and in April 1987 it admitted three individuals, whom Fatah considered to be Muslim Brotherhood representatives, into the membership of the council.[85] Fatah also named Dr. Muhammad Siyam, the former acting president of the Islamic University in Gaza and one of the Muslim Brotherhood leaders, as a representative of the PLO to the Islamic World League. This appointment occurred following Dr. Siyam's departure from the Gaza Strip at the end of July 1988.

Finally, in this respect one cannot ignore the clear Islamic reference in the Declaration of Independence which was issued by the PNC in November 1988: "The National Council declares, in the name of God, and in the name of the Arab Palestinian people, the establishment of the state of Palestine on our Palestinian territory, with its capital, Holy Jerusalem." Furthermore, the Declaration ended with the following Koranic verse: "Say: Oh God, Owner of the kingdom. Thou givest the kingdom to whom Thou pleasest, and takest away the kingdom from whom Thou pleasest, and Thou exaltest whom Thou pleasest and abasest whom Thou pleasest. In Thine hand is the good. Surely, Thou are the Possessor of Power over all things." [Koran 3:26]

Relations between Fatah and the Muslim Brotherhood in the Occupied Territories can generally be described as cooperative and coordinated at times, and ridden with disputes and confrontations at other times. Evidence of this can be seen in the coordination between Fatah and the Muslim Brotherhood in arranging the attack on the Red Crescent headquarters in Gaza on January 7, 1980. As stated by one of its leaders, Fatah had a hand in this incident.[86] Nevertheless, Fatah publicly criticized it.

Following the secession that occurred within the Fatah movement in the spring of 1983, supporters of Fatah and the Brotherhood found themselves in the same camp. Both took a hostile position toward Syria. The Brotherhood's sympathy with Fatah was evident in the society's condemnation of the secessionists, who were described as criminal. The Brotherhood accused the Fatah secessionists of being tools manipulated by Syria and Libya to gain control over the Palestinian decision. The society also attributed the secession to the presence of Western ideologies inside the PLO and to a plot by Palestinian leftist forces, Arab Marxists, and the Soviet Union, in addition to Syria and Libya. The Muslim Brotherhood pointed out that the goal of these forces was to tear down Fatah from within, liquidate the Palestinian issue, and nullify the military option. The Brotherhood criticized Arafat for allying himself with leftist forces, cooperating with the Soviet Union, and establishing relations with Syria and Libya. The society saw the secession as "a first step in the process of finishing off the followers of Islam in the Occupied Territories and an attempt to abort the Fatah leaders' efforts to get closer to the Islamic movement. Therefore, the Brotherhood leadership urged Fatah to purge its ranks of Marxist elements, to be aware of the futility of secularism, and to cooperate closely with the Islamic groups."[87]

The ouster of Arafat from Damascus on June 24, 1983, had angered the Islamists in the Occupied Territories. In mass rallies at al-Aqsa Mosque in Jerusalem, Sheikh Sa'd-al-Din al-'Alami, chairman of the Higher Islamic Council, condemned the Syrian action and declared that the killing of President Hafiz al-Asad was a duty of every Muslim. It is not known whether this position was motivated by the Islamic movement's hatred of the Syrian regime or was meant to show genuine solidarity with Arafat, or both. Sheikh al-'Alami is not a Muslim Brotherhood member, but only a leading Islamic figure.

It is rumored that in the 1986 elections of Birzeit University, supporters of the Fatah movement asked students of the Islamic Bloc to vote for Fatah so that the latter could achieve victory over a leftist bloc composed of the PFLP, the DFLP, and the Palestine Communist Party (PCP), who all formed an alliance to challenge Fatah. However, the Fatah Student Youth movement denied that the Islamic Bloc actually helped the movement win the elections and indicated that the Islamic Bloc had hoped to win the election itself, in the absence of unity between the nationalist factions.

The Brotherhood is not inclined, even for tactical purposes, to surrender power or leadership to any other group. The society believes in assuming responsibility and power, as expressed by a prominent Muslim intellectual: "The strategy of the Islamic movement must include the desire to assume the responsibility of achieving its program of Islamic rule. . . . Assuming power is not something to escape or renounce, as some think. . . . The world and history do not know any movement whatsoever that gave the sap of its struggle to anyone other than those who believe in its goals and who join its paths to the battle and struggle."[88]

Acceptance of the PLO by the Muslim Brotherhood will materialize only if and when the PLO becomes a part of the Islamic movement. An article published in one of the local publications of the Muslim Brotherhood outlined a list of actions it feels that the PLO leadership must take:

1. The PLO must renounce every commitment it has made to Arab regimes, whether in the summit conferences or in bilateral agreements, especially as regards the political solution or the so-called peaceful solution.
2. The PLO must extricate itself from the international political efforts that all world powers are making, because those efforts will only achieve the best interests of those powers.
3. The PLO must oust from its ranks every group belonging to those ruling regimes or those oppressive international powers.
4. The PLO must reorganize itself, so that it becomes a resistance movement, not a political organization with party cadres and regular armies. It must return to covert operations in all Palestinian, Arab, and international arenas, and abandon overt actions.
5. The PLO must forget the battle for its own interests, and enter the battle stemming from its cultural dimension, committing itself to the nation's religion, thought, program, and doctrine.
6. The PLO must go back to view the Palestinian issue as an issue of occupied territories and a refugee people, and not an issue of leaders devoting themselves to agreement and disagreements, exacting for this disagreement or that agreement a price paid by the nation's efforts and the blood of its sons.

7. The PLO must consider itself the representative of all the Palestinian people, including those who adhere to Islam and who are committed to it.
8. The PLO must include in its fold every son of the Islamic nation, and must consider all Islamic movements that are committed to Islam its strategic depth in its battle for civilization.[89]

These demands, which reflect a great deal of ideological purity and political idealism, fall within the Muslim Brotherhood's prescription to Islamize the PLO. But the Brotherhood's stand toward the PLO began to change after the society's decision to participate in the Palestinian *intifada* of 1987. For that purpose, the Palestinian Brothers have established the Islamic Resistance Movement (Hamas). Following their participation in the *intifada,* the Muslim Brothers began to realize that actual involvement in politics requires more than romantic stands.

Furthermore, both the Brotherhood and Hamas, which is a wing of the Brotherhood, are in essence political movements that embrace an Islamic ideology. As a political movement, the Brotherhood was bound to respond to and interact with changing political realities. During the *intifada,* Hamas has engaged in discourse and conduct that reflects political realism and even pragmatism. In its charter, Hamas has indicated that it "considers the PLO to be the closest to the Islamic Resistance Movement and regards it as a father, brother, relative or friend."[90]

Furthermore, on more than one occasion, Hamas forged alliances with some PLO factions vis-à-vis others. Reference in this context can be made to statements issued and signed jointly by Hamas, the marxist Popular Front for the Liberation of Palestine (PFLP) and the Democratic Front for the Liberation of Palestine (DFLP) in protest against Palestinian participation in the peace process that started with the Madrid Peace Conference in October 1991. This participation was championed by the mainstream Fatah movement.[91]

Hamas's political pragmatism has become more evident as the movement's strength versus the PLO has grown. Five years after the eruption of the *intifada,* the Hamas leaders have expressed preparedness to join the PLO if the organization becomes more democratic and conducts elections inside and outside the Occupied Territories to elect a new Palestine National Council, the Palestinian parliament in exile.

The Hamas leaders also indicate that Palestinian withdrawal from the peace negotiations is not a prerequisite for Hamas's joining of the PLO. According to Muhammad Nazzal, a prominent leader and the movement's representative in Jordan, Hamas will accept the establishment of a Palestinian state on part of Palestine as a first step toward the liberation of the Occupied Territories from Israeli rule. But the Hamas leader also indicates that while his movement accepts this interim solution, it will not recognize Israel.[92] This position of Hamas reflects some accommodation to the PLO political program, which calls for a two-state solution to the Palestinian-Israeli conflict.

3

The Intifada

■ In December 1987 a Palestinian popular uprising, an *intifada*, broke out in the Occupied West Bank and Gaza Strip. The eruption of the *intifada* was a function of a combination of root and immediate causes as well as catalysts.

Causes and Catalysts

The root causes of the uprising were embedded in twenty years of Israeli occupation and Israeli policies aimed at undermining the material and national existence of the Palestinians in their own land. The Palestinians believed that under the guise of maintaining its security, Israel had pursued a host of policies detrimental to Palestinian society. Israel had confiscated Arab land and launched an aggressive settlement policy that had left the West Bank and Gaza fragmented both geographically and demographically. Israeli "iron fist" policies—marked by repressive measures and human rights violations—had resulted in loss of life, imprisonment, detention, house or town arrest, demolition of dwellings, deportation, fines, interrogation, travel restrictions, curfews, closures of educational institutions, unjust taxes, economic hardships, and the like. Hardly a single Palestinian household had been left untouched.

Unlike classical patterns of colonialism, the Israeli occupation failed to win the sympathy or support of any meaningful sector of the occupied population. Even those social classes that have traditionally allied themselves to foreign occupation in other colonial settings found themselves in the Palestinian context at constant odds with the Israeli occupation. Under an active policy of land confiscation and Jewish settlement, major Palestinian landholders were the big losers. Even the leading Palestinian merchants were restricted and had to contend with unfair competition from their Israeli counterparts, who enjoyed differential treatment from their government.

Such attempts to undermine the material existence of the Palestinian people were compounded by continuous Israeli denial of Palestinian national aspirations, which included self-determination and an independent Palestinian state in the West Bank and Gaza. Israeli denial was perceived by the Palestinians as a deliberate attitude that blatantly ignored international recognition of legitimate Palestinian rights.

National and political awareness among the Palestinians had gradually evolved throughout the twenty years of Israeli occupation. The Palestinian national movement and the process of Palestinian nation-building had contributed to the evolution of this awareness. When harsh Israeli occupation policies entered a collision course with this heightened state of national awareness among the Palestinians, twenty years of seething discontent ripened into an uprising.

The uprising did not happen in a vacuum. It was dormant, awaiting the appropriate historical moment to erupt. In fact its manifestations and attributes were already somewhat visible and indicated that the uprising itself was imminent. Those who monitored the situation in the Occupied Territories closely and saw events in continuum were bound to come to this conclusion.

In the three years preceding the uprising, forms of popular resistance to the Israeli occupation were enforced. The setting for the December uprising was being prepared. One can even venture to suggest that the uprising had actually started, though partially, long before December 1987. The tactics and forms of confrontation employed by the Palestinians in the uprising and Israeli retaliatory measures were in fact in place before the eruption of the uprising. One can find evidence in both Israeli and Palestinian sources.

In his 1987 report, Israeli researcher Meron Benvenisti, director of the West Bank Data Project, indicated that in the period between April 1986 and May 1987, 3,150 violent demonstrations had taken place, of which 1,870 included stone throwing, 60 involved the setting of stone roadblocks and tire burning, and 665 involved the raising of Palestinian flags, leaflet distribution, and writing of nationalist graffiti on walls. During the same period there were 65 incidents involving firearms use, explosives, or stabbings, and 150 cases involving Molotov cocktails. All in all, 9 Palestinians were killed by the Israeli army (7 of them during demonstrations) and 67 were injured. Two Israelis were killed and 62 injured. On the other hand 3,000 Palestinians were arrested for their participation in demonstrations, and 1,550 others were arrested because of their involvement in "terrorist acts."[1] Palestinian sources indicate that between 1985 and 1987, 115 Palestinians were killed and 828 were injured while resisting Israeli occupation.[2] These figures seem to include Palestinian casualties inside and outside the Occupied Territories.

The objective conditions for the eruption of an uprising within the Palestinian society were ripe. The language and discourse of the uprising were in use before the uprising itself began. A leaflet distributed in the Occupied Territories by the Fatah movement on November 2, 1987, only five weeks before the uprising, commemorating the anniversary of the Balfour Declaration, read as follows:

> The colonizer wanted the 2nd of November to be an ill-omened promise targeting the people, land, civilization, and tradition of Palestine. . . . That was the dirty Balfour Declaration. . . . As for the people of heroism and martyrs, the brave people of the revolution, the anniversary is a fire that burns, kills, and bleeds all the enemies. . . . Let us fulfil the promise of the revolution and the people . . . and defend our holy land. . . . Let us protect Palestine by blood, fire, and arms. . . . Yes, revolutionary brother . . . think carefully, choose the appropriate time and place . . . mask yourself . . . carry your bomb and hit the target you have selected, hit the military patrol or the car of the murderous invading settlers . . . if you are in a remote area choose a dirty traitor . . . make sure that he is a traitor and attack him, burn him . . . he does not deserve to belong to our great people.[3]

Twenty years of occupation produced a state of deep anger and frustration among the Palestinians. Though initially internalized, these pent-up emotions sought an outlet through which to explode. The scope, magnitude, and persistence of the uprising attests to the depth and intensity of that anger and frustration. A number of developments in the Palestinian, Arab, and Israeli arenas found their way into the consciousness of the Palestinian people under occupation. These developments came to provide the immediate cause for the intifada.

In the Palestinian arena, the PLO and its leadership were unable to deliver on their promises. Just prior to the uprising, the PLO had reached its lowest ebb. Armed struggle was reduced to an empty slogan. The evacuation of the PLO's military forces from Lebanon highlighted an unprecedented degree of weakness. Splits and lack of meaningful national unity among the PLO factions only exacerbated this weakness. The Palestinians in the West Bank and Gaza gradually began to realize that they could no longer count on the Palestinian "exterior" alone for their salvation, and that they had to be more self-reliant.

Apart from their growing alarm at the PLO's increasingly obvious military weakness, the Palestinians in the West Bank and Gaza were further alienated by the PLO's persistent attempts to bypass them politically and to abort whatever national gains they had achieved over the previous twenty years. American notions of "improving the quality of life" for Palestinians in the West Bank and Gaza and the "Jordanian Development Plan" were viewed in this light and therefore rejected.

In the Arab arena, the Palestine problem sank for a number of reasons to a position of secondary importance. Among these reasons were the weakness of the PLO itself, the problem of Lebanon, the Iran-Iraq war and the Arab preoccupation with it, and a variety of particular problems facing each Arab nation-state. The Amman Summit Conference of November 1987 fully reflected growing Arab negligence of things Palestinian. The conference was called primarily to address the Iran-Iraq war. Although the Palestinian question was later added to the agenda, no major resolutions regarding Palestine were issued.

In the Israeli arena, Israeli intentions regarding the future of the Occupied Territories had become crystal clear, as manifested in the active Jewish settlement of the West Bank and the Gaza Strip. Palestinian frustrations, doubts, and fears were perpetuated and reinforced by the clear and significant Israeli voices calling for the "transfer" of Palestinians in the Occupied Territories to the East Bank of Jordan or for the establishment of an "alternative homeland" (*watan badil*) for them in Jordan. The transfer and the "alternative homeland" were perceived as Israeli attempts to confront the Palestinian demographic factor that threatened the homogeneity of the Jewish state and its Zionist nature should Israel decide to annex the West Bank and Gaza. According to Benvenisti, Palestinians and Jews in "Eretz Yisrael" would reach demographic parity in the year 2010.[4]

Israeli voices calling for the "transfer" were not taken lightly by the Palestinians, since they were no longer isolated voices. When Meir Kahane first called for the expulsion of the Arabs from "Eretz Yisrael," apologists claimed that Kahane represented only himself. Just a few years later, important figures, political parties, and a large segment of the Israeli society in fact came to embrace Kahane's views. References can be made in this regard to former minister without portfolio Yosef Shapira, former deputy minister of defense Michael Dakel, and most important, former defense minister Ariel Sharon, a leading figure in the Likud party. The Tehiya party, Gush Emunim, the majority of settlers, and over thirty percent of the Israeli population simply did not object to the idea of "transfer."[5]

Furthermore, Israeli intransigence had seemed to increase over time, despite what the Palestinians perceived as Palestinian and Arab concessions, represented, for example, in the 1982 Fez Peace Plan. The Fez Plan speaks of Arab willingness to recognize Israel as part of a comprehensive peace settlement in the region. What is especially significant about the plan, which accepts Israel's right to exist within secure borders, is the fact that it was authored by the Arabs themselves and not by a third party, as had been the case with previous peace plans.

The Palestinian-Jordanian Accord of February 1985 was perceived by Palestinians in the same conciliatory light. The accord made no unequivocal reference to an independent Palestinian state. It also spoke of Palestinian self-determination only within the framework of a Jordanian-Palestinian confederation. Yet Israel adamantly refused to recognize any fundamental change in the Arab/Palestinian position. The net effect was growing Palestinian certainty that Israel was not interested in a meaningful peaceful settlement to the conflict.

Apart from the causes—both root and immediate—a number of developments acted as catalysts in precipitating the outbreak of the *intifada*. Shortly before the uprising, a state of anxiety and psychological mobilization prevailed in the Gaza Strip, where the uprising initially erupted. This state of anxiety and mobilization emerged in the wake of the successful escape of six members of the Islamic Jihad movement from the Gaza central prison. This escape aroused nationalist sentiments and created a sense of mobilization and alertness among the population.

A short while later it was realized that members of this group were not only still in Gaza but were also responsible for a number of daring operations launched against the Israeli occupation. One such operation was the assassination of Captain Ron Tal, head of the Israeli military police in Gaza. After this incident, for which the Islamic Jihad claimed responsibility, a state of tension and anxiety prevailed until the outbreak of the uprising.

Just prior to the uprising, a bloody confrontation between the Israeli security forces and a group of Islamic Jihad members, which resulted in the death of four Palestinians and one Israeli intelligence officer, provoked an unprecedented display of highly charged nationalist sentiments. Demonstrators took to the streets in a number of areas in the Strip, and in a show of solidarity thousands of people visited the homes of the dead to offer condolences and express support.

Sympathy with, and admiration for, the Islamic Jihad reached a climax. One day before the uprising an Israeli was stabbed to death in Gaza, and the next day an Israeli truck hit two vehicles carrying Gaza workers. A number of workers were killed and others injured, most of them residents of the Jabaliya refugee camp. When the news reached Jabaliya, demonstrations erupted, marking the actual beginning of the uprising. It was rumored that the accident had been deliberate and was meant to avenge the death of the Israeli who had been stabbed in Gaza.

A number of other factors also served as catalysts for the uprising. A Palestinian hang-glider operation against an Israeli military camp in the Galilee on November 25, which resulted in the death of six Israeli soldiers and the injury of seven others, stirred feelings of pride among the Palestinians. The operation demonstrated that Israel— even with its strong army, advanced weapons, and elaborate security measures—was not invincible. It further served to highlight Palestinian courage.

Immediately after the Israeli citizen was stabbed to death in Gaza the day preceding the uprising, Israeli foreign minister Shimon Peres suggested that Israel consider the idea of demilitarizing the Gaza Strip. This announcement did not pass unnoticed by the people of Gaza and was perceived as a consequence of their acts of resistance. It also indicated that Israel could be forced to yield.

The Muslim Brotherhood Society and the *Intifada*

Despite claims to the contrary, the eruption of the *intifada* caught the Muslim Brotherhood Society by surprise, the way it caught the factions of the PLO in the Occupied Territories. Although the Muslim Brotherhood and the PLO each claim that it was behind the eruption of the *intifada,* the fact of the matter is that the *intifada* erupted without any political decision by any organized group.

The *intifada* marked the beginning of a new phase in the evolution of the Muslim Brotherhood Society in the West Bank and Gaza. This phase, characterized by actual resistance to the Israeli occupation, may be seen as a beginning of the actual *jihad* by the society. One of the leaflets issued by the Islamic Resistance Movement (Hamas) expressed this new direction: "What is happening today in this blessed land is but a new creation of the Islamic *umma* and of the Muslim generation that carries the banner of Islam."[6]

The leaders of the Brotherhood in the Occupied Territories accepted the notion of transition into a new phase with some variation of opinion. Sheikh Ahmad Yasin, the spiritual leader of Hamas, stated that "every movement passes through stages. Shifting from one phase to another is done in accordance with the decision of those in charge. Obviously, the practical reality indicates that *jihad* has moved to an active phase in confronting the occupation. The size of action and participation in this phase depends on the nature of available resources."[7] In his reply to a question about the possibility of the Muslim Brotherhood engaging in armed resistance to the occupation, Yasin said: "*Jihad* is a duty on every Muslim if the Muslims' land is violated."[8] Sheikh Bassam Jarrar argues that the adoption by the Brotherhood and the Islamic Resistance Movement of the Hamas Charter is an indication of the fact that the Brotherhood has entered a new phase.[9]

Sheikh Ibrahim al-Quqa, a deported Hamas leader, states that the *intifada* is "a phase, and a prelude to a more serious process of getting rid of the nightmare of the Zionist presence on this land."[10] Some Muslim youth leaders in the Occupied Territories think that Muslim Brotherhood participation in the *intifada* is an indicator of a new stage, and that the *intifada* is a mechanism to mobilize the masses, in order to create a generation of *jihad* to fight Israel. They also suggest that the *intifada* is one form of *jihad* and a prelude to armed *jihad* action and, accordingly, is considered a part of a new phase.[11] Yusuf al-'Azm, a Muslim Brotherhood leader in Jordan, says that the *intifada* has moved the Brotherhood from one stage to a new one in "a natural child-birth and not a Caesarean."[12]

The Muslim Brotherhood claims that it laid the groundwork for the *intifada* and is directly responsible for its outbreak. In this regard, the society points to the participation of the Islamic student blocs in the violent demonstrations which took place against the occupation in the Palestinian universities prior to the *intifada*, and especially to the role of the Islamic University in Gaza. The Brotherhood refers to a statement published on October 16, 1986, calling for a one-day general strike to protest the abuse and punishment practiced by the Israeli occupation authorities in the Gaza Strip. The society emphasizes the importance of this appeal in the preparation for the *intifada*. Furthermore, the Brotherhood claims that the *intifada* began as a result of a decision made by the society.[13] Ibrahim al-Quqa says that the Muslim people rose up "at the decision of the Islamic Resistance Movement (Hamas), which set the precise zero-hour in the sanctuaries of the mosques."[14] Sheikh Yasin says that the Brotherhood was the party which unleashed the *intifada,* and it is the party which leads it."[15]

Regarding the role of the Brotherhood in the *intifada,* Hamas leader Dr. 'Abd-al-'Aziz al-Rantisi suggests that the *intifada* began "with one fixed outcry, *allahu akbar* [God is great], and took off from the mosques, where the Koran was being read, and the Islamic songs sung, and the people provided with guidance. The [Israeli] detention camps have been filled with Muslim youth who have converted them into mosques. The streets and mosques have been filled with the pamphlets of the Islamic Resistance Movement, to which the people reacted remarkably. Those who will monitor the various political and press statements will note that these statements indicate the fact that the Islamists are behind the *intifada*."[16]

Regarding his explanation of the reasons for the outbreak of the *intifada,* al-Rantisi notes: "Our people had lost confidence in the [political] proposals by the different parties which raise slogans causing the people to bleed and to be weakened by wounds. Such proposals enforced the loss of our people's rights, and strengthened the occupation forces which weighed heavily upon our people's chest for many long years. Our people had become insecure in themselves, their sons, religion, values, authenticity, ethics, land, and crops. Our people hated being shackled indefinitely, without identity or state. This *intifada* came as a gift from God."[17]

Sheikh al-Quqa points out that the *intifada,* which has been undertaken by the Muslim people in occupied Palestine, was born as a result of the interactions that have accumulated in the Islamic mentality and psyche inside the Occupied Territories. Al-Quqa summarized these interactions as follows:

- The true and profound Islamic consciousness, created by the Islamic mosques, pulpits, centers and institutions, and the strong Islamic groupings in the universities and colleges of occupied Palestine.
- The Muslim generation, which is committed to its religion after a long alienation where it counted on earthly flags that were eclipsed by the 1967 defeat.
- The silence that prevailed in the region, in the midst of attempts to remove the Palestinian issue from the consciousness and the memory of the people, after they had waited for the 40 years of UN resolutions, Arab summits, and false promises, which ended with the Jews swallowing up the rest of Palestine.
- The repressive practices by the Israeli occupation authorities, which came to us bearing the hatred of history, the complex of Nazism, and the thirst for blood, in revenge for Khabir Qainaqa', the Bani-al-Nadhir, and the Bani-Qaridha [the three pre-Islamic Jewish tribes in Medina who were defeated by Muslims].
- The barbaric practices directed at each individual in Palestine, in the various social classes.
- The bankruptcy, negativism, and the end of the road to which the [Palestinian] organizations came; these organizations which raised non-Islamic slogans, abandoned the *jihad* and the determination to liberate all of Palestine.[18]

Egyptian Islamic writer Dr. Hilmi Muhammad Qa'ud, attributes the outbreak of the *intifada* to the disappointment of the Palestinian people in their outside organizations, after they had been disappointed in an effective support from other Arab nations. The Palestinian people had to take the initiative into their own hands, after everyone else had backed away, and they had to "declare their true identity without shame, and to say to the whole world: we are a Muslim people. . . and Palestine is Muslim."[19]

There are some Islamic writers who cast the *intifada* and its continuation, and the Islamic Resistance Movement (Hamas) in a divine light. One of these writers says: "The will of God hurled the stone in order to upset the balance of international peace in accordance with a precise divine order. The continuation of the *intifada* is divine destiny reflected in the will of the Palestinian Muslim people who know that stopping the *intifada* is the trap that God's enemies at home and abroad have planned, in order to besiege this people, and then to destroy and exterminate it. However, the Palestinian Muslim people will never, God willing, stop the *intifada,* not out of fear or faint-heartedness or cowardice, but in submission to God Almighty, and out of love for martyrdom on His path. God's will will prevail, but most people do not know."[20]

With reference to the rise of Hamas, the same writer continues: "Perhaps the most important event in this century is that the Islamic Resistance Movement emerged in this place, at this time . . . in the heart of Palestine, Jerusalem, the Aqsa mosque. . . . Jerusalem was the first *qiblah* [direction for prayer] for Muslims. Why is it not also the first *jihad qiblah* in this era, so that it can be the first spearhead of the establishment of the Islamic state?"[21] This writer also suggests that Hamas "has appeared by divine will and timing and, therefore, God will protect it from all its enemies, defend it and make it victorious."[22]

Regarding the goals of the *intifada,* Ibrahim al-Quqa sees them as follows: "The *intifada* is not aimed at toying with the Palestinian issue in the circles of politics, or raising and discussing this issue in conferences or organizations, but is aimed at liberating the land, all the land, and the honor and creed. It is aimed at the comprehensive and extensive liberation [of Palestine] from the hands of the imperialist oppressors and at restoring the cause to its free and independent Islamic framework."[23]

Concerning the importance of the *intifada,* an Islamic writer says that it "exposes the opportunistic regimes and organizations, which made capitulation a strategy and concessions a tactic, and which aimed from the beginning at using the *intifada* to polish the fading faces of some Palestinians at home, so that they can be the nucleus of the unilateral Jewish-Palestinian solution, which is based on autonomy as it is perceived by Shamir and his colleagues, and to pave the way for the international conference. . . . The Palestinian Muslim people know that the PLO will ride the wave of the *intifada*, as is its custom, in an attempt to turn it to its advantage politically and for propaganda purposes, while it has no actual claim to it. Let the *intifada*, God willing, be the death of every defeated coward."[24]

The Founding of the Islamic Resistance Movement (Hamas)

As a response to the eruption of the *intifada*, the Brotherhood in Gaza began to draw up contingency plans to deal with the new and sudden development. These contingency plans started with a meeting held in the house of Ahmad Yasin on December 9, 1987. Present at the meeting were the most prominent leaders of the Islamic Center in the Gaza Strip. In addition to Yasin, six other figures were present. Those were 'Abd-al-'Aziz al-Rantisi (a physician), Ibrahim al-Yazuri (a pharmacist), Sheikh Salah Shihada (a staff member of the Islamic University of Gaza), 'Issa al-Nashshar (an engineer), Muhammad Sham'a (a teacher), and 'Abd-al-Fattah Dukhan (a schoolmaster).[25] This group comprised the first Hamas leadership that had established leadership wings or committees in the political, security, military and information spheres.

The foundation of the Islamic Resistance Movement (Hamas) was not a clear-cut conscious decision, but rather a decision that evolved over time. The purpose of the December 9, 1987, meeting was to discuss ways to manipulate an incident that took place on December 8 of the same year, one day before the meeting. In this incident, a number of Palestinian workers were killed after an Israeli truck hit two cars carrying workers from Gaza. Discussion in the meeting revolved around the need and the means to seize this catalytic event to charge and arouse religious and nationalist sentiments and to create popular disturbances.

On December 14, the Brotherhood leaders issued a statement calling on the people to stand up to the Israeli occupation. Hamas

retrospectively considered this statement the first of Hamas's seri-
alized leaflets. As the disturbances in Gaza and the West Bank
continued and expanded, Yasin and his colleagues continued to
meet. In the meantime, Sheikh Yasin established contact with Sheikh
Jamil Hamami, one of the young preachers of Al-Aqsa Mosque in
Jerusalem. Hamami, who coordinated very closely with Yasin and
acted as a liason between the West Bank and Gaza Brothers, formed
a parallel leadership body for Hamas in the West Bank. He also
acted as a link between Yasin and the leadership of the Muslim
Brotherhood in Jordan.

Sheikh Ahmad Yasin, the leader of the Muslim Brotherhood and
founder of the Islamic Center in Gaza, is also the leader and main
founder of Hamas. Yasin was born in 1936 in the village of Jora in
the northern part of the Gaza district in Mandate Palestine. He
came from a relatively prosperous middle-class land-owning family.
But when Yasin's family left Palestine in 1948, it settled in a refugee
camp in Gaza. The uprooting of his family would have a lasting
impact on young Yasin, and later on his adult life as well as on his
thinking and fundamentalist views. Yasin completed his preparatory
school education in the Gaza Strip. Between 1957 and 1964 he
worked as a teacher in government schools. In 1964 he was admitted
to the English department of 'Ayn Shams University of Cairo. After
completing the first year of study, he was prevented from returning
to Egypt because of his membership in the Muslim Brotherhood
Society. Yasin continued teaching until 1984, when he had to retire
because of physical disability.

Yasin was imprisoned by the Israelis on April 15, 1984, on a
charge of belonging to a hostile group and weapons possession. He
was sentenced to thirteen years in prison. After ten months in jail
he was released as part of a prisoner exchange that took place in
May 1985 between the Israeli government and the Popular Front
for the Liberation of Palestine-General Command (PFLP-GC).
When Yasin left prison, he decided to devote himself to education
and social work to raise religious consciousness among people, rather
than to violent resistance to Israeli occupation. He pursued his
activities from the main headquarters of the Islamic Center at Jawrat
al-Shams, the poor neighborhood in Gaza where he lived. Yasin's
priority at this time was to reform the Palestinian community from
within and to combat the secularism of the PLO factions that led
the confrontation with Israel.[26]

Yasin continued to act as the leader of the Muslim Brotherhood Society in Gaza. But as it later became clear, Yasin was not deterred by the Israeli authorities. During thie *intifada* he was implicated in the kidnapping and killing of two Israeli soldiers and other violent acts against Israelis and Palestinians collaborating with them. In May 1989, Yasin was arrested and was later sentenced to fifteen years in jail.

Although Yasin has become the most prominent Islamic figure in the Gaza Strip and perhaps in the West Bank as well, the underlying reasons for his prominence are political. The emergence of his Brotherhood movement as a rival to the uncontested secular PLO brought him attention and high visibility. His decision to participate in the *intifada* at a later stage and to engage the Israeli occupation increased that attention and visibility. But Yasin is essentially the product of this political setting. His prominence cannot be attributed to any significant theological or doctrinal contributions. He is not a Khomeini, a Shari'ati, or a Fadlullah. He is neither a Banna or a Qutb. Yasin should be seen in the political context of the Palestine issue, and not in any regional or global context.

From time to time, Hamas would reconstruct its leadership bodies because of the frequent arrests of its leaders. After the arrest of Sheikh Yasin in May 1989, Dr. 'Abd-al-'Aziz al-Rantisi became the most prominent Hamas leader in the Occupied Territories. But part of Hamas's influential leadership resides outside the Occupied Territories. Some of the known leaders are Dr. Musa Abu-Marzuq, the head of the Politburo of the movement, Ibrahim Ghusha, the official spokesman of the movement, Muhammad Nazzal, Hamas's representitive in Jordan, and Emad al-'Alami, the representative of the movement in Iran. There are other prominent leaders of Hamas whose names are not publicized and who reside in a number of Arab countries.

Hamas is virtually led by a consultative council (*majlis shura*), whose members reside inside and outside the Occupied Territories. And since the Muslim Brotherhood Society in Palestine belongs to the society in Jordan organizationally and otherwise, the Jordanian Muslim Brothers play an instrumental role in the leadership of Hamas. The Jordanian Brotherhood is the ultimate frame of reference for Hamas, although the attitudes and politics of the two movements may not be identical.

After more than five years of effective participation in the *in-*

tifada, Hamas managed to create several echelons of cadres or leading activists who had gained experience in the field or in Israeli jails and detention camps. Therefore, while the Israeli December 1992 collective deportations of the Hamas leaders and activists have emptied the Occupied Territories of the first, second, and perhaps third echelons of leadership, the movement has the human resources to produce, over time, a younger breed of leaders to fill the vacuum. This breed may be more militant than the politically seasoned older generation of leadership.

Hamas, which means "enthusiasm" or "zeal" and which is the acronym for *Harakat al-Muqawama al-'Islamiyya* [the Islamic Resistance Movement], was therefore established as a response to the eruption and continuation of the *intifada.* Hamas emerged in a context of disillusionment with the Palestinian secular political movements and with the frustrated hope of achieving salvation from the Israeli occupation through them. In addition to that, the popular turn to Hamas was motivated by the search for psychological comfort, strength, and endurance which a religious ideology usually provides. According to Yasin, "when all doors are sealed, Allah opens a gate."[27]

Furthermore, Yasin and Hamas offered the population a more appealing combination than that of the PLO: "[T]he fundamentalist groups offered a special kind of activism that combined patriotism with moral purity and social action with the promise of divine grace. Sheikh Yasin offered the young Palestinian something far beyond Arafat's ken: not just the redemption of the homeland, but the salvation of his own troubled soul."[28]

The Muslim Brotherhood had more than one reason to form Hamas. Yasin's stated reasons for the establishment of Hamas are consistent with the message of his movement. In his reply to the charge of having established the Islamic Resistance Movement, Yasin stated that the establishment of Hamas was not only his basic and natural right, but also his main duty as a human being, as a Muslim, as an Arab, and as a Palestinian, since he and large segments of his people have for decades been suffering under the yoke of an intruding and oppressive occupation. Yasin argues that Hamas is basically a political movement and its primary goal is to secure the legitimate and natural rights of the Palestinian people by ensuring them safe and peaceful existence on the land of Palestine.[29]

Yasin was initially cautious and reluctant in endorsing an all-out and full-fledged Brotherhood participation in the *intifada*. He was not very keen on dragging the Islamic Center and the Brotherhood as a whole into an uncertain confrontation with the Israeli occupation. But he could not, even if he wanted, sit on the side and ignore the internal pressures within his movement and the unprecedented events taking place around him. He was forced to make serious and risky decisions.

Like the other PLO factions, Hamas participated in the various activities of the *intifada*. But since it is larger in size, in terms of following, than any single PLO faction except for the Fatah movement, Hamas's participation in the *intifada* has been characterized by regularity, extensiveness, and multiplicity of forms. Hamas has relied on its substantial presence in the various areas of the West Bank and Gaza to ensure the continuation of the *intifada*. This kind of presence enabled the movement to absorb repeated Israeli strikes or arrests of its leaders and members without impeding its ability to continue its activities in the *intifada*. Furthermore, Hamas has not been preoccupied with participation in the peace process and could as such dedicate its efforts to the *intifada* and avoid the internal differences and change of strategies and tactics which other PLO factions had to go through in order to accommodate their involvement in the negotiations with Israel.

In addition to the regular activities of the *intifada* (demonstrations, strikes, stone-throwing, etc.) Hamas's resort to violent tactics against Israeli targets, including the use of firearms, has increased over time and exceeded in volume similar tactics undertaken by other factions. Hamas has established for this purpose a special militant body called Kata'ib 'Izz-al-Din al-Qassam (Regiments of 'Izz-al-Din al-Qassam). These regiments have targeted Israelis as well as Palestinians collaborating with the Israeli occupation.

Yasin, the calculating and astute politician, has his own way of doing things. He and his close associates in the Brotherhood had to find a way to join the *intifada* without putting their future and the future of the movement in jeopardy. It was Sheikh Yasin's idea to create a special organization from the Muslim Brotherhood in Gaza to take responsibility for the participation of the society in the *intifada*. Yasin's main concern was to protect the Brotherhood and the Islamic Center which he "had built with such effort and care."[30]

The Muslim Brotherhood probably thought that in case the *intifada* failed, Hamas would take the blame. But if it persisted, the Brotherhood could claim Hamas, as it did a few months later when the charter of Hamas, was issued declaring the Islamic Resistance Movement as a wing of the Muslim Brotherhood Society in Palestine.[31] But Yasin was mindful of other considerations. Like the PLO, the Brotherhood needed a parallel resistance body. And in the immediate sense, Hamas was the Brotherhood's parallel to the PLO's newly established Unified National Leadership of the *intifada* (UNL).

Furthermore, the participation in the *intifada* confronted the Brotherhood with an ideological dilemma. Until the day the *intifada* erupted, Yasin was arguing that the Brotherhood was still going through the phase of Islamic upbringing and preparation and that the time had not yet come for the actual *jihad*. A seemingly new framework such as Hamas was therefore necessary to justify the ideological shift by Yasin and the Brotherhood and the new direction they were taking. But due to the success and popularity of Hamas, the Muslim Brotherhood Society in the West Bank and Gaza would become gradually submerged in it. Hamas has become a credible and convenient name for a rehabilitated Muslim Brotherhood Society. The "new" organization has attracted followers and supporters who were not members of the Muslim Brotherhood.

The Brotherhood's participation in the *intifada* through Hamas was also politically motivated. Yasin sought to maintain his movement's position vis-à-vis other political factions in the Occupied Territories. Perhaps the Brotherhood has also intended by its participation in the *intifada* to establish a claim in any future political negotiations or settlement.

The establishment and consolidation of Hamas was a turning point for both Yasin and his movement. Contrary to PLO nationalists' claim that the Brotherhood had joined the *intifada* late and under pressure, the Brotherhood's participation has been both extensive and effective. Yasin himself claims that his movement was responsible for the eruption of the *intifada* and its leadership. When asked if the *intifada* was spontaneous, he replied: "I believe it happened as something destined by God. There is nothing called spontaneous in Islam."[32]

Because of its ideological and political beliefs, the Brotherhood's participation in the *intifada* was not meant to support the political program and goals of the PLO. This participation was intended to serve the political objectives of the Muslim Brotherhood. The main point of convergence between the Brotherhood and the PLO was the common goal of ending the Israeli occupation of the West Bank and Gaza. The views of the Brotherhood and the PLO diverged on most other issues.

The participation in the *intifada* publicized Yasin and the Brotherhood and enhanced their political clout. Yasin and his movement became more vocal and less discrete in terms of political visibility and stands. Because of this participation and the establishment of Hamas, Yasin could, with almost no negative political consequences for his movement, challenge the PLO and its leadership, the organization which thus far has been accorded the legitimate representation of the Palestinian people. Yasin and the Brotherhood began to contend with the PLO for the representation of the Palestinians in the Occupied Territories and managed over a relatively short period of time to become a force that cannot be ignored and has, in fact, become a serious challenge to the secular forces led by the PLO.

Since the beginning of the *intifada,* Hamas struggled to assert itself and achieve recognition as a major counterpart to the PLO's UNL of the *intifada.* Even after this concession was made by the UNL, Hamas continued to insist on distinguishing itself from the UNL. While Hamas and the UNL generally honored what was included in their respective *intifada* leaflets and bulletins, such as the strikes and other activities, Hamas seized every opportunity to demonstrate its independence and authority. All through the *intifada,* it called for comprehensive strikes on days that the UNL had not specified as general strike days. These days often coincided with religious anniversaries or historical events celebrated by Muslims.

The appeals of Hamas for strikes, especially in the Gaza Strip, were met with widespread popular response. The Brotherhood enjoyed greater influence in Gaza than in the West Bank. The prevailing conditions in the Gaza Strip were readily conducive to militancy. Pressure was already building up in Gaza prior to the *intifada,* and a number of dramatic incidents that took place in the preceding weeks created a state of tense anxiety and high mobilization among the population.

Another indication of the considerable practical and moral authority of Hamas and the Muslim Brotherhood in the Gaza Strip was the large number of people who repeatedly visited the leaders of the movement seeking assistance for their various problems. Since

June 1988, scores of people from all walks of life (religious and nonreligious, poor, well-to-do, educated and noneducated, merchants, businessmen, and even some Christians) visited the home of Sheikh Ahmad Yasin, the leader of Hamas, seeking his good offices on a daily basis. People resorted to such informal mediation because of the absence of authority structures that are usually entrusted with this role, or because of the lack of credibility on the part of these structures. During the *intifada,* most of the Israeli-controlled government structures and institutions, including courts, were practically shut down. The secrecy of the PLO factions and the fact that they do not enjoy spiritual authority increased the demand for the arbitration of the Hamas leaders. While the resort to Hamas undermined the authority of the Israeli occupation, it also undermined the authority of the PLO and nationalist institutions.

It is worth noting that those who visited the Hamas leaders believed that these leaders were able to arbitrate issues and make judgments and that they had the capability to implement them. In addition, the Hamas leaders settled disputes without receiving personal payment. When Sheikh Yasin was asked about the kind of authority he had to implement arbitration and *fatwa* [formal legal opinion in Islamic law], he said that he "does not implement arbitration, but rather, helps the oppressed."[33]

As a result of the influential position of Hamas and its attempts to stress its authority and to set special strike days, it was criticized publicly by the Unified National Leadership:

> Recently, the national movement has noted attempts by Hamas, which is a wing of the Muslim Brotherhood, to impose its authority on the national street and to arrange a general strike on Sunday, August 21, 1988. The masses of our people, with their accurate sensitivity, perceive in this attempt a step that contradicts the national program upon which their Unified National Leadership has agreed, a step that diverts the people's will from resisting the enemy. The Unified National Leadership stresses that any encroachment upon the unity of ranks would mean doing the enemy a significant service by undermining the *intifada.* We extend our hands to any force that wishes to share in the national work, and we do not exclude Hamas from our efforts to unify the fighting position. However, any attempts to impose positions by force on our masses will be resisted. But the clash will only be to the advantage of the enemy and its plans to strike at the *intifada.* Accordingly, we condemn attacks by arson and sabotage against certain commercial centers and the property of

citizens for not responding to Hamas' call. At the same time, we call on Hamas to strengthen the unity of position and not to destroy the consensus, and to contribute to the general national position by co-ordinating with the parties of the Unified National Leadership and its active forces. We praise the preachers of the mosques who do not cease their appeals to close ranks within the framework of national consensus, out of concern for the *intifada* and its continuity.[34]

Attempts have been made by the Hamas leadership and the Unified National Leadership to resolve their disputes and to contain the crisis and the negative effects that could emanate from it.

However, Hamas has continued to call for its own strikes without coordinating with the Unified National Leadership. Clearly the *intifada* had upset the old balance of power and the Islamic movement had become a political force that could not be ignored. Hamas has become a formidable rival to the PLO factions in the Occupied Territories. On a few occasions, violent clashes took place between the supporters of Hamas and those of the UNL.

When asked about cooperation between Hamas and the Unified National Leadership, Sheikh Yasin said: "There is a limited degree of cooperation, and only in certain cases. The relationship between the two sides is characterized by ups and downs and changes from one time to another.[35] Some Hamas sources in the West Bank say that there has been almost no coordination with the Unified National Leadership.[36]

Hamas demands that the PLO commit itself to an Islamic program as a precondition for serious alliance and cooperation. Sheikh Yasin says: "There must be a mutual common ground, based on commitment to Islamic values and principles, without violating them in times of resistance. There must also be prior agreement that after liberation, the state will be Islamic. We opposed the Palestine National Charter because if we had accepted the establishment of a secular state, we would have violated Islam. The Palestinian organizations were established for political and nationalist goals, the Muslim Brotherhood has political and nationalist goals, but they fall within a broader Islamic framework."[37] Hamas and the Muslim Brotherhood oppose the Palestine National Charter, but from a perspective that is different from Israel's. The Brotherhood does not oppose the charter because it calls for the destruction of the Zionist entity in Palestine, but rather, because it does not call for the establishment of an Islamic state in place of that entity.

On the eve of, and during the convening of the nineteenth

session of the Palestine National Council (PNC) in Algeria (November 12–15, 1988), relations between Hamas and the PLO deteriorated once again when Hamas openly attacked the program that the PNC intended to adopt in this emergency session: "We wish to emphasize to you that any plan labelled 'transitional government' or 'independence document' or 'government in exile,' and whatever settlement plan that entails, is nothing but a plan to discredit the *intifada,* and stab the children of the stones in the back, and to prevent our sons from resuming the struggle and martyrdom."[38]

In response to the Unified National Leadership's leaflet number twenty-eight entitled "Proclamation of Independence," in which the UNL called upon the inhabitants of the West Bank and the Gaza Strip to hold mass rallies and celebrations to mark the convening of the PNC session and the declaration of independence,[39] Hamas appealed to the people to turn the days in which the PNC was in session into "days of confrontation, opposition, and rejection of peace with the murderers. . . . Let us tear down all appeals for capitulation and let us put an end to toying with the cause by weaklings and those who are betting on the enemy's elections."[40]

In response, the UNL urged the Islamic Resistance Movement to stop opposing the PLO decisions: "The Unified National Leadership calls on certain fundamentalist quarters to put the national interest of our people over their partisan principles and interests, and to stop casting negative positions, which by necessity serve the enemy."[41] Muslim Brotherhood sources indicated that Yasir Arafat asked the general guide of the Muslim Brotherhood in Egypt, just before the convening of the PNC's nineteenth session, to support the resolutions that the PLO leadership was about to adopt, to intervene with the Muslim Brotherhood leaders in Jordan and the Occupied Territories in order to narrow differences between Hamas and the UNL, and to avoid any conflict between the two sides.[42]

The appeal fell on deaf ears. Hamas considered the declaration of the Palestinian state to be premature. Sheikh Yasin argued: "We have not liberated any part of our country upon which we could found our state. We are still under occupation, and we have not yet put an end to it. In what place would we establish the state? . . . We must have land upon which we can stand in freedom and establish our state without prior conditions and without concessions."[43] Hamas's leaflets that were issued after the PNC session expressed a similar position.

However, the position of the Muslim Brotherhood in Egypt regarding the PNC resolutions was somewhat different from the position of the Brotherhood in the Occupied Territories, but with qualifications. A statement issued by the society in Egypt said:

> The Muslim Brotherhood declares its welcome and support for the declaration of the independent Palestinian state. The Muslim Brotherhood emphasizes that the sole basis for that is the natural right of the Palestinian people to establish their state and their government on Palestinian land. The UN resolutions that try to bestow legitimacy on the Zionist control over any part of the blessed Palestinian soil are of no consequence, since the UN does not have the right, nor does anyone else, even the Palestinian people themselves, to concede any inch or speck of this soil. . . . If the Palestinians are able, with God's help, to establish an independent free Palestinian state in the West Bank and the Gaza Strip, it must be stressed that that does not in any case mean the end of the road, but is only a step on the path to the total liberation of Palestine, as has been previously emphasized.[44]

On November 15, 1988, the PNC declared the establishment of the state of Palestine. The declaration was based on the UN Partition Plan of 1947, which divided Palestine into two states, UN resolutions 242 and 338, and the need to ensure the legitimate national rights of the Palestinian people, including the right to self-determination. Subsequent to the PNC session, Arafat held a press conference in Geneva in which he recognized the existence of Israel, accepted UN resolutions 242 and 338, and renounced terrorism. By doing that, Arafat fulfilled the United States's preconditions to open a dialogue with the PLO. Like the PNC resolutions, Arafat's "concessions" were attacked by Hamas.

When dialogue between the PLO leadership and the American government was initiated, Hamas demanded an end to this dialogue with "the American enemy who has proved to us that it is maneuvering for time to benefit the Zionists, so that they can defeat the will of our people in the Occupied Territories, tranquilize the Muslim Arab people around us, and remove them from the scene of the battle."[45]

Hamas also rejected the April 1989 proposal of Israeli Prime Minister Yitzhaq Shamir for elections in the Occupied Territories. It considered the proposal a ploy to cripple the *intifada* and to gain a public relations victory: "Our enemy will not concede anything to us except by force. We call on our sons to be fully on guard against anything our crafty enemy proposes. Let our slogan be 'No!' to the initiatives of Rabin and Shamir and 'No!' to elections until the occupation is banished."[46]

Hamas's repeated appeals urged the PLO leadership not to rely on America or on attempts to negotiate with Israel and to stop making concessions: "They must reconsider their positions while they are in the middle of the unknown road to concessions, and ask themselves candidly about where they are heading. Not a single day goes by without hearing about a Palestinian step by which we concede part of our right . . . while our enemy does not waver. For how long are the concessions going to continue? What will we gain from them? We warn you against falling into America's trap and its policies which are based on asking for gradual concessions, but only by one side."[47]

The Muslim Brotherhood stresses the importance of the continuation of the *intifada* until its causes, represented in the Israeli occupation itself, vanish. The appeals of Hamas and the statements of its leaders in this regard point an accusing finger at PLO leaders: "The *intifada* will go straight ahead until the usurper is ousted and the land of prophets is liberated from the defile of the occupier. This is the voice of the entrenched and no attention will be paid to the empty talk which aims at burying the stone and the will for a mirage of false promises from the protectors of Israel in the East and the West. . . . It is rumored that our people have given enough, and that the time of harvest has come. This tune aims at diverting the course of the *intifada,* and at blowing up the Palestine National Charter which stipulates the liberation of all of Palestine."[48] Sheikh Yasin states that Hamas is responsible for the eruption of the *intifada* and its continuation, even if the other groups decide to end their participation in it. It is not, however, certain that Hamas can sustain the *intifada* without the involvement of other Palestinian groups.

After the PLO's decision to sanction Palestinian participation in the Madrid Peace Conference of October 29, 1991, and the subsequent Palestinian-Israeli negotiations in Washington, the prospects for direct clash between Hamas and the Fatah movement, the largest of the PLO factions, loomed on the horizon. In July 1992, Fatah and Hamas supporters clashed with each other in several areas of the Gaza Strip, where scores of people were injured. Clashes between the two sides lasted for several days but were finally contained through the mediation of prominent Palestinians in the Occupied Territories.

Although it is still premature to determine how far Hamas would go in its opposition to the ongoing Palestinian-Israeli peace negotiations, it has been evident that the opposition of Hamas is tempered by a realization of the hardships facing the Palestinians in the Occupied Territories. Despite vocal opposition, Hamas does not wish to project itself as an obstructionist force when there may be a chance, even a slim one, to explore the possibilities of finding a solution to the Palestinian problem. Lack of alternatives on the part of Hamas and its awareness of the Palestinian internal balance of power also mitigate its opposition to negotiations. But as it became evident that the peace negotiations were not yielding any tangible results more than one year after their initiation, the Palestinians have become more disillusioned with these negotiations. Being aware of this disillusionment, Hamas was emboldened and became more aggressive in its opposition to the PLO and its tactics against Israel.

Hamas's influence and popularity have also increased since the beginning of the peace process.[49] Fatah and its following could not reconcile themselves to the emergence of a rival force that could challenge the mainstream faction. Fatah's high perception of itself and its influence clashed with the new reality of Hamas. The clashes that took place between the two movements came against this background. In this test of wills, Hamas emerged as an equal counterpart to the Fatah movement.

The leaders of the Muslim Brotherhood inside and outside the Occupied Territories say that their opposition to the PLO will be democratic. This position comes against the backdrop of the Brotherhood's realization that the balance of power at the present time is still in favor of the PLO. Sheikh Yasin notes: "We differ with regard to means of reaching the truth, but we differ in a democratic way. We reject inter-fighting because of our differences."[50] The Gaza Islamic University president Dr. Saqr says that Hamas will not accept any political settlement that runs counter to the principles of the Islamic movement, even if the PLO accepts such a settlement. However, the Islamists, according to Saqr, will be bound by the rules of the political game and will oppose in a civilized fashion.[51] This Palestinian attitude is similar to the positions of the Muslim Brotherhood Societies in Egypt and Jordan toward their respective governments, which are characterized by coexistence.

During the *intifada*, some Hamas leaders have occasionally

voiced ideas that reflect moderation. For example, one Hamas leader once outlined the possibilities and ways for resolving the conflict with Israel. Dr. Mahmud al-Zahhar, from the Gaza Strip, authored a scenario as to how and by what steps the Palestinian-Israeli conflict can be settled. Al-Zahhar submitted this scenario to Yitzhaq Rabin, the Israeli minister of defense at the time, in a meeting on June 1, 1988. The proposed solution discusses several stages:

1. A preparatory stage in which Israel declares its intention to withdraw from the Occupied Territories, release the detainees, and restore Palestinian rights. The actual withdrawal is to take place in the course of a few months. The occupied areas are to be turned over to a neutral party, such as the UN, the European Common Market, the Arab League, or the Organization of African States.
2. The Palestinian people will name their representatives by means that will satisfy everyone, without Israel having the slightest right in this matter, unless the Palestinian people are granted the right to name Israeli representatives.
3. The stage of final settlement will be concluded by negotiations between the parties concerned in order to define the nature of relations among these parties.[52]

Sheikh Yasin himself made a statement in which he indicated for the first time the willingness of the Brotherhood to negotiate with Israel, but under certain conditions. These conditions stipulated that Israel must "first acknowledge the Palestinian people's right to self-determination and right of return to their land. After that other issues can be discussed."[53] On a different occasion, when Yasin was questioned about negotiating with Israel, he replied: "Yes, if Israel acknowledges our full rights and recognizes the Palestinian people's right to live in its homeland in freedom and independence. But the Islamic movement will not negotiate as an alternative to the PLO. . . . I do not want to destroy Israel. . . . We want to negotiate with Israel so the Palestinian people inside and outside Palestine can live in Palestine. Then the problem will cease to exist."[54] These utterances of Yasin, and similar utterances by other Brotherhood leaders, may only be tactical.

When Yasin was asked if a Palestinian state and an Israeli state could live in peace side by side, he replied: "No. This situation will be temporary. If that happens the conflict will be resumed after a while in a more intense fashion. Palestine is a holy place for the Jews, the Christians, and the Muslims. The solution, therefore, lies in living together in one state."[55] Clearly, Yasin believes that this state has to be Islamic where the "people of the Book," the Jews and Christians, are treated according to Islamic teachings: "I personally prefer that Islam dominates in a state like this one."[56]

Additional statements were also made by Mahmud al-Zahhar and Ibrahim al-Yazuri regarding the Brotherhood's position on the convening of an international conference to settle the Arab-Israeli conflict: "The international conference must be looked at and studied from an Islamic perspective."[57]

Clearly, such ideas and positions contradict the traditional Islamic position with regard to ending the conflict with Israel. Perhaps the *intifada* was the reason that impelled some Hamas leaders to contemplate "realistic" positions, such as the positions the PLO leaders adopted in the nineteenth PNC session in Algiers in 1988.

In the course of the *intifada*, Hamas relied on a number of mechanisms and methods to mobilize popular support and participation in the various activities of the *intifada* and vis-à-vis the Israeli occupation. The mosque in particular played a significant role as a rallying point and as a place for launching demonstrations and other *intifada* activities. Hamas used the mosque as a platform and turned it from a place of worship into a center of learning, and later on a place for political organization. The pro-PLO nationalists did not possess a parallel mechanism of equal function and significance. Mosques are scattered across the West Bank and Gaza.

The Islamic movement has also relied on leaflets and graffiti. The leaflets are statements or bulletins that contain an agenda for the *intifada* activities for a period of time ranging from one to two weeks. In the course of the *intifada*, the Islamic Resistance Movement has issued scores of these leaflets. The first leaflet carrying the name of Hamas was dated January 1988. But the Hamas leaders argue that the movement issued its first leaflet on December 14, 1987, five days after the eruption of the *intifada*.[58] Hamas did not number its leaflets serially, except at a later date, when it began with the number 23, issued on June 15, 1988. Perhaps Hamas started with this number to keep up or compete with the leaflets of the Unified National Leadership, which has numbered its leaflets from the beginning. Hamas's leaflets differ in content from those of the

UNL. They reiterate the political goals and positions of the Muslim Brotherhood that are at odds with those of the UNL, especially Hamas's opposition to the idea of establishing a Palestinian state on a part of Palestine and concluding peace with Israel or recognizing it. On the other hand, most of Hamas's leaflets, in contrast to the leaflets of the UNL, have lacked an integrated plan of action for a specific time frame in terms of activities and appeals to escalate the *intifada,* especially during the first stages of the uprising.

Hamas's leaflets usually begin with and contain several Koranic verses and are full of Islamic historical and religious practices.[59] They call for opposing the Israeli occupation and its policies and criticize Arab rulers, referring to their responsibility for Arab defeats and the loss of Palestine.[60] The Hamas leaflets have attacked political initiatives and plans which sought to find a solution to the Palestinian-Israeli conflict: "Today, the American plot appears once more in order to abort your Muslim *intifada* through the Arab kings, presidents, and rulers under false slogans such as the exchange of land for peace and the umbrella of the international conference. This is only a mirage and delusion, and a containment to your *intifada* and your emotions."[61] But as the *intifada* progressed, the Hamas leaflets, which by mid-1993 numbered about a hundred, became more militant in content and in the tactics they prescribed, especially with regard to armed attacks against Israeli targets and opposition to the peace process.

Hamas also resorts to graffiti to express its political positions. Some of this graffiti has read as follows: "No to the Zionist entity," "Our land is Islamic, this is the identity," "Islam is the way to return," "O Jews, leave our land," "Islam is the solution," "The international conference is treason," "Down with the Camp David Accords and autonomy," "Yes to the blessed *intifada,* yes to the Islamic Resistance Movement," "Khaibar, Khaibar, O Jews, Muhammad's army will return," "The land of Palestine is an Islamic waqf, Islamic law forbids its abandonment or bargaining over it," "The destruction of Israel is a Koranic imperative," "Revolution, revolution, against the occupier, there is no solution except by the Koran," and "The Koran is the sole legitimate representative of the Palestinian people," in addition to other graffiti that condemns the peace negotiations with Israel and Palestinian participation in these negotiations.

During the *intifada,* Hamas has also resorted to the use of violence and firearms. As its involvement in the *intifada* intensified, Hamas was being gradually radicalized. Harsh Israeli measures to suppress Hamas contributed to this radicalization. Hundreds of Hamas activists have been detained, and many of its leaders have been deported. With the decline of mass demonstrations and other peaceful activities of the *intifada*, the tendency within Hamas toward violent tactics has increased. Some of the Hamas leaders were charged in Israeli military courts for establishing a military wing of the Hamas movement. This evolution in orientation was also inspired by a conscious decision on the part of the Hamas leaders. If the Hamas activists were looking for religious or political reference to engage in violence, they could readily find the justification they need in the utterances of their leader, Sheikh Ahmad Yasin.

Yasin always argued that the way to regain Palestine is through the exercise of *jihad*. When asked about his willingness to resort to *jihad* as a means to realize his aspirations, Yasin replied: "What is the other alternative available to those who cannot regain their rights by peaceful and non-violent means?"[62] Yasin argues that the Palestinian people preferred, and still prefer, the pursuit of peace and not violence in order to realize their objectives. But he adds that if the Palestinians resort to violence, then it is forced on them for self-defense and because the Israeli occupier understands the language of violence and force only. Under such circumstances, "the gun is the only means that should be used in addressing the enemy."[63] As a people under occupation, the Palestinians, according to Yasin, chose the means of resistance that were available to them. This may account for the various tactics, violent and nonviolent, used by Yasin's Islamic Resistance Movement during the *intifada*.

According to Yasin, the resort to war and violence has one sole objective, which is the removal of oppression and corruption and the establishment of justice, and not the destruction of human beings who engage in them. Those who defend oppression and try to sustain it are equal in the eyes of Islam, regardless of their religion or beliefs.[64] Based on that, when Yasin and the Brotherhood resorted to firearms, they used them against the Israeli authorities who defended oppression (the occupation) and tried to sustain oppression by the force of arms.

The articulations of Yasin and the Brotherhood on the issue of *jihad* vary and are sometimes contradictory. While Yasin argues that *jihad* should start after the completion of Islamic transformation of the Palestinian society, he and the Brotherhood believe that the Muslims who are silent about the occupation of Palestine are committing a sin because Islam requires them to engage in holy war. Failure to act is considered "fatal treason," and any philosophy that justifies submission and does not urge the sacrifice of souls and resources is "heretical."[65] Yasin argues that if the Muslims are not now doing what they should with respect to the exercise of *jihad*, time is bound to change this situation.

On August 18, 1988, the Islamic Resistance Movement issued a charter in which it outlined its philosophy and explained its raison d'etre and positions regarding a variety of issues. The charter derived most of its principles from Muslim Brotherhood ideas. Ziad Abu-Ghanima, a Muslim Brotherhood spokesman in Jordan, says that Hamas is not a new movement except in name only and that it is not new in its thinking or leaders: "The mother movement to which Hamas belongs is the Muslim Brotherhood Society which has been digging its roots into Palestinian soil for decades before the establishment of the occupying Zionist entity."[66]

The publication of the Hamas Charter is considered an important and fundamental indication of the establishment of Hamas as the resistance wing of the Muslim Brotherhood Society. With the foundation of a resistance wing the Brotherhood became, in a way, similar to the nationalist factions comprising the PLO. Despite the fact that this charter does not represent a coherent and sophisticated political or ideological program, compared to programs of other political parties, or even the programs of the PLO factions, its publication does define once more the ideological and political positions of the Muslim Brotherhood Society in the Occupied Territories.

According to the charter, the "Islamic Resistance Movement is a wing of the Muslim Brotherhood in Palestine, and the Muslim Brotherhood movement is a world organization."[67] The charter also states that the "Islamic Resistance Movement is a distinct Palestinian movement that gives allegiance to God, takes Islam as a way of life, and works to raise the banner of God over every inch of Palestine."[68] The charter ads that Hamas is "a world movement . . . and it must be considered and evaluated, and its role recognized on this basis. Belittling Hamas or failure to support it is like quarreling with destiny. Those who close their eyes to the truth intentionally or unintentionally will wake up to find that events have overtaken them and made it impossible for them to justify their positions."[69] The charter reiterates the Brotherhood's well-known motto: "God is the goal, the Prophet is the model, the Koran is the constitution, the *jihad* is the path, and death on God's path is our most sublime aspiration."[70]

With regard to the Islamic Resistance Movement's strategy toward Palestine, Hamas believes, as the charter states, that "the land of Palestine is an Islamic *waqf* for Muslim generations until the day of judgement. It is inadmissible to abandon it or a part of it, or to concede it all or a part of it. No Arab state or all Arab states, or a king or president, or all the kings and presidents, have that right. No organization or all the organizations, whether Palestinian or Arab, have that right either, because Palestine is an Islamic *waqf* for the Muslim generations until the day of judgement. Who has the right to decide on behalf of the Muslim generations from now until the day of judgement?"[71]

About peaceful solutions, initiatives, and the international conference, the charter states: "Initiatives, so-called peaceful solutions, and international conferences to solve the Palestinian issue are at variance with the doctrine of the Islamic Resistance Movement. Abandoning any part of Palestine is an abandonment of a part of religion. The patriotism of the Islamic Resistance Movement is a part of its religion. Only the *jihad* can solve the Palestinian issue. Initiatives, proposals, and international conferences are a waste of time and an exercise in futility. The Palestinian people are too precious for anyone to play with their future, their rights, and their destiny."[72]

The charter of the Islamic Resistance Movement talks about three factors related to the liberation of Palestine: the Palestinian factor, the Arab factor, and the Islamic factor. Each one of these three factors has its role in the struggle with Zionism.[73] The charter also refers to Hamas's position regarding other Islamic and nationalist groups on the Palestinian scene: "The Islamic Resistance Movement looks at the other Islamic groups with respect and esteem. If it differs with them in a given aspect or idea, it agrees with them in general aspects and ideas. It looks at those movements as being covered by the principle of *ijtihad* [Islamic legal judgment], as long as they are sincere and well intended, and as long as their actions remained within the bounds of the Islamic framework. Each *mujtahid* [an Islamic legislator formulating independent decisions] has a reward. . . . The Islamic Resistance Movement considers those movements its assets, and prays to God for divine guidance for all. Hamas will continue to raise the banner of unity and try hard to achieve it on the basis of the Koran and the sunna."[74]

As for the nationalist groups, the charter states that Hamas "exchanges respect with them and appreciates their circumstances, the factors surrounding them, and the impact of these factors. Hamas presses on their hands, so long as they do not give their allegiance to the communist East or the crusader West." Hamas "assures all nationalist trends active in Palestine that they have its support and assistance for the purpose of liberating Palestine. Hamas will do nothing other than that, in word and deed, and in the present and the future. It will unite and not divide, preserve and not dissipate, consolidate and not fragment, value every good word, sincere effort, and good offices, close the door to side disputes, and disregard rumors and ill-intended words, with the understanding that it has the right to self-defense."[75] Hamas, according to the charter, is prepared to discuss "objectively the new developments on the local and international scenes concerning the Palestinian issue, in order to determine the extent to which these developments serve or hamper our interest from an Islamic perspective."[76]

As regards the PLO's positions, the charter reflects some kind of evolution in the Muslim Brotherhood position. It says that Hamas "considers the PLO to be the closest to the Islamic Resistance Movement and regards it as a father, brother, relative or friend. Can the Muslim be alienated from his father, brother, relative or friend? Our nation is one, our misfortune is one, our destiny is one, and our enemy is one." But the charter also reiterates the traditional Brotherhood reservations vis-à-vis the PLO: "The PLO endorses secular ideas. . . . Secular thought is incompatible with religious thought, completely incompatible. Upon ideas are based positions and actions, and decisions are made. . . . Accordingly, and with our esteem for the PLO . . . and what it may evolve into, and without belittling its role in the Arab-Israeli struggle, we cannot abandon the present and future Islamism of Palestine, so that we can endorse secular thought. The Islamism of Palestine is a part of our religion, and those who abandon their religion, will lose. . . . the day the PLO adopts Islam as its way of life, we will be its troops and the fuel for its fire that burns the enemy. . . . Until that happens . . . and we ask God that it is near, the Islamic Resistance Movement's position toward the PLO is the position of the son to the father, the brother to the brother, the relative to the relative, and the one who feels the pain of the other, encourages him to confront the enemy, and wishes him divine guidance and support."[77]

Finally, with regard to the position of Hamas vis-à-vis the Arab and Islamic states, the charter says: "The Arab states surrounding Israel are asked to open their borders for the *mujahidin* of the Arab and Muslim peoples, so that they play their role and add their efforts to the efforts of their brothers, the Muslim Brotherhood in Palestine. . . . As for the other Arab and Islamic nations, they are asked to facilitate the *mujahidin's* movement. This is the very least to be done."[78]

An accurate reading of Hamas's charter reveals that some of its sections and ideas were written cleverly and can be interpreted in different ways. Perhaps the motives behind that were political, taking into account the circumstances under which the charter was formulated and published, illustrated by the absence of certainty and lack of definitive knowledge of an unfolding situation as well as by the circumstances of the continuing Israeli occupation of the West Bank and the Gaza Strip. It is also obvious that the charter is loaded with rhetoric and idealism. The subsequent conduct of Hamas following the issuance of the charter has not exactly reflected what was articulated in the charter, especially with regard to the PLO.

The *intifada* has been a catalyst for a process of differentiation and debate within the Muslim Brotherhood Society in the Occupied Territories. The Brotherhood's decision to take part in the *intifada* was made against the backdrop of a debate that was taking place within the leadership of the movement. The question debated was whether it was incumbent upon the society to delay the *jihad* against the Israeli occupation until an Islamic society is founded, or whether it was the Brotherhood's duty to enter into the confrontation immediately. Traditional Brotherhood leaders were not enthusiastic about an early participation in the *intifada*, but the young leaders were able to impose their will and vision in this regard.[79] On the leadership level, the *intifada* has widened the differences between the traditional Brotherhood leaders, who are linked to Jordan by virtue of being *waqf* employees receiving their salaries from the Jordanian government, and the young Muslim leaders, who began to emerge after 1967. The *intifada* has also forced the Brotherhood to define more clearly than ever its position toward the Israeli occupation and the way to deal with it, as well as the means and tactics that should be employed in opposing it.

The differentiation process and the debate can, in fact, be traced back to the second half of the 1970s. After the Islamic revival that began during that time, especially in the universities of the Occupied Territories, scores of the graduates of these universities were Brotherhood members or sympathizers. Many of them occupied functional positions in society. Some junior leaders, who enjoyed credibility and who were prepared to take risks and make sacrifices, advanced to the second tier of leadership in the Brotherhood. These young leaders gradually began to take the initiative in the actual leadership of the Brotherhood. They adopted positions that were popular and nationalistically appealing. Unlike the traditional leaders, they demanded that the issue of nationalism be given more emphasis by the society, in terms of thought and practice, and that the nationalist issue be considered a matter of priority. They also supported the idea of cooperation and coordination with the factions of the nationalist movement instead of an antagonistic relationship. The young leaders argued that failure to reassess all positions, especially those pertaining to the Palestinian issue, could stimulate differentiation within the ranks of the Brotherhood. The emergence of the Islamic Jihad movement, which is a splinter group from the Muslim Brotherhood, can be viewed as one form of this differentiation. The Brotherhood will find itself facing the same position it encountered after the emergence of the Islamic Jihad, where the society was disrupted and had lost part of itself, if it fails to devise ideological and political views on Palestine that are acceptable to the rank and file of the society.

One major manifestation of the differentiation process in the ranks of the Muslim Brotherhood leadership was related to the position the Muslim Brotherhood had to take vis-à-vis the *intifada*. Some traditional Brotherhood leaders were skeptical and questioned the wisdom of taking part in the *intifada*, on the grounds that non-Islamic parties could be the ones to reap the fruit of the *intifada* and use it for political goals that are not acceptable to the Muslim Brotherhood agenda. The traditional leaders also argued that the Brotherhood would not be able to guide the *intifada* in a direction that was compatible with its positions. In contrast to this position, the society's young leaders saw that it was the Brotherhood's responsibility to participate in the *intifada* and to strive to guide it in the direction that the Islamic movement desired, without consideration for the goals of other groups, or for the fact that the *intifada* could be used for certain political purposes.

The *intifada* and Hamas provided the Muslim Brotherhood with renewed doctrinal conviction and credibility. Putting the Islamic principle of *jihad* into practice, though in a modest form, had a reviving effect on the followers of the Brotherhood. It also had a similar effect on other Islamic movements outside the Occupied Territories. Through the *intifada,* the Brotherhood as well as the Islamic Jihad have been transforming Islam, long accused of conformity to the status quo, into a liberation theology. By becoming popular itself, Hamas has increased the popularity of political Islam in the Occupied Territories. But no conclusive estimate of this popularity or of the actual weight of Hamas vis-à-vis that of the PLO can be given without conducting free and democratic elections for the mass of the Palestinian population in the West Bank and Gaza. However, reference can be made to a number of criteria which would reflect the relative strength and popularity of Hamas:

1. Participation in the *intifada:* Hamas's participation in the *intifada* indicates an actual presence of the movement in every part of the West Bank and Gaza. The net effect of Hamas's participation presents the movement as the second largest political faction, after the Fatah movement.

2. The number of Hamas prisoners and detainees in Israeli jails and detention camps: Various estimates point out that Palestinian prisoners and detainees accused of membership in Hamas are the second largest in number after those prisoners who belong to the Fatah movement.

3. Political and moral presence: Hamas enjoys a great deal of political and moral presence among the Palestinians of the Occupied Territories. Hamas, and even the smaller-in-size Islamic Jihad movement, could call on the Palestinians of the West Bank and Gaza to observe a comprehensive strike and get a positive response. It is doubtful that any PLO faction, except perhaps for Fatah, could do the same and find a similar response. Hamas's moral and political influence has also increased in the absence of any tangible progress in Palestinian-Israeli peace negotiations, which Hamas opposes, and also in the aftermath of the Israeli deportation in December 1992 of more than four hundred Hamas and Islamic Jihad leaders and activists to southern Lebanon because of the movement's escalating resistance to the Israeli occupation.

4. Change in the national discourse: Hamas's influence and the change in the balance of power between the Islamists and the PLO nationalists have also been evident in the changing nationalist discourse. Mindful of the growing Islamic influence and the rising role of Islam as an effective factor in mobilizing the masses, the nationalists have resorted to the frequent use of Islamic references. The leaflets of the *intifada* that are issued by the Unified National Leadership, as well as the other nationalists' statements, contain Koranic verses and other religious indications. In the 1992 elections to the Chamber of Commerce of the city of Nablus in the West Bank, the PLO nationalists ran under the name of the "Muslim Nationalist Trend."[80]

5. A drift toward conservatism: Social relations and conduct in the Palestinian society in the Occupied Territories during the years of the *intifada* reflect a drift toward conservatism. More and more people frequent the mosques across the West Bank and Gaza, and more women wear the veil. Conditions of oppression and hardship and the daily human and material losses sustained by the Palestinians under Israeli occupation have created a sober national mood and have contributed to the spread of a religious climate. At times of national threat people tend to seek solace in religion as an ultimate haven.

   Furthermore, the abandonment by PLO factions of ideological and revolutionary discourse and their turn to political realism and pragmatism have created an ideological and doctrinal vacuum. After the demise of secular ideologies, Islam became the only readily available doctrine that could fill this vacuum in order to maintain the ideological and psychological equilibrium in society.

6. Sectoral elections: The prevailing assumption in the Occupied Territories indicates that the PLO still enjoys the upper hand over Hamas. These assumptions are based on the sectoral elections that are conducted in Palestinian institutions, trade unions, professional associations, student councils, and chambers of commerce. These elections demonstrate that Hamas usually enjoys 35 to 45 percent of the popular vote.[81]

The rise in Hamas's influence and popularity has also been linked to an extensive network of foreign relations, which provide the movement with all forms of doctrinal, political, moral, and material support. Hamas enjoys the support of Islamic movements in Jordan, Egypt, Saudi Arabia, the Gulf states, Sudan, Algeria, Tunisia, and elsewhere. Muslim communities and organizations in the United States and Europe also extend support to Hamas.

After the eruption of the *intifada* and the formation of Hamas, the relationship of the Palestinian Muslim Brothers with Iran improved. Iran viewed favorably the Brothers' engagement in resisting the Israeli occupation. But this improvement also came against the background of a rapprochement between Iran and the Muslim Brotherhood Society in Jordan. During the Gulf crisis and the Gulf War of 1991, Hamas's relationship with Saudi Arabia and the Gulf states deteriorated. It seems that Hamas was keen to find new allies, hence the improvement in relations with Iran and Hamas's appointment of a permanent representative for the movement in Tehran.

In its funding, Hamas draws on a number of sources including the following:

1. Donations collected in the Occupied Territories: These donations are collected from Hamas supporters and the public in general and come in the form of alms (*zakat*) or charity. Hamas also receives donations in return for mediation efforts and the resolution of disputes among the people in the Occupied Territories. The money that Hamas collects goes to needy families and to the construction of mosques, kindergartens, health centers, and the like. Such activities have a moral and religious appeal among large segments of the population.

2. Islamic movements abroad: Motivated by Islamic brotherhood, Islamic movements in countries such as Jordan, Saudi Arabia, and the Gulf states, among others, provide Hamas with financial assistance. These movements enable Hamas to resist Israeli occupation and are eager to strengthen the movement's position vis-à-vis secular forces in the Occupied Territories.

3. Informal donations from other countries: Supporters of Hamas collect money for the movement from Muslims in Arab and Muslim countries, Europe, and the United States. As the Muslims in the past offered financial support to the *mujahidin* in Afghanistan, the "*mujahidin* in Palestine" are viewed in

the same vein. Furthermore, Islamic funds and organizations in several countries extend financial support to the Palestinian Muslims through Hamas.

4. Governments supportive of Hamas: Despite denials from the Hamas leadership that the movement receives financial support from governments, the widespread belief is that Hamas has received money from the governments of Saudi Arabia and some Gulf states. It is also believed that these governments have continued to provide Hamas with financial support after the Gulf war as a way of punishing the PLO for its support of Iraq during the Gulf crisis. The support to Hamas may also be aimed at appeasing the Islamic movements in these countries.

   After the rapprochement between Hamas and Iran, the Iranian government began to extend several forms of support to the movement, including financial assistance. This assistance is estimated at tens of millions of dollars. Iran also provides logistical support to Hamas and military training to its members.

5. The PLO: The PLO leadership has in the past extended financial support to Hamas. On at least one occasion, PLO Chairman Yasir Arafat authorized granting Hamas over one hundred thousand dollars.[82] It is not known if any payments were extended to Hamas after the rise of sharp differences between the movement and the PLO.

6. Investments: In order to ensure its financial needs, Hamas is believed to have financial investments in projects. While the leadership of the movement denies engagement in such projects, several unofficial Hamas sources confirm the movement's resort to investment to generate income.[83]

Unlike the PLO, Hamas does not possess a complicated or extensive bureaucracy. Therefore, its financial responsibilities are considerably less than those of the PLO. It is also known that Hamas's style of spending is modest and far from being extravagant or corrupt. Hamas's popularity among the Palestinians of the Occupied Territories cannot be attributed to the movement's financial capabilities, since those capabilities cannot be compared to the relatively huge resources the PLO musters and the organization's extensive financial penetration of the Palestinian society.

Worth mentioning, however, is that the PLO's financial responsibilities cover the Palestinians in the Occupied Territories and several communities in the diaspora.

The political gains accrued as a result of participating in the *intifada* and the foundation of Hamas have been an eye-opener, especially for the Muslim Brotherhood in the Occupied Territories. The society has realized that it did not require much to establish itself as a serious contender and rival to the PLO and as a source of trouble to the Israeli occupation. It is true that the leaders and followers of the Islamic movement have been subjected to imprisonment, death, and other forms of punishment from the Israeli authorities, but considering the political gains achieved, this price can be tolerated. The Muslim Brotherhood has broken the barrier of fear vis-à-vis Israel and has emerged as a major challenger to the PLO. With Hamas in the forefront, the Brotherhood could achieve, in less than four years, the kind of credibility, popularity and legitimacy the PLO has earned over two decades. Through its participation in the *intifada* and the sacrifices that participation entailed, the Muslim Brotherhood, together with the Islamic Jihad, have established a record of Islamic resistance that can be claimed and drawn upon, and have built a tradition that can be used as a source of inspiration for future generations.

4

The Islamic Jihad

The Founding of
the Islamic Jihad

Context

■ The Islamic Jihad movement started as a splinter group of the Muslim Brotherhood Society. The 1967 war was a pivotal point in the evolution of the Muslim Brotherhood Society and the changes it went through. This war, from the standpoint of one of the Islamic Jihad founders, did not put only nationalist and secularist ideological orientations into a self-questioning posture. It also put the traditional religious orientation, led by the Muslim Brotherhood Society, in the same posture of self-questioning. The Muslim Brotherhood Society was held accountable and was not absolved of the burden of negligence and defeat. Despite the overwhelming influence of Islam in Arab culture and society, the Brotherhood, which was established in 1928 in Egypt, was not successful in countering the nationalist and secularist trends, or in preventing the defeat.[1] The 1967 defeat, from a viewpoint of the Islamic Jihad, was tantamount to a "second catastrophe" following that of 1948, and it was a complete collapse for the socialist revolutionaries, in terms both of their regimes and their programs.[2]

According to the Islamic Jihad movement in the Occupied Territories, the Muslim Brotherhood has gone through three stages. The first was the Hasan al-Banna stage (1928–1949), known as the "stage of insurrection." The second was the "stage of ordeal and retreat" (1949–1967). This stage witnessed the development of the society after Hasan al-Banna, the rise and fall of its influence, and the changes in its domestic and external relations. The third stage was the "stage of differentiation" within the society (1967–present).[3]

Following the 1967 war, intellectual and ideological differentiation within the Muslim Brotherhood Society began to emerge in a limited way, at least on the individual level. This war caused a severe shakeup within the Brotherhood and posed several questions pertaining to the crises of the society that were still unanswered. The search for solutions and alternatives continued for more than a decade. The Islamic revolution in Iran in 1979 came to offer an Islamic model that could be emulated. The Islamic Jihad movement in the West Bank and Gaza was the product of these factors. The Islamic model in Iran had great influence on the movement but it was not the only one.

The Beginnings

The official founding of the Islamic Jihad movement in Palestine took place against a backdrop of differences of opinion and the emergence of certain trends within the Muslim Brotherhood Society in Egypt. The founders of the Islamic Jihad were very much aware of these trends. While attending university in Egypt, the founders of the Islamic Jihad were exposed to militant Islamic groups such as *al-Takfir wal-Hijra* [the Atonement and Holy Flight] and the *Tandhim al-Jihad* [the Jihad Organization], both of which emerged from the Muslim Brotherhood ranks in the mid-seventies. There was also the Salih Sirriyya group, which was affiliated with the Islamic Liberation party and which in 1974 attacked the Egyptian Military Technical Academy.[4] The Jihad movement considers Sirriyya one of the first founders of the Islamic *jihad* tradition.

One of the first Islamic figures in the Occupied Territories to call publicly for *jihad* against the Israeli occupation was Ya'qub Qirrish, who was connected with the Fatah movement. Qirrish tried in 1977 to set up an organization to resist the Israeli occupation. He was arrested in early 1979 and expelled to Jordan. Although Qirrish's efforts were not sufficient to crystallize the new trend of thought in Islamic ranks, his endeavor contributed new ideas and set a precedent. Other Islamic figures followed suit later. Muhammad Abu-Tayr, another Fatah affiliate from Jerusalem, was arrested and sentenced to life imprisonment on charges of being engaged in military action. Abu-Tayr was released from prison in a prisoner exchange in 1985 between Israel and the Popular Front for the Liberation of Palestine-General Command (PFLP-GC). A third Islamic figure initiating the Islamic *jihad* trend in the Occupied Territories was Sheikh As'ad Bayoud al-Tamimi, the imam of al-Aqsa Mosque. Al-Tamimi had called for "the destruction of the Jewish state"[5] and for fighting the Jews "in an Islamic battle that will end your state, so that it will become part of history's residue."[6] Al-Tamimi, who was prevented by the Israeli authorities from returning to the West Bank in 1970, was a source of inspiration for all those who believed in the idea of *jihad* against Israel.

In Israel itself, a trend calling itself *Usrat al-Jihad* (the Family of Jihad) emerged from within the Muslim Brotherhood Society. This trend appeared in 1979, the year the Islamic revolution erupted in Iran. Sheikh 'Abdallah Nimr Darwish, the spiritual leader of the Family of Jihad, led this new trend. After he was jailed for three years on charges of belonging to an organization hostile to the state of Israel and carrying out several military operations, Darwish gave up his Islamic revolutionary ideas and visions. He returned to advocating religious education as a means of spreading the Islamic call and thereby moved closer to the traditional ideas of the Muslim Brotherhood. Darwish abandoned the idea of establishing an Islamic state in Palestine and criticized the ideas of Sa'id Hawwa, which call for an Islamic revolution, describing these ideas as inappropriate for the Muslims in Palestine.[7] Darwish also called for coexistence between the state of Israel and a future neighboring Palestinian state.[8]

The establishment of the Family of Jihad in Israel might have some relationship with the emergence of the Islamic Jihad in the West Bank and the Gaza Strip, but there is no evidence to indicate that there was a direct connection between Darwish and the founders of the Islamic Jihad. Darwish may, however, have offered another example to emulate for those who later founded the Islamic Jihad in the Occupied Territories.

After 1970, a number of Palestinian students from the West Bank and the Gaza Strip went to attend Egyptian universities. These students included members of the Muslim Brotherhood. The presence of these students in Egypt, close to the Muslim Brotherhood's mother organization, played an important role in crystallizing new ideas in their minds. The Palestine question and the Brotherhood's lack of satisfactory answers vis-à-vis Palestine sparked a search by these young students for an alternative. This search caused some of these students to break away from the Muslim Brotherhood.

In the period between 1967 and 1970, questions arose within the Brotherhood about the society's position towards the Israeli occupation and how to combat it. The issue of armed struggle was also debated. The Brotherhood leaders' response then was that the society should focus on the raising of an Islamic generation. These leaders justified noninvolvement in armed resistance against the occupation on the grounds that "the leadership of the struggle was not in Islamic hands."[9] Such answers were not satisfactory to the dissenting young Muslims.

In addition, there were other factors that motivated the breakaway from the society. The young Muslims believed that the society was ridden by "moral bankruptcy," notably the absence in the society of the spirit of criticism and new thinking and openness. According to the Jihad, the Islamic revival that started in the mid-seventies came partly as a reaction to the weakness of the Islamic movement and was the "natural and practical response to the previous stages, which had led our *umma* to two terrible catastrophes in less than 20 years,"[10] the catastrophes of the 1948 and 1967 defeats.

The Formal Emergence of the Islamic Jihad

The year 1980 is considered the official date of the founding of the Islamic Jihad movement in Palestine. The founders of this movement were two men from the Gaza Strip, Fathi al-Shaqaqi and 'Abd-al-'Aziz 'Auda. Al-Shaqaqi is one of the movement's most important thinkers, while 'Auda is the movement's spiritual leader. Al-Shaqaqi's family came from the village of Zarnuqa in the Ramla district of Palestine. In 1948, his parents fled to the Gaza Strip where they lived in a refugee camp in Rafah in the southern part of the Strip. Al-Shaqaqi's family came from modest socioeconomic origins. His father was a laborer. Al-Shaqaqi attended Birzeit University in the West Bank, graduated from the mathematics department, and worked as a teacher. While working, he studied for a second diploma and was admitted to the medical school of Zaqaziq University in Egypt. After graduation, al-Shaqaqi returned to work as a doctor at the Muttala' Hospital (Augusta Victoria) in Jerusalem. Later, he moved to work in the Gaza Strip.

During his university studies in Egypt, al-Shaqaqi was arrested twice in 1979. He was also imprisoned in Gaza in 1983 for eleven months. In 1986, he was again jailed and sentenced to four years of actual imprisonment and another five years of suspended sentence on charges of incitement against the Israeli occupation, transporting weapons to the Gaza Strip, and belonging to the Islamic Jihad movement. A short time before the completion of his prison term, the Israeli authorities deported him directly from prison to outside the Occupied Territories on August 1, 1988.

Prior to 1967, al-Shaqaqi was a Nasirite. The 1967 defeat had such an impact on him that he changed his orientation and joined the Muslim Brotherhood Society. However, by the end of 1974 and the beginning of 1975, al-Shaqaqi began to differ with the Muslim Brotherhood. His different political and ideological views were expressed in his book, *Al-Khomeini: al-Hall al-'Islami wal-Badil [Khomeini: The Islamic Solution and Alternative]*, published in 1979.

'Abd-al-'Aziz 'Auda's family came to the Gaza Strip from the Wadi al-Hasa area in the Bersheba district of Palestine in 1948. They lived in the Jabaliya refugee camp in the northern part of the Strip. 'Auda earned a degree in Arab and Islamic studies from Dar al-'Ulum in Cairo, as well as a diploma in the Islamic *shari'a*. When 'Auda returned to the Gaza Strip in 1981, he worked as a lecturer in the Islamic University in Gaza. In 1984, the Israeli authorities arrested 'Auda on charges of incitement and sentenced him to eleven months in prison, and in November 1987, the Israeli authorities deported him to Lebanon. 'Auda has an outstanding ability to preach and speak. While still in Gaza, 'Abd-al-'Aziz 'Auda earned the respect of many people in the Occupied Territories. Until their deportation, al-Shaqaqi and 'Auda were considered the two principal leaders of the Islamic Jihad movement in the Occupied Territories.

Leadership and Following

The leaders of the Jihad come from a new Islamic generation; they are young men in their thirties or early forties. The first founders and leaders of the movement, like 'Auda and al-Shaqaqi, came from the ranks of the Muslim Brotherhood, while others were originally members of the PLO factions and were recruited by the Islamic Jihad inside Israeli prisons. Jabr 'Ammar, a former officer in the Popular Liberation Forces (PLF) of the Palestine Liberation Army, was a founder of *al-Jama'a al-'Islamiyya* in the Israeli jails. This group had also set the stage for the emergence of the Islamic *jihad* tradition in Palestine. 'Ammar was arrested in the early seventies and sentenced to life imprisonment. He was released in a prisoner exchange in 1983 and was sent to Egypt. However, it was not long before he was deported from Egypt because of his antiregime activities.

Another leader of the Islamic Jihad is Ahmad Mahanna, a former officer in the PLF. Mahanna was one of the prominent Jihad leaders in the Israeli prisons. He was sentenced to life and then released in a prisoner exchange in 1985, but he was arrested again in 1986, on the charge of leading one of the Islamic Jihad's military groups. In jail, he was isolated from the rest of the detainees and was deported from the country on December 31, 1988. Other leading figures were Muhammad al-Jamal and Misbah al-Suri, who were former members of the PFLP and the PLF, respectively. Al-Jamal and al-Suri were recruited by the Jihad during their imprisonment in Israeli jails.

Some Jihad leaders were even secularists before they converted to fundamentalism. Among those leaders are Ramadan Shallah, Suleiman 'Auda, Fayez Abu-Mu'ammar, Nayef 'Azzam, Fayez al-Aswad, and Ahmad Mahanna.[11] A small number of the Jihad's founders were former activist students who had been expelled from Egyptian universities because of their underground activities there.

Followers of the Jihad are recruited in mosques and university campuses and through social activities. The Islamic Jihad members are known for their good organization, strict discipline, and absolute secrecy, especially with regard to armed activities. They are young Palestinians who were attracted to the militant positions embraced by the Islamic Jihad and were impressed by its violent activites. They were adherents to a new way of thinking characterized by enlightenment, debate, and heightened awareness. The Islamic Jihad followers go through hard ideological indoctrination and training.

Israeli jails have been a good place for recruiting new members for the Islamic Jihad movement. Islamic Jihad leaders in the Israeli jails were successful at recruiting many new members. Perhaps this was one reason why the Israeli authorities began to deport the Jihad leaders instead of keeping them in jail.

Members of the Islamic Jihad are religious fundamentalists who do not hesitate to carry out actions that they know in advance are dangerous. Khalid al-Ju'aidi, a Jihad member who took part in killing two Israelis, said during his trial: "We, the members of the Islamic Jihad Movement, show more interest in death than we do in life. We shall either liberate our land or die bravely in the attempt."[12]

The majority of Jihad followers come from modest social origins and live in poor neighborhoods and refugee camps. This following is primarily concentrated in the Gaza Strip. But the movement's small presence in the West Bank is constantly growing. Israeli security sources announce, from time to time, the discovery of secret cells of the Islamic Jihad.

Before the *intifada,* the Islamic Jihad members controlled four mosques in the Gaza Strip. One of these mosques, the 'Izz-al-Din al-Qassam Mosque, served as the headquarters of the Islamic Jihad's spiritual leader, 'Abd-al-'Aziz 'Auda. Two of the other mosques are also located in the city of Gaza, and the fourth mosque is in Rafah. The Islamic Jihad supervised a sports club which was frequented by youths sympathetic to the movement.

In the Islamic University in Gaza, the Islamic Jihad has a few hundred supporters among the student body, and it has a small but growing number of supporters in other universities of the Occupied Territories. There are also a number of Muslim Brotherhood members who have strong leanings toward the Islamic Jihad movement without openly declaring their sympathy.[13]

In the West Bank, the Islamic Jihad movement was responsible for the famous Gate of Moors operation on October 15, 1986. In this operation, three hand grenades were thrown by Islamic Jihad members at Israeli troops (conscripts from the Israeli Giv'ati Brigade) during a graduation ceremony near the Wailing Wall. About seventy soldiers were wounded and the father of one conscript was killed. The three youths who carried out the operation were Tariq al-Huleisi, 'Abd-al-Nasir al-Huleisi and Ibrahim Hasan I'liyyan.[14]

The members of the Jihad cell that planned to detonate a booby-trapped car in September 1987 inside Israel came from the areas of Nablus, Tulkarm, Qalqiliya, and Bethlehem. In August 1988, cells belonging to the Islamic Jihad had been discovered in the Hebron area.[15] In subsequent years, Islamic Jihad supporters, despite their small numbers compared to Hamas, were found all across the West Bank and Gaza. In any case, it is difficult to determine the actual size of the Islamic Jihad following and their areas of concentration because of the secrecy of the organization.

Doctrine and Ideology
The Islamic Jihad movement derives its ideology and political ideas from the Islamic tradition in general. Nevertheless, there are

three Islamic figures who enjoy special status among the leaders and followers of the Islamic Jihad and are considered worthy of emulation. They are Hasan al-Banna, Sayyid Qutb, and 'Izz-al-Din al-Qassam, in addition to the Ayatollah Khomeini, the leader of the Islamic revolution in Iran.

The Islamic Jihad views Hasan al-Banna as an Islamic leader who founded an Islamic renaissance movement by reconciling two Islamic orientations, one Salafi and the other reformist. Al-Banna's importance, from the Islamic Jihad's point of view, lies in three aspects that he emphasized in his attempt to revitalize the Islamic call. They are revival, organization, and upbringing. Hasan al-Banna's personality and the various roles he played provide a source of inspiration for both the supporters of the Muslim Brotherhood Society and the Islamic Jihad movement. He was the "founder of the Society, the builder of the organizational structure, the delineator of the content of the call, its goals and means, and the general overseer of guidance and implementation and all the work the [Islamic] call required."[16]

Sayyid Qutb occupies a special place for the Islamic Jihad movement. He is credited for his intellectual and ideological qualities and his ability to crystallize the aspects of the challenge that Muslims face, as well as his ideas regarding the way to confront that challenge. Qutb embodies the position of active oppposition to, and noncooperation with, the existing order, in contrast to Hasan al-Banna, who is known for his moderation. Qutb is a model for the Islamic fundamentalist leader and is considered by the Islamic Jihad movement a true symbol of revolutionary Islam. Qutb talked about an "Islamic vanguard," without which the Islamic renaissance will not be achieved. The Islamic Jihad sees in itself this vanguard. Moreover, Qutb led a new direction within the Muslim Brotherhood Society in his time, and today the Islamic Jihad movement sees itself as carrying out the same role.

Sayyid Qutb's books are sources of education and indoctrination for the Islamic Jihad movement. His book, *Ma'alim 'ala al-Tariq [Signs along the Way]*, is a piece of revolutionary analysis advocating a new Islamic way, different from the traditional one: "Today, we are in an age of ignorance like the ignorance which existed prior to the coming of Islam, and even worse. There is ignorance all around us, in the ideas of the people and their beliefs, customs and traditions, the sources of their culture, arts and literature, and their religious and secular laws. Much of what we regard as Islamic culture, Islamic philosophy, and Islamic thought is derived from this ignorance."[17]

The prominent Egyptian writer Hasan Hanafi refers to *Ma'alim 'ala al-Tariq* as a basic turning point in the development of Muslim Brotherhood thought. This book stresses the existence of a "severe contradiction between two thoughts, two concepts, two societies, two systems, and two truths: Islam and ignorance, belief and heresy, truth and falsehood, good and evil, the rule of God and the rule of man, God and Satan. . . . The existence of the one requires the destruction of the other. There is no way to compromise or mediate between the two."[18] According to this book, change cannot come about except through the overthrow of authority, the destruction of the imams of nonbelief, and putting the imams of belief in their place. There are no phases and no gradual progress in the process of change: "As the revolution in the person occurs through divine guidance, it occurs in society through the change of authority."[19] As for the mechanism of change, or the party that should implement this change, it is the "'believing elite,' a new Koranic generation (such as the generation of the first companions of the prophet Muhammad) that is capable of leading the society of belief against the society of nonbelief."[20] The Egyptian writer Muhammad Ahmad Khalafallah wrote that the ideas of Sayyid Qutb "are the foundation of Islamic consciousness and are the cause for the divisions within the Muslim Brotherhood Society and the emergence of splinter groups from it."[21]

Sheikh 'Izz-al-Din al-Qassam is the main source of inspiration for the Islamic Jihad movement. Al-Qassam is considered the movement's first pioneer. He is viewed as the first leader of the Palestinian armed resistance in the history of modern Palestine and the true father of the armed Palestinian revolution. Al-Qassam is an exalted and revered symbol. The Islamic Jihad's supporters have elevated him almost to a saintly status.[22]

Sheikh 'Izz-al-Din al-Qassam was a Syrian, born in the town of Jabla in Latakia in northern Syria in 1881. He received his education at al-Azhar, Egypt, where he was a student of Sheikh Muhammad 'Abdu. 'Abdu left his mark on al-Qassam's philosophy. As a result of al-Qassam's participation in the resistance to French colonialism in Syria, he was sentenced to death in absentia and fled to Haifa, Palestine, where he worked as a preacher in a mosque there. From the beginning, al-Qassam called for resisting British colonialism and

Zionist settlement in Palestine. His message was clear: "Jihad against Britain and its Zionist agents."[23]

There are a number of similarities between what al-Qassam and his supporters did in opposing Britain and what the Islamic Jihad is doing in its stuggle against the Israeli occupation. Al-Qassam, who is thought of as a symbol of belief, consciousness, and revolution, combined the call for *jihad* for the sake of God with the call for *jihad* for the sake of the country, raising the slogan "God's book in one hand, and the rifle in the other."[24] Al-Qassam believed that blood and revolution are the way to freedom and independence; therefore, he raised the banner of armed struggle instead of passive resistance.

The Islamic Jihad movement has emulated al-Qassam by selecting its followers with great care. A prospective member is carefully observed and put on probation before he is placed in a secret cell, composed of a small group of individuals who do not know one another.[25] Al-Qassam believed that the peasants and other poor classes in Palestine were the ones to be entrusted with carrying out the *jihad*. Perhaps that explains why the Islamic Jihad movement today is oriented toward the disadvantaged in the Occupied Territories.

Just as 'Izz-al-Din al-Qassam embarrassed the traditional leaders of his time with the pursuit of the *jihad*, the Islamic Jihad had embarrassed the Muslim Brotherhood Society before the *intifada*. The Islamic Jihad has engaged the Israeli occupation in armed resistance, while the Brotherhood avoided this kind of resistance. Al-Qassam, who was martyred in a confrontation with the British forces in 1935, understood that the pursuit of the *jihad* would end with his martyrdom. This is the same spirit that dominates the young men who join the ranks of the Islamic Jihad today.

Al-Qassam saw Britain and Zionism as two faces of the same coin, and the Islamic Jihad sees Israel and America in the same way. Al-Qassam believed that the Muslim Arabs in neighboring countries were a strategic depth for the Palestinian people and their revolution, but that the Palestinian people must depend on themselves first because those countries were under the oppression of imperialism.[26] Similarly, the Islamic Jihad movement believes that *jihad* for Palestine must be waged by the Palestinians without waiting for the prior victory of the Islamic call.

There are other similarities between al-Qassam's movement and the Islamic Jihad. Just as the battle of Ya'bad in Jenin was the real spark for the revolution that erupted in 1935 and continued until 1939, supporters of the Islamic Jihad believe that the daring operations that they carried out against the Israeli occupation shortly before the *intifada* were the spark that ignited this *intifada*. And just as al-Qassam and his colleagues rejected the principle of dialogue with Britain, in contrast to other nationalist groups and traditional political parties in the thirties,[27] the supporters of the Islamic Jihad refuse dialogue with Israel and the United States.

As it was not possible to ascertain the true number of al-Qassam's followers because of the secrecy of his organization, so too it is not possible to learn the number of the Islamic Jihad's following. Al-Qassam's followers were active inside prisons, and so was the Islamic Jihad, whose members recruited Palestinian prisoners in Israeli jails to their movement's ranks. Despite the fact that Islam is the primary and ultimate frame of reference for both al-Qassam's movement and the Islamic Jihad, the two movements embody a unique relationship between religion and nationalism. There is no doubt that al-Qassam's character, experience, and leadership left a lasting impact on Palestinian political culture.[28]

Al-Qassam was admired by non-Islamists for being a symbol for the poor and for embodying what they believed to be the path to salvation for the majority of the Palestinian people. He also personified two other dimensions, one nationalist and the other socialist. Al-Qassam was a Syrian Arab who opposed British imperialism and Zionism in Palestine, just as he had resisted French colonialism before in Syria. On the other hand, Al-Qassam was a protector and ally of the poor. He saw "the workers and peasants to be the most sincere groups, who were willing to work and sacrifice."[29]

The Islamic Jihad movement rejects putting a social class stamp on al-Qassam's ideas and practices: "We must forget the idea that the main motive behind the actions of al-Qassam and his followers was economic; they did not come from the most economically suffering class. He who can arm himself is economically able, and al-Qassam himself enjoyed a stable economic condition. Belief was the driving force of this vanguard, and awareness of the dangers of resistance and battle was the most important underlying factor in the making of the *jihad* tradition."[30]

With regard to the impact of the Islamic revolution in Iran on the doctrine and ideology of the Islamic Jihad movement, this revolution was a source of inspiration in terms of ideas and practice. From the outset, the Jihad's founders looked to Ayatollah Khomeini as a symbol and leader of the Islamic revolution and revival, not just in Iran but everywhere.[31] They tried to learn from the Iranian revolution and to apply its lessons in the Palestinian context. Until the eruption of the Islamic revolution in Iran, Islam was, from the Islamic Jihad's point of view, absent from the battlefield. This revolution proved to the Islamic Jihad that Islam was the solution and that *jihad* was the way.[32]

In addition to al-Qassam's experience, the Islamic Jihad also derived inspiration for its position on the issue of *jihad* in Palestine from the Iranian revolution, the Muslim Brotherhood tradition, and the experience of the Jihad Organization in Egypt. Islam, according to Khomeini, is "the religion of the *mujahidin* who want truth and justice. It is the religion of those who demand freedom and independence."[33] The founders of the Islamic Jihad in Palestine have been influenced by the Jihad Organization's experience in Egypt, by virtue of living this experience at close range. The Jihad Organization in Egypt believes that *jihad* is the only means of achieving the Islamic state. The Muslim Brotherhood's experience in the war of Palestine is recalled, but the articulations of Sayyid Qutb regarding *jihad* are considered a frame of reference.

Muhammad 'Abd-al-Salam Faraj's book *Al-Farida al-Gha'iba [The Absent Duty]* is considered the most important of the *jihad* literature. Faraj was the leader of the Jihad Organization and was responsible for issuing the order to assassinate President Sadat. In the words of Hasan Hanafi, this book has had an important influence on youth, because it reinforces the "self-confidence versus loss, pride versus submission, dignity versus humiliation, and power versus failure."[34] Dr. Hanafi describes the book, which totals no more than fifty pages, as having the potential of changing the face of Egypt and of upsetting the balance of power in the region.[35] Among the ideas contained in this book is that "learned men of religion today have ignored *jihad*, despite their knowledge that it is the only way to restore and raise the edifice of Islam again, and despite their awareness that the idols on this earth can only be removed by the power of the sword."[36]

The Islamic Jihad theoreticians believe that the danger of Israel lies not only in its occupation of Palestine, which is part of "*Dar al-Islam* (House of Islam), and the humiliation of its people, but also in the spread of Jewish corruption in it. Israel is a central part of a plan to fragment the Islamic *umma*, to westernize it, to subjugate it, to enslave it, to paralyze its will, and to cast an eternal yoke over its neck. . . . The planners wanted Israel to be a military power from which the [Arab] governments of partition will recoil and will wish to have a truce with, so these governments would surrender leadership to America to avoid Israel's evil . . . until this surrender brings subjugation and subordination and even leads to implementing the plans of the East and West in fighting Islam and the Muslims."[37] But the Islamic Jihad concludes that Israel is condemned to destruction and that it was born to be annihilated.[38] The movement agrees with Khomeini that the Islamic states, and all the Muslims in general, must "eliminate the element of corruption, Israel."[39]

From the point of view of the Islamic Jihad, Muslims who have ousted Israel from South Lebanon are the best Muslims. Fighting the "Torah adherents to the bone" can only be done through the "Islamic doctrine and the war of popular liberation."[40] Islam alone as a religion, as a history, as a culture, as a way of life is "capable of facing up to the crisis, of understanding it, of leading the struggle, and concluding it. . . . Islam represents the awareness of the *umma*."[41] In his book, *Khomeini: al-Hall al-Islami wal-Badil,* Fathi al-Shaqaqi cites a *fatwa* issued by Khomeini indicating that the endeavor to eliminate the "Zionist entity" is a religious duty.[42]

According to the Islamic Jihad, suicidal attacks are acts of martyrdom. These attacks comprise one of the principal ways in the tradition of *jihad.* They assume a special importance because of their symbolism as well as the other effects they have: "Perhaps it is a blessing of God Almighty bestowed upon one *mujahid* or two *mujahidin,* enabling him or them to charge against the enemy's position, or against a concentration of enemy military forces on a martyrdom mission, assaulting with explosives, smashing down everything around them, inflicting the heaviest losses, breaking down the enemy's morale and determination in the face of this Islamic spirit of martyrdom which cannot be resisted. At the same time, it increases fear of the Muslims after a long period of weakness and humiliation, and it increases the outpouring of new bloods which seek *jihad* for the sake of God."[43]

According to the spiritual leader of the Islamic Jihad, the problem of Muslims today lies in the new Western challenge they face. While facing this challenge, the Muslims strive to realize "objectives and goals." These objectives are "maximum" objectives represented in creating an Islamic revival in the world. As for the goals, they are lesser than the objectives, and are composed of "a long-range goal" aimed at "overcoming the crisis of the modern Western challenge" and "a short-range goal" aimed at "establishing the Islamic state and establishing the Islamic political power." All of these matters are related, "establishing the state, overcoming the crisis and creating the Islamic revival all come under the umbrella of pleasing God."[44]

As for Palestine and its liberation, the Islamic Jihad's philosophy is a distinct one, which does not restrict Islam's role to the mosque, as is the case in traditional Islamic practices. The Muslim Brotherhood, from the Islamic Jihad's point of view, concentrates on religious upbringing and education, in contrast to the nationalist factions of the PLO, which concentrate on struggle. The Muslim Brotherhood has chosen the "path of belief," and did not choose the "path of *jihad*." The nationalists chose the "path of *jihad*," and have avoided the "path of belief." The uniqueness of the Islamic Jihad movement lies in forging a dialectical relationship between the path of *jihad* and the path of belief.[45] In this sense, the Islamic Jihad blends religion and nationalism in its endeavor to annihilate Israel, combat Zionism, and establish an Islamic state in Palestine. These ideological positions are reflected in the Jihad movement's practices and activities. On one occasion, the flag of Israel was discovered in Gaza with "*allahu akbar* [God is great], death to Israel, the destruction of Israel is a Koranic imperative" written on it. In the middle of a Palestinian flag that was planted in the form of an arrow in the Star of David on the Israeli flag, the words "Islamic Jihad" were written.[46]

Unlike the Muslim Brotherhood Society, the Islamic Jihad is not a transnational movement in the organizational sense. However, the movement does have organizational following outside Palestine. It also has political and ideological affiliations and certain forms of coordination and cooperation with other Islamic organizations.

The Islamic Jihad does not have major local publications in the West Bank and the Gaza Strip. On certain occasions, the movement issues statements or pamphlets to clarify its position regarding a specific issue. However, there are certain Islamic publications which, to a considerable degree, reflect the Islamic Jihad's points of view. They are published abroad, but they find their way to the Occupied Territories. Among these publications is *Al-Tali'ah Al-Islamiyya,* a monthly magazine published in London and reflecting the line of the Islamic revolution in Iran. This magazine began publication in 1982 but ceased to appear a few years later. Another publication is *Al-Mukhtar Al-Islami,* also a monthly magazine, published in Cairo, expressing the opinions of the radical Islamic trend in Egypt. A third publication is entitled *Al-'Islam wa-Filastin* and is published in Cyprus. After the eruption of the *intifada,* the Islamic Jihad began to publish its own bulletin, *al-Mujahid,* which comes out of Lebanon.

With the founding of the Jihad movement, a new type of political Islam and Islamic leaders began to emerge in the Occupied Territories. From the outset, the Islamic Jihad and its leaders provided a new formulation in which religion and politics were directly and practically linked. Therefore, the Jihad movement constituted a challenge, not only to the Muslim Brotherhood Society, but also to the rest of the Palestinian nationalist factions inside the Occupied Territories. The Islamic Jihad was able, by presenting Islam as a force of resistance, to attract the sympathy and acceptance of a growing number of people. The case of the Islamic Jihad may prove that linking Islam with the rifle is a major formula to gain popular support.

The special nature of the Islamic Jihad movement lies in its being an organization that was founded and developed inside the Occupied Territories. By virtue of its ideology and the nature of its leaders, membership, strategy, and tactics, the Jihad movement seemed to have a potential no other group has. In contrast to the Muslim Brotherhood Society and the PLO factions, the Islamic Jihad movement does not subject itself to the political and diplomatic considerations to which the rest of the organizations do. It does not receive directions from abroad that might contradict reality at home. However, the Islamic Jihad has not so far achieved the expected takeoff. The rise of the movement was curbed essentially by harsh Israeli measures and by the rise of Hamas as a competitive militant force.

Strategy vis-à-vis Palestine

The Islamic Jihad movement considers Palestine its central issue, in contrast to the Muslim Brotherhood Society, which regards the victory of the Islamic call as the central issue and the prelude to resolving the Palestinian problem in an Islamic way. Sheikh 'Abd-al-'Aziz 'Auda says "I am a Palestinian Muslim; I consider Palestine the most important nation in the Islamic world. I hope that an Islamic state will be established there; we dream of this."[47] Like the Muslim Brotherhood, the Islamic Jihad sees the Palestinian problem as an Islamic problem and not a national or pan-Arab nationalist issue that concerns the Arabs only, but rather a problem that concerns the entire Islamic nation. As for the most appropriate solution to this problem, the Islamic Jihad believes in an Islamic popular war of liberation, resulting in the destruction of Israel and the creation of an Islamic state in Palestine.[48]

The Islamic Jihad thinks that Palestine has come to its present condition because of the role of "the opportunistic non-Islamic leaderships, which successively led the masses, or which seized power following the defeat of the Islamic state at the beginning of this century."[49] The Islamic Jihad believes that the Arab nationalist movement "was a legitimate son of the Western assault against the Islamic nation," and the the Zionist movement also began "as an authentic part of that attack."[50] The failure of the non-Islamic leaderships, according to the Islamic Jihad, was repeated in 1948 and 1967 and is reflected in the inability of these leaderships to continue, and to truly understand, the struggle. This failure is evident today in the practices of "those who claim to lead the Palestinian people" and in the plans that they put forth to solve the Palestinian issue.[51]

A publication that reflects the Islamic Jihad's views describes what happened in 1967 in the following way:

On the Jewish side stands an individual [the Jew] with a long, historical and doctrinal identity, with his war for the land, the land of Palestine, as part of that identity. Moreover, the Jew in Israel is an integral part of a modern, materialistic culture, or rather, he is its true essence, who possesses its tools, its way of life, values, and methods, and who supports it totally. . . . On the other side stands a human being whose [political] regimes divested him of his true, historical and doctrinal identity, and divested him of 13 centuries of history and culture, and gave him 50 years or less of intellectual distortion, anxiety, and a contradictory and alien sense of belonging. On this side stands the individual of the Islamic homeland, on whose face they tried to put the mask of the Western culture, without being able to fit the mask around the original features. The [Islamic] nation did not turn out for battle with the tools of the Western culture, and its approach and methods. Nor has it turned out with its own traditional features, and authentic approach.[52]

In his booklet *Ma baʿd al-Nakbatayn [After Two Catastrophes]*, published in 1968, the Islamic writer Tawfiq al-Tayyib wrote that the disaster of 1948 was a defeat for liberal Arab thought, whereas the rout of 1967 was a defeat for Arab socialist and revolutionary ideas. This booklet is considered by the Islamic Jihad leaders in Palestine as one of the most important Islamic documents to be published after the 1967 defeat.[53] Al-Tayyib believes that the Arab catastrophe was in essence an intellectual catastrophe, a catastrophe of modern Arab thought: "The disaster in our ideas came before the disaster in our land . . . and was the prelude, and the long term cause, for the disaster in the land."[54] The Zionist presence in Palestine, according to al-Tayyib, is "an embodiment of the modern Western challenge, and an evidence that this challenge still exists. . . . The natural reaction to the challenge lies in the Islamic trend which constitutes the defense line. And despite our harsh criticism of this trend, it has played a historic role in the restoration of the psychological balance of both the Islamic community and of the educated Muslim."[55] According to this position, the Islamic solution continues to be the final and divinely guided solution, which is bound to fill the vacuum in the ongoing ideological and political struggle.[56]

The Islamic Jihad movement believes in the armed struggle as a strategy for political action. Contrary to the Muslim Brotherhood's point of view, the Islamic Jihad does not insist on the Islamic transformation of society as a prerequisite to the liberation of Palestine and the establishment of an Islamic state in it.[57] The Brotherhood believes that Islam must prevail in society before the struggle for Palestine starts. The Islamic Jihad's position gives priority to the elimination of Israeli rule. This goal can only be achieved through *jihad,* which cannot be delayed under any pretext. Like the Brotherhood, the Islamic Jihad rejects any form of recognition of Israel and opposes all proposed political settlements.

The Islamic Jihad has focused its activities on armed struggle against the Israeli occupation. The Jihad differs in this context from the rest of the factions that adopt this tactic. When it started its operations against Israeli targets, the Islamic Jihad refrained from claiming responsibility for these operations, in order not to give the Israeli authorities any justification to prosecute its members. Despite that, the Islamic Jihad left its special mark on the operations it undertook. The Islamic Jihad attacks were usually noted for their effectiveness and success. After repeated Israeli blows prior to and after the outbreak of the *intifada*, the Islamic Jihad began to claim responsibility for operations it undertook in order to prove its continued existence.

Among other spectacular operations of the Islamic Jihad, in addition to the Gate of Moors attack, was the successful escape from the Gaza Central Prison of six Jihad members, the killing of Captain Ron Tal, commander of the Israeli military police in the Gaza Strip on August 2, 1987, and the violent clash between Jihad members and the Israeli security forces in the al-Shija'iyya area of Gaza city on October 6, 1987, which resulted in the death of an Israeli security officer, in addition to the four members of the Jihad cell.

In its military operations, the Islamic Jihad uses knives and daggers, as well as firearms. The Jihad obtains its weapons from different sources. These weapons are smuggled in from Jordan or Egypt or by sea, stolen from the Israeli army, or purchased from the underworld in Israel. Certainly, obtaining weapons from the underworld carries security risks. This way of obtaining weapons can provide Israeli security forces with leads to members of the Jihad.

Members of the Islamic Jihad are usually subjected to the harshest punishments. They are perceived by the Israeli authorities as highly dangerous. The military court in Gaza on March 12, 1987, sentenced 'Abd-al-Rahman Fadl al-Qiq and Khalid Mutawi' al-Ju'aidi to life imprisonment, after convicting them of killing three Israelis with knives.[58] Before the outbread of the *intifada*, there were fifty to sixty members of the Islamic Jihad incarcerated in Israeli jails for carrying out armed actions or attempting to carry out such actions against the occupation.[59]

Despite severe Israeli punishment, which included long-term imprisonment, deportations, and in a few cases, killings, the material presence of the movement, contrary to some expectations, has not been destroyed. On the first anniversary of the famous al-Shija'iyya operation, the Jihad followers distributed a statement in the Gaza Strip calling on the people to observe a strike. This appeal received a widespread response from the various nationalist forces and the population at large. On the same day, Jihad members threw hand grenades at an Israeli military patrol in the Sheikh Radwan neighborhood in Gaza, and wounded two Israeli soldiers.

Subsequently, the Islamic Jihad movement in Palestine claimed responsibility for a series of operations against Israeli targets, such as the hand grenade attack against an Israeli patrol in Khan-Yunus in the Gaza Strip on August 4, 1989, in which four Israeli soldiers were wounded.[60] There was also the firebombing in Ramallah on August 14, 1989, of an Israeli Civil Administration vehicle, in which four Israeli tax collectors were injured.[61] Nidal Zallum, who carried out a knife attack on several Israelis on Jaffa Street in West Jerusalem on May 3, 1989, killing two and injuring three others, belonged to the Islamic Jihad. A faction of the Islamic Jihad headed by Sheikh As'ad Bayoud al-Tamimi claimed responsibility for the attack on the Israeli tourist bus on the Isma'iliyya-Cairo road in January 1990 in which eight Israelis were killed and a few others were injured. Other spectacular operations claimed by the Islamic Jihad include the July 7, 1989, derailment of an Israeli bus on the Tel-Aviv-Jerusalem highway by a member of the Jihad, killing 14 Israelis and injuring several others, as well as several knife attacks resulting in the death of a number of Israelis. As described by an Israeli journalist, "the Islamic Jihad is a plant that, as soon as it is cut off, it grows bigger and stronger once again."[62]

The Islamic Jihad and the PLO

Until the *intifada,* there was no direct coordination or cooperation between the Islamic Jihad movement and factions of the PLO, with the exception of the Fatah movement. Islamic Jihad supporters do not agree with the secular orientation of the various PLO factions, expecially those factions with Marxist beliefs. The Islamic Jihad regards the PLO's goal of establishing a secular democratic state in Palestine as incompatible with the Islamic view of history.[63] However, the Islamic Jihad's positions toward the PLO and its factions can generally be described as ambiguous and two-faceted. This attitude reflected to a considerable degree the position of the Iranian revolution vis-à-vis the PLO, which started as being supportive, but soon became ambivalent when the PLO failed to toe the line of the Islamic revolution.

The Fatah movement is the closest of the PLO factions to the Islamic Jihad. The fact of the matter is that there is some affinity between the two organizations. Fatah's ideological view of the Palestinian issue is closer to the Islamic Jihad's view than it is to the Muslim Brotherhood's. The Jihad movement views Fatah positively, because of the Islamic background of Fatah's first founders. Fatah, in the view of the Islamic Jihad, was "born out of an Islamic attempt to respond to the crisis of the Islamic trends in 1955–58."[64] Fatah was tempered in "the furnace of *fedayeen* operations in Gaza in the years from 1954–66, and it was born from the womb of the Muslim Brotherhood experience, and in the backdrop of the political and intellectual struggles, which the Brotherhood lived in that period."[65] As for those who are in charge of Fatah, the Jihad argues that all of them were the sons of the Islamic movement: "Yasir Arafat, Khalil al-Wazir, Salah Khalaf, 'Abd-al-Fattah al-Hmud, Kamal 'Udwan, Muhammad Yusef al-Najjar, Mamduh Saydam, Mahmud Abbas, and Salim al-Za-'nun. One should not forget that the first military communique issued by al-'Asifa forces [military wing of Fatah] began with the mention of the name of God, followed by a verse from the Koran."[66]

According to the Islamic Jihad, Fatah embodied the aspirations of the Palestinian people: "The Fatah Movement is not only the largest of the Palestinian movements, and not only the mother of the contemporary armed revolution (since its inception in 1965), but it is also a microcosm of the Palestinian people at home and abroad, in all their past and present interactions, struggles, sensitivities, and contradictions. . . . Because of that, Fatah is constantly at the center of the concerns of the Palestinian people of all affiliations."[67]

However, the Islamic Jihad does not hesitate to criticize Fatah. This is reflected mostly in voicing differences on the ideological and political levels, especially after Fatah had changed into a "mixture of Islam, nationalism, liberalism, and finally leftist ideas."[68] After the Fatah leadership changed into "a nationalist leadership of the same mold as other liberation movements in Third World countries, and began to fluctuate between Islam and nationalism, it became a mixture of tradition, liberalism, and nationalism, and turned away from its Islamic essence. This change has forced Fatah to adopt a policy of maneuvers, parallel positions, balances, and domestic and foreign bargains to maintain equilibrium and safeguard itself and the accomplishments it achieved! This policy has prevented any possibility for an Islamic evolution within the Fatah movement, and has changed those who yesterday were Muslim leaders into professional politicians, and dignitaries competing for influence and status."[69]

In a clear reference to Fatah, Sheikh 'Abd-al-'Aziz 'Auda wrote: "We do not accept the slogan raised by the PLO's main faction with regard to noninterference in the internal affairs of the Arab countries. We regard the Arab regimes and rulers as a reason for enforcing the backwardness and defeat in the Arab world. We do not accept a truce with them. We believe that the Palestinian revolution is the most important and most active national liberation movement in the region, and that this revolution must strengthen its alliances with the Iranian revolution, the true ally of the Palestinian revolution. Despite that, we see the Palestinian revolution, as well as the Muslim Brotherhood, attacking the Iranian revolution. But our political and ideological differences with the PLO do not justify the use of violence against the nationalist forces. We respect the views of the main faction [Fatah] and all nationalist forces, because we believe in dialogue as the only means to reach a mutual understanding. Our main dispute is with the Israeli occupation."[70]

It is not easy to determine the nature of the relationship between Fatah and the Islamic Jihad and whether this relationship does in fact exist as a coordinated strategy, or just a functional relationship between groups or wings in the two movements. The Islamic Jihad rejects Fatah's claims about its relationship with the Jihad and points out that Fatah and others try to gain credibility through linking their names with the Islamic Jihad. They want to take the credit for the achievements of the Palestinian Islamists:

> Most of the Palestinian Marxist and secular organizations have claimed responsibility for the Islamic Jihad's operation (the Gate of Moors) as their own, in an attempt to get themselves through the doors of the masses and, consequently, to market themselves in the Palestinian political marketplace. These organizations trade in the blood of the Muslim people in Palestine. For example, Yasir Arafat announced from Kuwait that the Islamic Jihad was responsible for the (Gate of Moors) operation, but he falsified the facts by his erroneous claims that the Islamic Jihad organization was a religious organization that belongs to the Fatah Movement, and that he founded this organization for the purpose of *jihad!* This is not the

first attempt by Mr. Arafat. Before that, he tried to profit from the Islamic resistance in South Lebanon, in order to cover up the criminal negotiating role the Palestinian leadership was undertaking with the Zionist left, and to justify the negotiations and meetings with the butcher of Amman (King Hussein) and to distort the truth about the Islamic Jihad Movement. His number two man in the Fatah movement, who is known as Abu-Iyad, has maneuvered and camouflaged the truth from the masses, in an attempt to adopt the Islamic Jihad, after the failure of the Palestinian revolution inside Palestine.[71]

But Fatah sources define the relationship with the Islamic Jihad as one of cooperation. These sources suggest that the Fatah leaders, especially Abu-Jihad, encouraged the idea of Islamic *jihad,* particularly after the Islamic movement had become an effective force in the Occupied Territories. Abu-Jihad was aware of the religious propensity of the Palestinian people and fully understood the role of Islam as a driving force in society. Abu-Jihad believed that if Islam could be manipulated, it would become a formidable force in confronting the occupation. During the *intifada* in particular, the Islamic character of resistance to the Israeli occupation became more apparent. The nationalists have become aware of that, and the leaflets of the United National Leadership of the *intifada* began to include many religious references.

Even before the *intifada,* Abu-Jihad tried to win over a group of young Muslims who were disenchanted with the nationalist factions as well as with the Muslim Brotherhood. Since 1982, he encouraged a trend within Fatah to extend all forms of support to those Palestinian Islamists who believed in the idea of *jihad* in Palestine. This trend was led by Muhammad Basim al-Tamimi (Hamdi), who is considered one of the prominent military leaders in Fatah. Hamdi was one of the three Palestinians assassinated in Cyprus on February 14, 1988. The Israeli Intelligence was accused of this assassination.[72] A publication that reflects the views of the Islamic Jihad stated that Hamdi and Muhammad Bahais (Abu-Hasan Qasim), who was also assassinated in Cyprus with Marwan Ibrahim al-Kayyali, "saw the Palestinian issue in essence and first and foremost as an Islamic issue."[73]

It is believed that Fatah did provide military and logistical support to the Islamic Jihad before the movement diversified its sources of support to include Iran and Islamic groups in some Arab countries.

Radio Israel reported that individuals of the Islamic Jihad cell, who planned to detonate a booby-trapped car in front of a government building in West Jerusalem in September 1987, had received their military training in several Arab countries, including Jordan, Iraq, Syria, and Algeria, and that each of them received individualized training. One of the cell members, Suleiman Zahiri, an engineer from Tulkarm, had received his training in Pakistan in a camp belonging to the Afghani Resistance. The report added that the cell members had received instructions from Amman, indicating that the Islamic Jihad had some kind of connection with Fatah.[74]

While the Islamic Jihad received support from Fatah and maintained a relationship with it, the movement was eager to maintain its independence and its distinct ideological and political views. However, after the eruption of the *intifada,* the Islamic Jihad was more willing than the Muslim Brotherhood to coordinate with Fatah and the Unified National Leadership of the *intifada,* despite its refusal to join the UNL formally.

Like the Muslim Brotherhood, the Islamic Jihad calls upon Fatah to return to Islam before it is too late. The movement states that the revolutionary Islamic position "makes it incumbent upon us to be concerned about Fatah so it does not become a scapegoat for Arab and international intrigues, which would force the movement to drop the rifles which it is raising against the enemy."[75] The Jihad movement goes on to say: "Once again the region looks as if it is returning to the time of the collapse of the Army of Salvation, and the battalions of the Holy Jihad, in 1948. Arafat in his tragic situation looks like Hajj Amin [al-Husseini], deported, and banished without being pursued, far from his country. The pieces of the long dream have fallen on the steps of the deteriorating reality."[76] The only solution from the Islamic Jihad's point of view lies "in the advance of the forces of revolutionary Islam to occupy the lost space, on the basis of *jihad* against the enemies. . . . Between the end of the forties and the beginning of the eighties are thirty years, a thousand experiences and another generation on the move."[77]

The Islamic Jihad's position toward the PLO faction is defined in a book published by one of the movement's leaders in Palestine. The book, circulated on a limited scale in the Occupied Territories, indicates that these factions, which have damaged "our people, our cause and our *umma,*" because of their leadership of the Palestinian people, were able to do so because of "the Islamists' absence."[78]

The book also states the following:

> We Islamists neither hate nor reject these organizations, groups, and political parties, nor oppose them because they are carrying arms against the Zionist foe, but because they are not carrying Islam, nor ruling by the Koran. . . . We want these organizations and groups to discard all the anti-Islamic ideas, doctrines, programs, and slogans. . . . We want them to be committed to Islam, to the Koran and the Sunna, in word and deed, in everything, small and large, and to adopt the Islamic doctrine and carry weapons simultaneously. However, and regrettably, we note that these organizations have categorically rejected, and still reject commitment to Islam, from their inception until today. They have adopted constitutions, principles, charters, and manmade doctrines which have no relationship to Islam. Based on that, we will not accept, and our Muslim people will not accept, and our *umma* will not accept the leadership of these organizations.[79]

Other PLO factions may view the Islamic Jihad with anxiety. The daring attacks of the Jihad on Israeli targets have embarrassed those factions that could not match the movement in this sphere. It was therefore natural for some of these smaller factions to cast doubts on the Islamic Jihad. A publication reflecting the views of a marginal Palestinian Communist group, the Revolutionary Workers party, which is supported by Fatah, stated:

> Despite the tangible progress in the Islamic Jihad's positions, particularly in its struggle against the occupation which, from the political standpoint is inspired by the Palestinian nationalist position, the Jihad's tactics towards the United National Leadership and, consequently, the PLO, allude to what these tactics hide. The position of the Islamic Jihad is still one of opposition to the democratic and secular nature of the PLO. The Jihad attempts to Islamize the PLO, even though it does not state this goal explicitly. On this basis, the leaders of this movement express their willingness to cooperate and coordinate only with Fatah and not with the other Palestinian organizations. This position reveals the attempt by this movement to attain a level of achievement that would enable it to compete with the democratic nationalist orientation which the PLO represents.[80]

The leftists believe that the ideological position of the Islamic Jihad does not differ from the Muslim Brotherhood's position, especially with regard to the PLO. While the Jihad does not object to co-operation with Fatah, it, like the Muslim Brotherhood, refuses to join the PLO.

The Islamic Jihad movement argues that there is room for all to pursue the struggle: "The Islamic Jihad is keen on avoiding any clash with any other Palestinian force, whether Islamic or secular, and believes that the battlefield is wide enough for all."[81] In a clear reference to the Muslim Brotherhood and their position regarding secularist factions, one Islamic source wrote that the Islamic Jihad has "efficiently and consciously sidestepped a trap into which other Islamists operating in Palestine have fallen, by getting involved in unfortunate clashes with some Palestinian secularist factions."[82]

But the most important nationalist endorsement for the Islamic Jihad came from George Habash, the leader of the Popular Front for the Liberation of Palestine, the second largest faction in the PLO after Fatah. Habash stated: "Let me stress my warm welcome to the Islamic Jihad inside occupied Palestine. This phenomenon has struck painful blows at the Zionist enemy. I declare that we extend our hand to this movement, in order to establish various forms of cooperation in opposition to the Zionist enemy, who occupies our land and oppresses the masses of our people."[83] Habash differentiated between the Islamic Jihad movement and the Muslim Brotherhood. He stated that while the Islamic Jihad focused its attention on Israel and directed its military attacks against it, the reactionary trends in the Islamic movement intentionally manufac-tured confrontations with nationalist and progressive forces.[84] Re-garding the future of the Islamic trend in the Occupied Territories, Habash said: "I believe that the religious trend will be able to take over in the event the PLO ceases to pursue armed struggle and continue to proceed on a course of deviation and capitulation. In this event, the Palestinian masses which seek the liberation of Pales-tine will rally behind those forces that they feel are capable of continuing the struggle to achieve this goal."[85]

The Islamic Jihad and the *Intifada*

Islamic Jihad members were among the first elements to partic-ipate in the *intifada*. There is sufficient evidence to suggest that they were extremely active in ensuring its continuation, especially at its early stages. However, the active participation did not continue for long, because of the repeated blows they suffered at the hands of the Israeli authorities. These blows prevented the Jihad from attaining more tangible influence among the population, despite the clear sympathy the movement had won. The Islamic Jihad resorted to violent tactics to make up for the decline in its participation in the activities of the *intifada*.

In the early pamphlets it had issued, as well as in its graffiti, the Islamic Jihad had avoided taking any stands against the positions of the Unified National Leadership. In fact, some sort of coordination has taken place between the Jihad and the UNL, especially during confrontations with the Israeli troops. In contrast to the Muslim Brotherhood, the statements of the Islamic Jihad did not in the beginning directly reject the idea of a Palestinian state. These statements also refrained from making any mention of the PLO. Without a doubt, the Jihad movement's initial participation in the *intifada* reinforced its status, especially in contrast to the Muslim Brotherhood Society. The Jihad was taking a middle-of-the-road position. An Islamic Jihad leader said: "The Jihad is the only organization capable of bringing the traditional Muslim trend into the *intifada*. Even now, the Israelis are doing everything in their power to create opposition between the Islamists and the nationalists, especially in Gaza. But we represent the intersecting point between the two trends."[86]

The incompatibility between the positions of the Islamic Jihad and those of the PLO began to emerge more clearly during and in the aftermath of the resolutions of the PNC's nineteenth session. While the council was in session, the Jihad issued a statement in which it opposed the political plans submitted to the council. After the resolutions were adopted, the Islamic Jihad issued another statement condemning the acceptance of UN resolution 242 and stating that the acceptance of that resolution meant conceding an important part of Palestine. This "comes after years of placating and deceiving the people, even at the last minute, since the Document of Independence [issued by the PLO] is merely a show."

The Jihad statement added that acceptance of resolution 242 "shifts the future of the battle from a battle against the enemy to a battle on the Palestinian scene itself," and that the Palestinian state, if established, "would not only be separated from the rest of

Palestine, but rather, would not be a state for all the Palestinian people, especially those who are scattered in the diaspora or who are still within the 1948 borders [Israel]. . . . Finally it would form a true bridge for the expansion of Zionism throughout the whole region."[87] The statement added that the recognition of resolution 242 comes in the absence from the council of the fighting groups, and in the absence of an important segment of the Palestinian people, the segment of political Islam "which is always present on the Palestinian battlefield."[88] The Islamic Jihad also warned against transforming the *intifada* from a tool of liberation into a tactical maneuver to stir the Palestinian issue, as happened after the October 1973 war, when Egyptian president Anwar al-Sadat exploited the results of the war to stir the Arab-Israeli issue, and not to liberate the land.[89]

The Islamic Jihad regards the actions of the PLO leadership as tantamount to political suicide: "The political suicide into which the PLO leadership is plunging is similar to the step-by-step approach that begins with exploiting the *intifada,* and ends with aborting it through the undoing of the elements of its strength, unity, and cohesion, and the use of its remnants to sign an agreement that, in the best of cases, will not go beyond autonomy which is included in the Camp David Accords."[90] The Jihad also expressed its reservations over the attitude of the PLO leaders toward the Palestinian issue in the aftermath of the PNC resolutions: "This attitude continues to be known today in the official political dictionary of the Palestinian leadership as realism and rationalism. It derives its strength from the weakness of the *umma*. The weakness of the *umma* is being used as a pretext to emphasize this official position. And instead of looking at the weakness of the *umma* as a strong reason to identify the causes of this weakness . . . [that] weakness was made a strong pretext to carry through the policy of the *fait accompli*."[91]

In a later statement, distributed by the Islamic Jihad on March 20, 1989, the movement declared that it was "innocent before God of all bargaining over our rights in all of our homeland, or of willingness to renounce any inch of our holy land. . . . We are innocent before God of any call for the so-called elections or for the so-called international conference or any formula that brings down on the owners of those rights the curse of conceding their rights."[92] Finally, the Islamic Jihad movement wonders whether it was possible to remove or wrest away the representation the PLO leadership has exercised throughout the last two decades. The Jihad's answer is that the PLO leadership is "like the cat which licks the wound. . . . While it was enjoying the taste of its own blood, it believed that it was drinking the blood of someone else."[93]

Undoubtedly, the Islamic Jihad movement, as a concept and as an organization, has dug its roots inside the Occupied Territories as a political force. This movement embodies a form of political Islamic resurgence more than it embodies a revival of religious practices or moral conduct. By its daring actions against the Israeli occupation, the Islamic Jihad argues that it played a role in restoring confidence among the people following a period of decline, indifference, and recess of Palestinian nationalist struggle.

However, the future of the Islamic Jihad movement does not depend only on the quality of its own performance. Rather, this future will also be determined by four other factors. The first factor is the Muslim Brotherhood's position toward the Palestinian issue and the changes that may occur in this position. The second factor relates to the performance of the PLO factions and their success or failure in maintaining their support among the Palestinians of the Occupied Territories. The third factor is the reaction of the Israeli authorities and the means these authorities will use in dealing with the Islamic Jihad. The fourth factor is the level of support the Islamic movements outside Palestine are willing to give the Islamic Jihad.

The Islamic Jihad and the Muslim Brotherhood

The Islamic Jihad movement and the Muslim Brotherhood Society share the broad lines of the Islamic ideology. Both groups seek to establish an Islamic state and apply Islamic principles in an Islamic society as an ultimate goal. The differences between the two groups are not epistemological or doctrinal, but rather emanate from their different understanding and interpretation of the doctrine in the way it deals with the various Islamic issues, in particular, the political and the social.

Islamic writers who are sympathetic to the idea of the Islamic

Jihad argue that the Muslim Brotherhood has lost the living and correct perspective of history and deals with this history as if it were scattered events, not governed by a framework or law. Consequently, the Brotherhood does not understand the reality around it. It is not completely aware of how to define the basic features of history and sometimes does not understand the need to search for them. The society has lost the correct vision and does not "sense the Israeli era which is creeping everywhere. It inflates small issues while the large issues are marginalized."[94]

In its criticism of the Muslim Brotherhood, the Islamic Jihad relies on the writings and ideas of Islamic writers such as the prominent Muslim thinker Fathi Yakin. Yakin writes: "The battle that is going on today between Islam and the *jahiliyya* [pre-Islamic age of ignorance] is no longer waged on the level of pure scientific discussion or within the bounds of purposeful, intellectual debate. . . . The struggle has become bloody and fierce in the real sense of the word."[95] Yakin adds: "The Islamic movement ought to be the academy that produces the *mujahidin* and heroes, before being an intellectual academy propagating culture and pure Islamic concepts among the people. . . . We need consciousness, profoundness, and wisdom, just as we need courage, sacrifice, and boldness. . . . The tyranny of the principle of seeking safety and exaggerating this principle and adopting it as a permanent policy at all times and in every circumstance and on all levels, will only result in the permanent killing of the spirit of sacrifice in individuals and will transform the Islamic movement into a theoretical school or simply into one orientation of thinking."[96]

Yakin also writes: "In order for the Islamic movement to shoulder its responsibilities, it must reconsider its basic principles . . . its internal structure, educational programs, direction, means of operation, and methods of confrontation . . ."[97] because "the methods the Islamic movement had relied upon throughout the past years always lacked the exploration and evolution required to cope with the Islamic cause and the events and circumstances that surrounded it. If the Islamic orientation needs to develop its methods and programs, it is even in greater need to explore the value of planning and its role in enabling the Islamic cause and the Islamic movement to achieve their goals and objectives. . . . The failure and the setbacks that afflicted the Islamic movement stemmed in particular from confusion in the methods of learning and the negligence in the areas of planning."[98]

Fathi Yakin concludes: "There is another justification that necessitates the establishment of one international Islamic movement. The challenges facing Islam come in fact from international movements, such as Zionism, Masonry, communism, and the crusading missionary movements. . . . These international movements, with their vast human, material and technical capabilities and resources, cannot be matched except by equivalent means and levels. Failing to do so will mean nothing but retreat and destruction."[99]

Fathi al-Shaqaqi, leader of the Islamic Jihad movement in Palestine, says that "if the Islamic movement's absence was understandable and justified during the fifties and sixties (because the battle had not yet been determined in favor of Islam as the sole and overwhelming choice), one cannot understand, nor justify today's baffling absence of the Islamic movement from occupying its true position in the leadership of this stage, directing its events and controlling its variables."[100]

Al-Shaqaqi holds the Muslim Brotherhood responsible for the indifference of the Islamic youth, putting the blame on the methods of formation the Brotherhood adopts. These methods are, in most cases, "static and detached from the ever changing social, political, economic and intellectual reality."[101] Al-Shaqaqi questions the ability of the traditional Islamic movement to "tear up its methodological, ideological, and political cocoon, in order to catch up with the movement of history, and join with the masses in their daily preoccupations and in all their small and large concerns."[102]

The Islamic Jihad movement considers Hasan al-Banna, the founder of the organization of the Muslim Brotherhood Society, a principal leader and a symbol for *jihad* as well as the inventor of new Brotherhood principles. In this respect, reference is made to the Brotherhood volunteers whom al-Banna dispatched to Palestine in 1947–1948. But the Islamic Jihad movement blames the Muslim Brotherhood for not having a correct understanding of what Hasan al-Banna represents, and for not being committed to the essence of his ideas and positions.

The Islamic Jihad stresses the difference in its interpretation of Islam vis-à-vis the Muslim Brotherhood's interpretation. Sheikh 'Abd-al-'Aziz 'Auda says: "Our interpretation of Islam is not engulfed in ambiguity. It is based on our understanding of the social, political, and economic dimensions of the lives of the people. As for the Islamic reform movement (the Muslim Brotherhood), it regards the use of words such as 'masses,' 'nation,' 'Palestine,' and the like, to be satanic. But what we understand is that Islam talks about the complaints of the masses and their needs."[103]

From the Islamic Jihad's point of view, the problems of the Arab society cannot be solved by gradual reform. Therefore, the Islamic Jihad rejects the Muslim Brotherhood's traditional ideas and practices in all aspects of daily life and argues that the alternative to that reformist approach is revolutionary action by an Islamic vanguard, capable of imposing an Islamic system that can launch an all-out war against Israel.[104]

Generally the Islamic Jihad movement regards itself as the antithesis of the reformist orientation of the Muslim Brotherhood Society. It represents a trend of "decisiveness and revolution," in contrast to the trend of "truce, patching and reform."[105] The Islamic Jihad considers itself a source of challenge to the Brotherhood, because of the latter's lack of commitment to an all-out battle against Israel. The Jihad movement blames the Brotherhood for its moderate positions and policies in this regard. The Jihad supporters wonder how the Brotherhood, which considers *jihad* to be one of the pillars of its doctrine, did not engage in armed struggle, while the secular nationalist factions engaged in this kind of struggle.

The Muslim Brotherhood can justify its position by resorting to the words of Hasan al-Banna, founder of the mother society:

> Many people ask: does the Muslim Brotherhood Society intend to use force to achieve its goals and attain its objectives? Does the Muslim Brotherhood think about the preparation for a general revolution against the political system or the social system? I do not want to leave these questioners in any doubt. I will take this opportunity to remove the veil from the straightforward answer to these questions, and say it clearly for those who wish to listen. As for force, it is the motto of Islam in all its rules and regulations . . . but the Brotherhood's thought is too deep and farsighted to be lured by the superficiality of ideas and deeds, instead of diving into the depth of things and weighing their results, meanings and purposes. The Brotherhood knows that the ultimate degree of force is the force of doctrine and belief; the force of the arm and weapons comes second. It is incorrect to attribute force to a group until all meanings of the word are acquired. If the force of the arm and weapons is used while the group suffers from incoherence, disequilibrium or weakness of doctrine, then the fate of that group will be destruction.[106]

The views of the Jihad movement and the Muslim Brotherhood differ concerning several issues, but the main differences between the two groups revolve around the Palestinian issue, the position that should be taken toward the existing Arab order, and the attitude toward the Islamic revolution in Iran. The Islamic Jihad believes that the Brotherhood's position toward the Palestinian issue is erroneous. It argues that the Brotherhood's position lacks criticism and analysis, particularly the society's belief that the "establishment of an Islamic state in the region would end the problem completely, resolve the long conflict, and restore Palestine to its people within hours. If you asked the Brotherhood about the Islamic state that it seeks, you would only hear one word from them: 'It is not our concern to think about it, or plan for it. We must work and work only.' Regrettably, the Brotherhood is ignorant of this stage and of its tools, because the Society is ignorant of the essence of the struggle that is now taking place on the Muslim homeland, and of the relationship of the Palestinian issue, and its place in this phase, and in the circle of struggle."[107]

The Islamic Jihad rejects the position of the Muslim Brotherhood Society toward the Palestinian issue and describes this position as being emotional, relying on rhetoric instead of the actual fight for the liberation of Palestine.[108] The Jihad considers this position as alien to the heritage of the Islamic movement, and incompatible with Hasan al-Banna's work, since he had emphasized actual struggle by dispatching Brotherhood members to fight in Palestine. When the Muslim Brotherhood sent its youth to Palestine between 1947 and 1948, the Islamic Jihad argues, it reinforced the awareness of the Palestinian issue as the Islamic movement's central issue.[109]

Al-Shaqaqi attributes the Muslim Brotherhood's crisis, regarding the attitude toward the Palestinian issue, to the society's failure to engage in the armed struggle: "Was not the withdrawal of the Palestinian Islamic leadership from the Palestinian battlefield, and their disavowal of 'national paganism' a reason for alienation and enmity between the youths of the Islamic movement and the majority of our people? . . . It is ironic that the theoreticians and writers of the Islamic movement, some of whom are Palestinian, are the ones who talk most, and sometimes exaggerate the Jewish plots and plans . . . yet, the Islamic movement in recent years has remained most distant from the confrontation with the Jewish entity in Palestine."[110]

In a clear reference to the Muslim Brotherhood, the following was published in one of the periodicals that reflect the opinions of the Islamic Jihad movement: "Even in the ranks of the Islamic movement, there are major tendencies and forces that pursue the same policy of Arafat: respect for the international game, the balances, the alliances, liberalism in practice and relations, financial and media power, status, and influence as an alternative to the continuing *jihad* and reliance on God and the power of the conscious Muslim masses."[111]

With regard to its position vis-à-vis the Arab regimes, the Islamic Jihad movement regards the Arab governments as an "actual security belt for Israel," and believes that these governments are hostile to the idea of *jihad*, because *jihad* would reveal the "falsehood of these governments and their slogans and ideas and would reveal their collusion, dependency, and connections with the Jewish and colonialist enemies of Islam. The exercise of *jihad* would reveal the true natures of these governments, which only serve the Zionist entity. The *jihad* would leave these governments naked before the masses which would see with their own eyes these governments' positions in light of our *jihad*, and the clash with the Zionist enemy that will ensue from it. The masses would recognize that these governments are the real guardians of the security of the Zionist enemy and that they are the real tools, which the Jews and colonialism used, and still use, to suppress the *mujahidin* movements."[112] The Islamic Jihad criticizes the Muslim Brotherhood for its position of truce and coexistence with these regimes, especially those which have strong ties with the West, such as Saudi Arabia, Egypt, and Jordan. One Jihad leader points out that the Muslim Brotherhood's coexistence with these regimes reflects the fact that the Brotherhood is out of touch with history, as well as the society's willingness to deal with the status quo.[113]

The Islamic Jihad rejects conciliation with Arab regimes and believes in the comprehensive struggle. It regards "the Arab regimes and Israel as two faces to the same coin; they are both the fruit of the Western invasion of the Arab world. The political programs of these regimes represent a peripheral challenge and a marginal struggle with this invasion. Islam is the real opposition."[114] A booklet entitled *Al-Farida al-Gha'iba [The Absent Obligation],* which reflects the opinions of the Islamic Jihad, describes the Muslim rulers today as being "in apostasy from Islam, raised at the dining tables of colonialism . . . be it the Crusades, communism or Zionism."[115]

It is worth mentioning that the Islamic Jihad movement views Hafiz al-Asad, Mu'ammar al-Qaddafi, King Fahd, King Hussein, and Saddam Hussein in the same vein.[116] After the deportation of its leaders from the Occupied Territories, the Jihad ceased to attack Hafiz al-Asad, since some of these leaders and some of their following reside in, or operate from, Syria and Lebanon.

In the Occupied Territories, the Islamic Jihad accuses the Brotherhood of direct collusion with Arab regimes. One of the pamphlets issued by a pro-Islamic Jihad student group in the Islamic University in Gaza claimed that the university's administration, dominated by the Muslim Brotherhood, was seeking, with the assistance of Jordan, to create centers of influence for Jordan in the Gaza Strip. The pamphlet also pointed out that "the American-Jewish-Saudi axis" was controlling the region.[117] In another statement, supporters of the Jihad movement accused the Muslim Brotherhood in the Gaza Strip of trying to link the Strip to the Jordanian regime, "as a card in the Jordanian king's hand with which to enter the tarnished American peace." Moreover, they accused the Islamic University's administration of working to "liquidate the aware and committed Islamic trend and every honorable Palestinian Muslim rejecting the administration's conspiracies."[118]

The Muslim Brotherhood, on its part, accuses the Islamic Jihad movement of being a Shi'ite movement allying itself with the Communists. The Jihad rejects such charges: "While everyone knows that in all of Palestine, from the river to the sea, there is not a single Shi'ite, we find those who lie to God and who lie to you, labelling the chastised youth who are willing to give up this life and give themselves to God and to death on His path . . . of being Shi'ite in an attempt to exploit the ignorance of some, and to besiege this Muslim voice. . . . They talk falsely about alleged alliances with other forces, exploiting the simplicity of some Muslim youth. But God knows, and they know, that they are lying."[119]

Regarding the attitude toward the Iranian revolution, the Islamic Jihad perceived this revolution as a beginning for comprehensive revolutionary change. The Muslim Brotherhood does not share this view, although it initially regarded the Iranian revolution favorably, but soon changed its position with the start of the Iran-Iraq war. The Muslim Brotherhood believes that despite the fact that this revolution stemmed from Islamic principles, it began to lose its Islamic appeal. The society argues that while the revolution succeeded in overthrowing the Shah's regime, it was "unable to claim that it had established an exemplary Islamic state that is founded on stable institutions. . . . An Islamic state which strives to absorb all Islamic potentials is supposed to embrace Islamic principles that would exceed sectarian differences. However, all can see the sectarian nature of the state, which is confirmed day after day through words and deeds inside and outside Iran."[120]

The Jihad movement believes that certain Arab antirevolutionary regimes could not openly stand against the Iranian revolution at the outset and that these regimes remained silent or even expressed support until the eruption of the Iran-Iraq war, when campaigns of incitement and scheming against the revolution then began. The Jihad indicates that the regime in Jordan played a role in pressuring the Muslim Brotherhood in Jordan to convince the Brotherhood in the Occupied Territories to change its position toward the Iranian revolution. The Islamic Jihad argues that the Brotherhood stirred up the issue of the dispute between Shi'ites and Sunnis as a pretext to embrace a hostile position toward the Islamic revolution in Iran.[121]

The Islamic Jihad movement indicates that the Muslim Brotherhood Society in the West Bank and the Gaza Strip held a hostile stand toward the revolution, while the other Islamic movements did not take such a stand. In this regard, the Islamic Jihad refers to the attitudes of 'Issam al-'Attar, a Syrian Muslim Brotherhood leader, and of Fathi Yakin, a noted Islamic thinker. It also refers to the position of the Muslim Brotherhood's International Organization and to al-Azhar's stance in Egypt, as well as to the positions of the Islamic groups in Pakistan and the prominent Islamic educator, Abu-al-A'la al-Mawdudi. All of these positions were cordial and reflected no hostility to the Iranian revolution.[122]

The Islamic Jihad is criticized by the Muslim Brotherhood for various reasons. The Jihad is accused of being part of the Fatah movement, the "Islamic Fatah," which suffers from duplicity in doctrine. The Jihad movement is also criticized for concentrating on the political matters, while ignoring the significance of Islamic education. The Brotherhood accuses the Jihad of following Iran's path and of being firmly linked to it. The Jihad is also labelled as a Shi'ite group, carrying out Iranian policies, which the Muslim Brotherhood rejects.[123]

The Islamic Jihad has defined its relationship with Iran in the words of the movement's spiritual leader, Sheikh 'Abd-al-'Aziz

'Auda: "The Iranian revolution is a serious and important attempt to achieve the Islamic awakening. Iran is now trying to unify the Islamic *umma* and unite the Sunni and Shi'ite schools of thought."[124] As regards the Jihad movement's position toward the Iran-Iraq war, Sheikh 'Auda stated: "Khomeini's decision to continue the war against Iraq was a wise decision. . . . We see the Iran-Iraq war as a classical war that will bring about unusual results and will alter the face of the entire region. Based on that, we believe that the continuation of the war will be for the benefit of the Palestinian cause."[125]

The Islamic Jihad believes that Islamic Iran is the state that is most committed to the Palestinian issue and that its victory over Iraq would create a new situation in the region on the way to the establishment of the Islamic state, which will in turn be an asset in the battle against Israel. The Jihad leaders draw an analogy between Sheikh 'Izz-al-Din al-Qassam and al-Hussein, son of 'Ali, who is venerated by the Shi'ites: "Like al-Hussein in the dawn of the first movement, al-Qassam was, in the twenties and thirties of this century, a symbol of belief, consciousness and revolution."[126] 'Ali is the first cousin of the prophet Muhammad. This kind of analogy may enhance speculation about the Islamic Jihad's pro-Iranian sympathies. The Jihad's position of unqualified support for Iran may have some negative effect on the movement, especially in light of the arms deals Iran has concluded with Western counties, as well as with Israel.

Sheikh 'Abd-al-'Aziz 'Auda points out that the campaign of siege which the Muslim Brotherhood launched against the Islamic Jihad since 1981 has hampered the movement's efforts to initiate armed action against Israel in an earlier period. 'Auda attributes the Brotherhood's negative position toward the Islamic Jihad to the society's fear that the Jihad may become an alternative to the Brotherhood.[127]

The Islamic Jihad notes that the Brotherhood's refusal to go into alliances with the nationalist factions stems from the Brotherhood's belief that such alliances would weaken the Brotherhood's influence as a distinct movement. Moreover, this refusal also stems from an inability to comprehend and analyze, and is a result of the type of mentality that dominates the Brotherhood. The Islamic Jihad cites the example of how the Syrian Muslim Brotherhood joined the National Front for the Liberation of Syria along with secular forces, while the Brotherhood in the Occupied Territories refuses to ally itself with similar nationalist forces, using the pretext that "the Muslim *ulema* of Syria are learned men and are better judges of their own situation."[128] From the Jihad movement's point of view this kind of attitude reflects the uncritical mentality of the Muslim Brotherhood.

Until the eruption of the *intifada,* the relationship between the Islamic Jihad movement and the Muslim Brotherhood Society could be described as negative and incompatible. No attempts until then were made at unification, serious reconciliation, or narrowing of major differences. Disputes between the two groups had at one point turned into violent clashes. The last of these clashes occurred when a group of pro-Brotherhood youths in the Islamic University attacked, a few days before the *intifada,* supporters of the Islamic Jihad in the university. The latter were demonstrating inside the university protesting the Israeli authorities' decision to deport Sheikh 'Abd-al-'Aziz 'Adua. Before that, other incidents and confrontations occurred between the two sides. The Islamic Jihad accused the Muslim Brotherhood of attempting to assassinate 'Auda on January 16, 1983, but the Brotherhood denied the charge.

Regarding the future relationship between the Muslim Brotherhood and the Islamic Jihad and the possibilities of unity between the two groups, the Brotherhood sees itself as the primary Islamic power and believes that cooperation with the Jihad would be acceptable only if it is done on the Brotherhood's terms. As an independent organization, the Brotherhood can make its own decisions and has no need to give concessions. On the other hand, the Brotherhood looks suspiciously at the Jihad's links with Fatah and Iran. The Brotherhood still recalls that the Islamic Jihad is a splinter group from the society and that it may still hope to dominate the Islamic movement in the Occupied Territories.[129] But prospects for mutual understanding became better during and in the aftermath of the Gulf crisis. The prevailing mood in the circles of both the Brotherhood and the Jihad favors a rapprochement between the two groups.

The Brotherhood's participation in the *intifada,* the formation of Hamas, and the application by Hamas of violent tactics against the Israeli occupation have narrowed the differences between the Brotherhood and the Jihad. During the Gulf crisis, the Brotherhood's attitude toward Arab regimes, especially Saudi Arabia and the Gulf states, has become closer to the critical positions of the Islamic Jihad toward these regimes. The Brotherhood, like the

Islamic Jihad, has established links with other Muslim fundamentalist groups in the Arab countries. Finally, the Palestinian Brotherhood has begun to take a more favorable view toward Iran. Both Hamas and the Islamic Jihad participated in a conference held in Iran to protest the convening of the Madrid Peace Conference of October 29, 1991. Discussions between Hamas and the Islamic Jihad are currently under way to explore the possibility of closer coordination and even unity between the two groups.[130]

Conclusion

■ While the Islamic movement in the West Bank and Gaza has made tangible gains by becoming a major political force in Palestinian society, this movement continues to face a number of major challenges. It is not yet clear whether this movement will ever be able to make Islam an alternative to the PLO and what it stands for, as a frame of reference for the Palestinian people in the Occupied Territories. This kind of accomplishment will depend on the Islamists' ability to prove the validity of their vision and the feasibility of their positions and policies with regard to the achievement of legitimate national goals of the Palestinian people. It will also depend on the extent to which the Palestinians are willing to take an Islamic identity and give this identity priority over their nationalist identity, as well as the ability of the Islamic movement to rekindle Islamic sentiments and beliefs.

In addition to skepticism about the Islamic movement's ability to become a viable alternative to the PLO, the strict and conservative social outlook of the movement creates anxiety among large segments of the population. Palestinian society has a strong secular tradition. This tradition can act as counterbalance to the expansion of Islamic influence. Secularist tendencies in the Occupied Territories are perpetuated through a large number of secular institutions, PLO factions, and the intelligentsia as a whole. There is also an active Christian minority that is centrally positioned in the cities of Jerusalem, Ramallah, and Bethlehem. Many members of this minority are influential politicians, businessmen, academicians, journalists, educators, and community leaders. Furthermore, Christian schools and kindergartens, which are attended by large numbers of Muslim students and children, play an important role in defining Palestinian national and political culture.

The Islamic movement in the Occupied Territories has few prominent leadership figures. A number of the Hamas leaders and virtually all known leaders of the Islamic Jihad have been expelled from the West Bank and Gaza. If the ailing Ahmad Yasin, who is serving a fifteen-year jail sentence, dies, the Brotherhood and Hamas will lose their most influential and charismatic leader. Such an eventuality will confront the movement with a leadership vacuum and crisis, since Hamas lacks leading figures with the same stature and caliber of Yasin. A leadership vacuum may open the way for a younger, less experienced breed of leaders who may be prone to internal divisions and splits or may be trapped in an untimely showdown with the Israeli authorities. This showdown could prove to be detrimental to Hamas and the Muslim Brotherhood Society as a whole. The December 1992 deportation of 418 Hamas and Jihad leaders and activists by the Israeli authorities should be seen in this context.

Moreover, the Islamic movement is not a homogeneous whole. The two major groups comprising this movement have varying views and positions, and within each group homogeneity is far from being total. In Hamas, for example, there are the fundamentalist, the political, and the opportunist. While still united vis-à-vis the PLO, no major differences within Hamas have yet emerged. But the challenges facing the movement, and conflicting views as to the best way to handle them, may give rise to differences and bring them to the fore. However, active involvement of the Jordanian Brotherhood in Hamas and Hamas's major reliance on the Muslim Brotherhood in Jordan may prevent the emergence of any significant crises within the movement.

Smaller factions have also split from the Islamic Jihad movement. Splits are motivated primarily by personal differences or by competition. Following a dispute over the leadership of the Islamic Jihad, As'ad Bayoud al-Tamimi split from the movement and formed a faction under his own leadership. Al-Tamimi, who heads the Islamic Jihad Movement-Beit al-Maqdis, currently resides in Jordan and maintains links with, and receives support from, the PLO, Iraq, and Iran.

A second splinter group is headed by Ahmad Mahanna, who

formed an organization called "Hizbullah Palestine." Mahanna is believed to be the person who masterminded an attack on an Israeli tourist bus in 1989 on the road between Cairo and Isma'iliyya in Egypt, before his split from al-Tamimi's group. In this attack, twelve Israelis were killed and seven others were injured. It is not clear what process of differentiation will take place within the Islamic groups, especially if the Islamic movement gains supremacy in the Occupied Territories.

Issues of democracy and pluralism have not so far been a matter of concern for the Islamic movement in the Occupied Territories. But failure to articulate acceptable positions on these issues may alienate significant segments of the Palestinian society and consequently undermine the Islamic movement and its influence. The problems Islamists in some other countries (Tunisia and Algeria, for example) are confronting may urge the Palestinian Islamists to address these issues. The Islamic movement in the Occupied Territories may be able to evade such issues for some time on the pretext that the pressing and immediate concern of the movement is national liberation from the Israeli occupation, and not the seizure of political power in society. But despite that, the Islamists need to define the basis for their dealings with other political groups and with society as a whole.

From a theoretical and doctrinal point of view, Palestinian Islamists dismiss the concept of democracy as a Western concept that has no place in a Muslim society. The Islamists argue that the Islamic doctrine provides principles that are more just and comprehensive. In an Islamic order, political parties that do not take Islam as a frame of reference will be prevented. But while the Islamic society and Islamic rule are not established, the Islamists favor the notion of democracy because they believe that Islam can thrive under democracy better than it does under dictatorship.[1] When Islamic rule is established, a prominent Islamist in the West Bank argues, this Islamic rule will have to decide whether it is more useful for the spread of the Islamic idea to allow the circulation of different ideas or whether these ideas should be banned.[2]

The PLO remains the major and more powerful challenge to the Islamic movement in the Occupied Territories. The Islamic movement does not have the solid nationalist record and legitimacy which the PLO has earned as a result of more than twenty-five years of nationalist resistance to the Israeli occupation. The PLO is accredited with reviving and crystallizing the Palestinian national identity and with defining the national rights of the Palestinian people. As long as the Islamic movement does not espouse a defined nationalist program that responds to the aspirations of the Palestinian people and stresses their right to self-determination and statehood, the movement may not be able to become an alternative to the PLO or even a serious contender for the legitimate representation of the Palestinian people. However, the Islamic movement will enjoy a larger measure of popular support if the PLO fails to achieve the national objectives it has defined for itself. The failure of the PLO to deliver will most likely translate into credit for the Islamic groups. Hamas gained the most when the PLO failed to deliver after all the concessions the PLO leadership has made. Hamas has been challenging the PLO to produce any tangible achievement as a result of these concessions. But these Islamic groups, especially Hamas, will be required to deliver and not to rely on the short-comings of others as a means of gaining influence. While the maximalist stands of the Islamic groups may be appealing to the Palestinians in the Occupied Territories, in light of increasing dis-illusionment with the PLO and its ability to offer tangible gains, the Islamists' high goals of establishing an Islamic state and society in Palestine, which are unattainable, at least in the short run, may produce the same kind of disillusionment.

The reluctance of the Islamic groups to work jointly with the PLO may alienate Palestinians who believe in the virtue of national unity. From the very start, the Muslim Brotherhood, and later Hamas, have refused to work with the PLO because of irreconcil-able ideological and political differences. Only in the aftermath of the eruption of the *intifada* did Hamas address this prospect. In reply to an invitation to join the PLO, Hamas requested as a precondition that it be given 40 to 50 percent of the seats in the Palestine National Council (PNC), the Palestinian parliament in exile. The PLO has refused to concede this request. If Hamas is given 40 to 50 percent of the PNC seats, it may become able to take over the PLO from within. In the aftermath of Israel's de-portation to southern Lebanon of 418 Hamas and Islamic Jihad leaders and activists in December 1992, Hamas has set down new conditions for joining the PLO. While no longer insisting on a specific number of seats in the PNC, Hamas requests the con-ducting of elections inside and outside the Occupied Territories to enable the Palestinians to elect their representatives in the PLO leadership bodies. The PLO has also refused to concede this demand, arguing that it is impractical under the circumstances. Hamas opposes the PLO's political program altogether. Joining a PLO that is secular and which has already recognized Israel would undermine the very raison d'être of Hamas and the mother organization of the Muslim Brotherhood Society. Therefore, it is not clear whether the Hamas terms to join the PLO are genuine or if they are only meant to make it extremely difficult for the PLO to accept them. Perhaps Hamas wishes to place the blame on the other side and would relieve itself from Palestinian public pressure for rejecting national unity and cooperation with the PLO. Hamas would probably join the PLO only if it is convinced that it has a chance to gradually control the organization and change its entire orientation.

The reaction of Hamas to Iraq's invasion of Kuwait on August 2, 1990, and the ensuing Gulf crisis was not very much different from the reaction of the PLO factions in the Occupied Territories. While Hamas opposed the Iraqi invasion of Kuwait, it strongly opposed the massive foreign military presence in Saudi Arabia and the "American occupation of lands sacred to Islam,"[3] and called on Iraq to "attack the heart of Tel Aviv if America attacked Baghdad."[4] According to Hamas, the Muslim nation was facing a wild crusade campaign and an imperialist offensive against the Muslim nation.

The Iraqi invasion of Kuwait and the Gulf crisis came to preoccupy Palestinians in the Occupied Territories and to divert their full attention from the *intifada*. The crisis mitigated the internal Palestinian debate on a variety of issues, including the relationship between the nationalist and the Islamic camps. Initially, the crisis tipped the balance of popular support between Hamas and the PLO in favor of the PLO, though temporarily. Hamas had to follow the lead of a nationalist, pan-Arab line, since the confrontation in the Gulf was perceived in the Occupied Territories primarily as one between the Arabs and the United States. Of course Hamas preferred to define this confrontation as one between the Muslims and the West and take the lead itself.

The Gulf crisis was a critical test for Hamas. It confronted the movement with a dilemma. With the kind of position it took vis-à-vis the crisis, Hamas risked alienating its allies and supporters in Saudi Arabia and the other Gulf states. The decline and loss of financial and political support may have cost the movement internal Palestinian popular support. Furthermore, it was doubtful that Hamas was eager to fight such a major and uncertain battle with much at stake, let alone under the leadership of a man, Saddam Hussein, whose Islamic credentials are not very impressive.

With the defeat of Iraq in the Gulf war, both the PLO and Hamas were held accountable by Kuwait and Saudi Arabia and their Arab and foreign allies for supporting Iraq. Iraq's defeat created a condition of objective weakness in the Palestinian arena for all the Palestinian parties involved. While both the PLO and Hamas have been weakened in the aftermath of the war, it is expected that Hamas will survive the defeat and emerge with less damage than the PLO. Hamas is better equipped than the PLO to survive this crisis, cope with its consequences, and rehabilitate itself for the following reasons.

First, Hamas does not have a strict and well-defined political program. It can claim, for example, that while the liberation of "Muslim Palestine" remains the ultimate goal, and *jihad* the ultimate means, the circumstances which the *umma* is going through require a temporary and tactical retreat. The Muslim Brotherhood did that in the past and for many years, until the eruption of the *intifada* in 1987. Hamas can use the example of the *intifada* to support an argument that when the time is opportune, the Muslims will engage the enemy as they did during the *intifada*. Hamas can rely on an Islamic doctrine that lends itself to more than one interpretation to justify shifts in attitudes.

In the meantime, the PLO cannot suggest to its following that self-determination, statehood on about 20 percent of the land of Palestine, the right of return, and PLO representation are no longer feasible and need to be postponed until further notice, and that the Palestinians should settle for whatever the Israelis are willing to offer. After all, the above-stated objectives have been the raison d'être of the PLO. The PLO will have a tough time making a case for a settlement that falls short of addressing its stated objectives or that does not have the prospects for achieving such objectives.

Second, unlike the PLO, Hamas has better prospects for reconciliation with the old Arab order, or even with a new one, in which the pro-U.S. Arab states become dominant. The Muslim Brotherhood Society and Hamas's political and ideological flexibility permits that kind of reconciliation. In addition, Islamic movements in other Arab states will be inclined to press for a sympathetic view toward their Palestinian brethren.

Third, Hamas will also be amenable to some kind of relationship with Jordan. It is worth mentioning that the Muslim Brotherhood in the Occupied Territories opposed King Hussein's disengagement from the West Bank in 1988. The Brotherhood and Hamas also favor a Palestinian-Jordanian confederation. In this regard Yasin argues: "Islam calls for unity. When we commit ourselves to Islam, we do not reject any unity, but this unity should be predicated on correct and equal basis."[5] With the Muslim Brotherhood in Jordan enjoying considerable political weight, Hamas can be assured that a relationship with Jordan is not going to be detrimental to the movement. Rather, such relationship is bound to strengthen the Brotherhood vis-à-vis the PLO nationalists.

Fourth, one reason for the radicalization of the Muslim Brotherhood in Palestine has been the competition with the PLO nationalist factions. If the nationalists are weakened, Hamas will feel less pressed to adopt radical politics to keep up with the competition. It is true that the weakening of the nationalists will translate into a relative strength for Hamas, but it will not necessarily mean the further radicalization of Hamas. A transition of Hamas from militancy to accommodation may not, however, be smooth. The movement may undergo splits of radical factions, as was the case in 1980 when the Islamic Jihad movement split from the Muslim Brotherhood Society.

The most serious challenge the Islamic movement will have to confront is the Israeli occupation. The way the Israeli authorities decide to deal with the Islamic movement will have a significant impact on the future of the movement. Israel has been subjecting the movement to harsh measures, especially when Islamic activists resort to violence in their confrontation with Israel. As a result of these measures, the movement has been weakened. In May 1989, about 260 Hamas activists, together with Yasin and his close aids, were arrested. The Islamic Jihad activists have been subjected to similar treatment. Ever since that date, Israel has managed to abort every attempt by the Islamic movement to regather its full strength. Thousands of Islamic leaders, activists, members, or sympathizers have been in Israeli jails or detention camps. The December 1992 deportation to south Lebanon of 418 Hamas and Islamic Jihad leaders and activists has been the most dramatic measure undertaken by the Israeli authorities.

Fear of Israeli wrath is likely to have a sobering effect on the Islamic groups. Hamas in particular may have to mitigate its rigid political and ideological stands and perhaps its violent tactics, since it is more exposed to the Israeli authorities than the secretive and smaller organization of the Islamic Jihad. Because of this fear, and in the absence of any effective means to seriously challenge the Israeli occupation, Hamas may shift back, perhaps tactically, to infrastructure-building and consolidation of internal influence within the Palestinian society.

Finally, the Islamic movement in the Occupied Territories is an integral part of the world Islamic movement. While this dimension may be an asset, since it would ensure different forms of support for Palestinian Islamists, it may also be a liability. The world Islamic movement, as well as the Muslim Brotherhood Societies in the Arab region, mainly in Jordan and Egypt, may, for certain considerations, restrain the Islamic movement in the Occupied Territories. Since the Islamic groups in the West Bank and Gaza lack decision-making authority, especially with regard to strategic matters, these groups may have to abide by decisions that are taken outside the Occupied Territories. Such decisions would take into account not only factors that are at play in the Occupied Territories, but also the circumstances and the interests of the Islamic movement in the region as a whole.

NOTES

Introduction

1. Isma'il Sabri 'Abdallah et al., *Al-Harakat al-'Islamiyya al Mu'asira fil-Watan al-'Arabi [Contemporary Islamic Movements in the Arab Homeland]* (Beirut: Markaz Dirasat al-Wahda al-'Arabiyya, 1987), p. 17. The initial and ultimate decline or failure of other non-Islamic doctrines and ideologies was not an outcome of the rise of Islamic fundamentalism, but rather a function of other external and internal factors.

2. Salah 'Abd-al-Maqsud, "'Ashar Ittihamat Muwajjaha ila al-Jama'a" [Ten Accusations Directed at Society], *Liwa' al-'Islam,* February 7, 1989, no. 11, p. 13.

3. Fathi Yakin, *Mushkilat al-Da'wa wal-Da'iyya [Problems of the Call and the Caller]* (Beirut: Mu'assasat al-Risala, 1981), p. 232.

4. "Al-Quwa wal-Hai'at al-Wataniyya wal-'Islamiyya al-'Amila Did al-Wujud al-Isra'ili fil-Aradi al-'Arabiyya al-Muhtalla" [Nationalist and Islamic Forces and Institutions Working against the Israeli Presence in the Occupied Arab Territories], *Qadaya Fikriyya,* April 1988, no. 6., p. 249.

5. David Shipler, *Arab and Jew: Wounded Spirits in a Promised Land* (New York: Penguin, 1987), p. 177.

6. "Al-Quwa wal-Hai'at," p. 249.

7. For more information about the reformist style of the Muslim Brotherhood Society in the West Bank and Gaza prior to 1967, see Amnon Cohen, *Political Parties in the West Bank under the Jordanian Regime, 1949–1967* (Ithaca: Cornell University Press, 1982), and Ziad Abu-Amr, *'Usul al-Harakat al-Siyasiyya fi Qita' Ghazza: 1948–1967 [The Origins of Political Movements in the Gaza Strip: 1948-1967]* (Jerusalem: Dar al-Aswar, Acre, 1987). For the period after 1967, see Ziad Abu-Amr, *Al-Harakat al-'Islamiyya fil-Daffa al-Gharbiyya wa Qita' Ghazza [The Islamic Movement in the West Bank and the Gaza Strip]* (Jerusalem: Dar al-Aswar, Acre, 1989).

8. As'ad Bayoud al-Tamimi, *Zawal Isra'il Hatmiyya Qur'aniyya [The Destruction of Israel Is a Koranic Imperative]* (no publisher or place of publication, 1988), p. 10.

9. Fathi 'Abd-al-'Aziz (al-Shaqaqi), *Al-Khomeini: al-Hall al-'Islami wal-Badil [Khomeini: The Islamic Solution and the Alternative]* (Cairo: Al-Mukhtar al-'Islami, 1979).

1. The Emergence and Evolution of the Muslim Brotherhood Society

1. Thomas Mayer, "The Military Force of Islam: The Society of the Muslim Brethren and the Palestine Question, 1945–1948," in Elie Kedourie and Sylvia G. Haim (eds.), *Zionism and Arabism in Palestine and Israel* (London: Frank Cass, 1982), p. 101.

2. Richard P. Mitchell, *The Society of the Muslim Brothers* (London: Oxford University Press, 1969), pp. 56, 97; Kamil Isma'il (al-Sharif), *Al-'Ikhwan Al-Muslimun fi Harb Filastin [The Muslim Brotherhood in the War of Palestine]* (Cairo: Dar al-Kitab al-'Arabi, 1951), p. 38; and 'Arif al-'Arif, *Al-Nakba: Nakbat Beit al-Maqdis wal-Firdaws al-Mafqoud 1947–1955 [The Disaster: The Disaster of Jerusalem and the Lost Paradise: 1947–1955]* (Sidon-Beirut: al-Maktaba al-'Asriyya, n.d.), p. 396. Al-Najjada, a paramilitary organization founded in late 1945, had centers in several Palestinian towns (Nazareth, Haifa, Nablus, Jaffa, Jerusalem, and Gaza). Muhammad Nimr al-Hawwari, a lawyer, headed this organization. Al-Futuwa was also a youth organization founded as a wing of the Arab party; Kamil 'Uraiqat was the leader of this organization, which paid allegiance to the party's leader, Jamal al-Husseini (Bayan Nuwaihid al-Hout, *Al-Qiyadat wal-Mu'assasat al-Siyasiyya fi Filastin: 1917–1948 [Political Leaders and Institutions in Palestine: 1917–1948]* [Beirut: Mu'assasat al-Dirasat al-Filastiniyya, 1986], pp. 508–11).

3. Omar al-Tilmisani, a former supreme guide of the Muslim Brotherhood, recalls that the number of Muslim Brotherhood volunteers killed in Palestine ranged between thirty and forty (Ibrahim Qa'ud, *'Umar al-Tilmisani Shahidan 'ala al-'Asr: al-'Ikhwan al-Muslimun fi Da'irat al-Haqiqa al-Gha'iba [Omar al-Tilmisani, Witness to an Era: The Muslim Brotherhood in the Circle of the Absent Truth]* [Cairo: al-Mukhtar al-'Islami, 1985], p. 70).

4. Al-'Arif, p. 399.

5. Isma'il, pp. 52–53.

6. Al-'Arif, p. 393.

7. Mayer, p. 109.

8. Ibid., p. 108.

9. Ibid., p. 109.

10. Ibid., p. 107.

11. Ibid.

12. Ibid., p. 103.

13. Amnon Cohen, *Political Parties in the West Bank under the Jordanian Regime, 1949–1967* (Ithaca: Cornell University Press, 1982), p. 145.

14. Ibid., p. 149.

15. Ibid., p. 146.

16. Ibid., p. 150.

17. A personal interview with Yusuf al-'Azm, a Muslim Brotherhood leader in Jordan and a member of parliament, Amman, May 30, 1989.

18. Mohammed K. Shadid, "The Muslim Brotherhood Movement in the West Bank and Gaza," *Third World Quarterly,* April 1988, vol. 10, no.

2, p. 662. Muslim Brotherhood members of parliament were Yusuf al-'Azm, Ahman al-Kufahi, 'Abdallah al-'Akayila, and Dr. Hafez 'Abd-al-Nabi al-Natsha.

19. Ibid.

20. Cohen, pp. 162, 164.

21. Ibid., p. 163.

22. Ziad Abu-Amr, *'Usul al-Harakat al-Siyasiyya fi Qita' Ghazza: 1948–1967 [The Origins of Political Movements in the Gaza Strip: 1948–1967]* (Jerusalem: Dar al-Aswar, Acre, 1987), p. 67.

23. Ibid., p. 69.

24. The terms of the treaty allowed Britain to return to the al-Tall al-Kabir base in Egypt, in the event of an attack against any Arab country or Turkey. Muslim Brotherhood sources say that the incident was planned by 'Abd-al-Nasir's regime to provide a pretext to strike at the Brotherhood because of the mounting disputes between the two sides, and in order to increase Nasir's popularity (Hasan Hanafi, *Al-'Usuliyya al-'Islamiyya [Islamic Fundamentalism]* [Cairo: Maktabat Madbuli, 1989], p. 42, and Mahmud 'Abd-al-Halim, *Al-'Ikhwan al-Muslimun: Ahdath Sana'at al-Tarikh [The Muslim Brotherhood: Events That Made History]* [Alexandria: Dar al-Da'wa, 1985], p. 46).

25. Abu-Amr, pp. 72–73.

26. Ibid., pp. 71–73.

27. A personal interview with a former Muslim Brotherhood leader in the Gaza Strip who asked that his name not be used, Gaza, October 1986.

28. This plan, agreed to in June 1953 by the Egyptian government and the United Nations Relief and Works Agency (UNRWA), was aimed at resettling 50,000 to 60,000 refugees from the Gaza Strip in an area in the northwestern Sinai desert, after reclaiming the land and supplying it with water from the Nile (Hussein Abu-al-Namal, *Qita' Ghazza 1948–1967: Tatawwurat Iqtisadiyya wa-Siyasiyya wa-Ijtima'iyya wa-'Askariyya [The Gaza Strip 1948–1967: Economic, Political, Social, and Military Developments]* [Beirut: Markaz al-Abhath, Munadhamat al-Tahrir al-Filastiniyya, 1979], p. 86).

29. The author of this plan was Lester Pearson, Canadian minister of state for foreign affairs, who in February 1956 proposed to the UN that the Gaza Strip be internationalized. The plan stipulated that the UN, after agreement with Egypt, would be responsible for establishing a civilian administration in the Gaza Strip, whose task would be "to achieve economic and social prosperity, and to safeguard law and order" (E. L. M. Burns, *Between Arab and Israeli* [London: George G. Harrap, 1962], pp. 253–54).

30. Abu-Amr, p. 65.

31. Al-'Azm.

32. Ibid., p. 69.

33. *Al-Haqiqa al-Gha'iba [The Absent Truth]*, a booklet published by the Muslim Brotherhood in the Occupied Territories (author, publisher, place and date of publication not given), p. 24.

34. Hanafi, p. 55.

35. Ibid., p. 63.

36. Ibid., p. 120.

37. Ibid., pp. 54–55.

38. Zakariyya Muhammad, "Al-Intifada wal-Islah al-Tandhimi fi Munadhamat al-Tahrir al-Filastiniyya" [The *Intifada* and Organizational Reform in the PLO], *Al-Fikr al-Dimuqrati,* Winter 1989, no. 5, p. 30.

39. Emile Sahliyeh, *In Search of Leadership: West Bank Politics since 1967* (Washington, D.C.: Brookings Institution, 1988), p. 143.

40. Ze'ev Schiff and Ehud Ya'ari, *Intifada: The Palestinian Uprising—Israel's Third Front* (New York: Simon and Schuster, 1989), p. 224.

41. Fahmi Huwaydi, "Ha'ula' al-'Usuliyyun fil-Ard al-Muhtalla" [These Fundamentalists in the Occupied Territories], *Al-Ahram,* Cairo, December 8, 1987.

42. This university was built with the assistance of the Islamic Development Fund, an offshoot of the Islamic Conference, established during King Faisal's reign in 1969. This bank donated $150,000 in 1978 to build the Islamic University (personal interview with Dr. Muhammad Saqr, president of the Islamic University in Gaza, Amman, May 29, 1989).

43. A personal interview with Sheikh Ahmad Yasin, leader of the Muslim Brotherhood Society, and founder of the Islamic Center in the Gaza Strip, Gaza, April 27, 1987.

44. *Al-Fajr,* English weekly, Jerusalem, September 6, 1987.

45. Elie Rekhess, "The Iranian Impact on the Islamic Jihad Movement in the Gaza Strip," a paper submitted to a conference entitled "The Iranian Revolution and the Muslim World," held in the Dayan Center, Tel Aviv University, January 4–6, 1988, p. 5.

46. *Al-Muntalaq,* February 1984, vol. 8, pp. 17–18.

47. *Al-Sha'b,* July 15, 1986.

48. Sources in the Islamic University who asked not to be named, Gaza, summer of 1988.

49. Sahliyeh, p. 145.

50. Shadid, p. 672.

51. Hala Mustafa, "Al-Tayyar al-'Islami fil-Ard al-Muhtalla" [The Islamic Trend in the Occupied Territories], *Al-Mustaqbal Al-'Arabi,* July 1988, no. 113, p. 82. Originally quoted from Jean François Legrain, "Islamistes et lutte nationale Palestinienne dans le territoires occupés par Israel," *Revue Française de Science Politique,* April 1986, vol. 26, no. 2.

52. *Al-Fajr,* September 7, 1986.

53. Sahliyeh, p. 142.

54. Ibid.

55. Ibid., p. 146.

56. Sa'id al-Ghazali, "Adwa' 'ala al-Harakat al-'Islamiyya fil-Daffa al-Gharbiyya wal-Qita'" [Lights on the Islamic Movements in the West Bank and the Gaza Strip], *'Abir,* September 1987, no. 14, p. 31.

57. *Al-Fajr,* June 9, 1987.

58. Avinu 'Am Bar Yosef, "Al-Jama'at al-'Islamiyya fi Ghazza fil-Kharita al-Siyasiyya," [Islamic Groups in Gaza in the Political Map], *Ma'ariv,* translated article, *Al-Quds,* August 8, 1987.

59. Shadid, p. 666.

60. A personal interview with Ahmad Yasin, Gaza, May 2, 1989.

2. The Muslim Brotherhood and the Palestine Question

1. Ahmad Nawfal, *Al-Tariq ila Filastin [The Road to Palestine]* (publisher, date and place of publication not given), p. 38. This is an edition printed in the Occupied Territories from an original copy.

2. Sa'id al-Ghazali, "Adwa' 'ala al-Harakat al-'Islamiyya fil-Daffa al-Gharbiyya wal-Qita'" [Lights on the Islamic Movements in the West Bank and the Gaza Strip], *'Abir,* September 1987, no. 14, p. 33.

3. Muhammad 'Ali Qutb, *Madhabih wa-Jara'im al-Tafteesh fil-Andalus [Massacres and Crimes of the Inquisition in Andalusia]* (Cairo: Maktabat al-Qur'an, 1985), p. 6.

4. Colin Legum, ed., *Middle East Contemporary Survey* (New York: Holmes and Meier, 1984), p. 372.

5. Nawfal, p. 39.

6. Ibid., p. 15.

7. Ibid., p. 20.

8. Nabil Shubaib, *Al Waqi' al-Qa'im wa-'Iradat al-Taghyeer [The Existing Reality and the Will to Change]* (Bonn: Al-Dar al-'Islamiyya lil-I'lam, 1983), pp. 9, 12.

9. Ibid.

10. *Al-Da'wa,* November/December 1985, nos. 110, 111, p. 14.

11. Abu-Mus'ab, "Filastin fi Fikr al-Imam al-Shahid Hasan al-Banna" [Palestine in the Thought of the Martyred Imam Hasan al-Banna], *Liwa' al-'Islam,* February 7, 1989, no. 11, p. 17.

12. Shubaib, p. 15.

13. *Al-Haqiqa al-Gha'iba [The Absent Truth],* a booklet published by the Muslim Brotherhood Society in the Occupied Territories (author, publisher, date and place of publication not given), p. 1.

14. Shubaib, p. 3.

15. Ahmad Bin Yousef, *Harakat al-Muqawama al-'Islamiyya [The Islamic Resistance Movement]* (Illinois: The Islamic Center for Research and Studies, 1990), p. 125.

16. Nawfal, pp. 67, 68.

17. Ibid., p. 47.

18. Shubaib, p. 115.

19. Ibid.

20. *Al-Muntalaq,* April 1984, no. 9, p. 17.

21. Ziad Abu-Amr, *'Usul al-Harakat al-Siyasiyya fi Qita' Ghazza: 1948–1967 [The Origins of Political Movements in the Gaza Strip: 1948–1967]* (Jerusalem: al-Aswar, Acre, 1987), p. 87, and "*Al-Haqiqa al-Gha'iba,*" p. 18.

22. In order to trace the relationship of several founders of the Fatah movement with the Muslim Brotherhood, see Abu-Amr, pp. 71–78.

23. *Al-Haqiqa al-Gha'iba,* p. 6.

24. Ibid., p. 54.

25. *Al-Fajr,* April 29, 1984.

26. *Al-Da'wa,* September 1986, no. 115, p. 35.

27. "Munadhamat al-Tahrir al-Filastiniyya: min Mihna ila Mihna" [The PLO: From One Ordeal to Another," *Al-Muntalaq,* November 1986, no. 16, p. 6.

28. *Al-Muntalaq,* June 1985, no. 14, p. 41.

29. Muhammad Hamid Abu-al-Nasr, "Al-'Ikhwan al-Muslimun wa-I'lan al-Dawla al-Filastiniyya" [The Muslim Brotherhood and the Declaration of the Palestinian State], *Liwa' al-'Islam,* December 11, 1988, no. 9, p. 5.

30. Ibid.

31. An election leaflet issued by the Islamic Bloc at Birzeit University entitled: "Difa'an 'an al-Kutla al-'Islamiyya" [In Defense of the Islamic Bloc], 1986.

32. A personal interview with Sheikh Ahmad Yasin, leader of the Muslim Brotherhood Society and founder of the Islamic Center in the Gaza Strip, Gaza, April 27, 1987.

33. *Al-Sha'b,* September 11, 1988.

34. Ibid.

35. Al-Ghazali, p. 33, and *Al-Haqiqa al-Gha'iba,* p. 43.

36. An interview by the Jerusalem newspaper, *Al-Nahar,* with Sheikh Ahmad Yasin, April 30, 1989.

37. A personal interview with Sheikh Ahmad Yasin, Gaza, May 2, 1989.

38. Al-Ghazali, p. 32.

39. A personal interview with Sheikh Bassam Jarrar, a prominent Islamic figure in the West Bank, al-Bireh, May 11, 1989.

40. A personal interview with a number of Brotherhood supporters, Ramallah, May 5, 1989.

41. *Al-Sahwa,* 1983, pp. 37–39.

42. Ibid.

43. Hilmi Muhammad Qa'ud, "Al-Tariq al-Sahih li-Tahrir Filastin" [The Correct Path to the Liberation of Palestine], *Al-I'tisam,* December 1988, no. 8, p. 13.

44. A leaflet issued by the Progressive Student Action Front—Birzeit University Branch, entitled "Limadha la Ya'tarif al-'Ikhwan al-Muslimum bi-Munadhamat al-Tahrir al-Filastiniyya?" [Why Does the Muslim Brotherhood Not Recognize the PLO?], September 1987.

45. Ibid.

46. A leaflet issued by the Islamic Bloc, "Dif'an 'an al-Kutla al-'Islamiyya" [In Defense of the Islamic Bloc].

47. Harakat al-Shabiba al-Tullabiyya, "Al-'Ikhwan al-Muslimun: ma Ashbah al-Yawm bil-Bariha" [The Muslim Brotherhood: How Similar Are Yesterday and Today], July 1985, p. 35.

48. Hasan Hanafi, *Al-'Usuliyya al-'Islamiyya [Islamic Fundamentalism]* (Cairo: Maktabat Madbuli, 1989), p. 65.

49. *Al-Haqiqa al-Gha'iba,* p. 51.

50. David Shipler, *Arab and Jew: Wounded Spirits in a Promised Land* (New York: Penguin, 1987), p. 177.

51. *Middle East Contemporary Survey,* p. 373.

52. Yasin, April 27, 1987.

53. The president of the Birzeit University's Student Council at that time recalls that the Islamic Bloc lost only one of its members in this demonstration, Jawad Abu-Silmiyya. The same source indicates that Sa'ib Dhahab was a member of the Fatah Student Youth movement at Birzeit University. The Student Council's president said that the Islamic Bloc took part in this demonstration, after it had been strongly urged by the Student Youth movement to do so, and after the youth movement assured the bloc, in a joint leadership meeting that the demonstration would take place under the slogan "Unity in Opposition to the Occupation." The same source recalls that the Islamic Bloc demanded that pro-PLO banners not be carried (personal interview with Marwan al-Barghuthi, former president of the Birzeit University Student Council, Amman, June 28, 1989).

54. A leaflet issued by the Islamic Bloc in Birzeit University, January 12, 1983.

55. *Al-Muntalaq,* February 1984, no. 8, p. 17.

56. Sheikh Yasin says: "The Hizbullah in Lebanon does not represent us; it does not represent the Muslims in Lebanon. Therefore, it only represents itself" (Yasin, *Al-Nahar*).

57. Sadat's assassination on October 6, 1981, was carried out by orders issued by Muhammad 'Abd-al-Salam Faraj to Khalid al-Islambulli. On March 6, 1982, Egyptian military courts decreed the execution of Muhammad 'Abd-al-Salam Faraj, Khalid al-Islambulli, Hussein 'Abbas, 'Ata Tayil, and 'Abd-al-Hamid 'Abd-al-'Al. Sources point out that, in the aftermath of the incident at the Military Technical Academy in 1974, the Egyptian press was filled with statements issued by Muslim Brotherhood leaders declaring their support for and allegiance to Sadat, such as the statements issued by Salih Abu-Ruqayyiq, Muhammad al-Ghazali, and Zaynab al-Ghazali (Al-Mahdawi, p. 130).

58. A personal interview with Yusuf al-'Azm, a Muslim Brotherhood leader and member of parliament in Jordan, Amman, May 30, 1989.

59. *Al-Haqiqa al-Gha'iba,* p. 33.

60. Nawfal, p. 44.

61. A personal interview with Dr. Muhammad Saqr, president of the Islamic University in Gaza, Amman, May 29, 1989. The prevailing belief is that Dr. Saqr is one of the Brotherhood's leaders, but he denies having an organizational relationship with the society.

62. Ibid., pp. 67–68.

63. Ziad Abu-Ghanima, "Filastin al-'Islamiyya hiya Filastin al-Muharrara" [Islamic Palestine Is Liberated Palestine], *Liwa' Al-'Islam,* January 9, 1989, no. 10, p. 25.

64. Ibid.

65. Fahmi Huwaydi, "Husn al-Qira'a Qabl al-Kitaba wal-Ittiham" [Good Reading Is Required before Writing and Accusing], *Liwa' al-'Islam,* February 7, 1989, no. 11, p. 25.

66. *Al-Haqiqa al-Gha'iba,* p. 25.

67. Ibid., p. 24.

68. Al-'Azm.

69. *Al-Haqiqa al-Gha'iba,* p. 23.

70. Ibid., p. 30.

71. Some of the participants in this meeting recalled that the meeting with Rabin had been misrepresented, since those invited to the meeting did not know in advance that they would be meeting with Rabin. They were initially told that they were to meet with the head of the Israeli Civil Administration in the Gaza Strip.

72. Salama Amin, "Al-Ittijahat al-Diniyya wa-Dawruha fil-'Amal al-Watani al-Filastini" [The Religious Trends and their Role in Palestinian National Action], *Tariq al-Intisar,* May 1, 1988, no. 199, p. 26.

73. Leaflet no. 3 issued by the "Central Leadership of the United Palestinian National Front," Gaza, June 8, 1983.

74. A leaflet issued by the Nationalist movement in the Occupied Territories, June 1983.

75. The Islamic Bloc at Birzeit University, "Bayan Hawl al-I'tida' al-'Athim 'ala al-Shabab al-'Islami fi Jami'at Birzeit" [Statement concerning the Criminal Attack on the Islamic Youth at Birzeit University], June 6, 1983.

76. Ibid.

77. A statement issued by the Student Council at Birzeit University (undated).

78. *The Jerusalem Post,* January 11, 1982. An Islamic source, who requested that his name not be used, said that Sawalha did not fall from the third floor, but jumped from the window of his office when members of the Islamic Bloc stormed the office.

79. *Al-Quds,* August 15, 1987.

80. A statement issued by the Islamic Center: "Suqut al-Aqni'a al-Shuyu'iyya" [The Collapse of the Communist Masks], Gaza, undated.

81. "Message of Brother Yasir Arafat, Chairman of the PLO's Executive Committee, Commander-in-Chief of the Palestinian Revolutionary Forces, on the 22nd Anniversary of the Outbreak of the Revolution," *Shu'un Filastiniyya,* nos. 166–167, January/February 1987, pp. 3–15, and "Message of Brother Yasir Arafat, Chairman of the PLO's Executive Committee, Commander-in-Chief of the Palestinian Revolutionary Forces, on the 23rd Anniversary of the Outbreak of the Revolution," *Shu'un Filastiniyya,* no. 178, January 1988, pp. 3–13.

82. *'Abir,* November/December 1986, pp. 15–17.

83. "Nash'at wa-Tatawwur al-Ahzab wal-Quwa al-Siyasiyya fil-'Urdun: al-Quwa al-Salafiyya" [Emergence and Development of Political Parties and Forces in Jordan: The Salafi Forces], *Al-Nashra,* no. 92, p. 25.

84. Dr. Saqr told the writer that a delegation from the Islamic University's board of trustees in Gaza, comprised of Ahmad Hasan al-Shawwa, Raghib Murtaja, Zari' al-Astal, and Habib Jarada, came to visit him in Amman and asked him to accept the presidency of the university. Dr. Saqr recalled that the delegation was accompanied by Kamil al-Sharif and Musbah al-Zumayli, both prominent Islamic dignitaries in Jordan. Dr. Saqr says that he does not know the reasons for choosing him president for the university instead of Dr. Riad al-Agha.

85. These three are Dr. 'Abdalla Abu-'Azza, 'Abd-al-Rahman Hurani, and Dr. Salim Amin al-Agha. They are all members of the Gaza Islamic University's Board of Founders. They were not included in the PNC as a result of an agreement with the Muslim Brotherhood. 'Abdalla Abu-'Azza entered the council as an Islamist, and not as a member of the Muslim Brotherhood. He resigned from the PNC and did not attend the nineteenth session in November 1988. 'Abd-al-Rahman Hurani was also an Islamic figure, but not a Muslim Brotherhood member. As for Dr. al-Agha, he had been a PNC member for a while before the eighteenth session and is still a member today. Al-Agha is considered to be reflecting the views of the Islamic Resistance Movement (Hamas) in the PNC. Therefore, in the nineteenth session, along with Hurani, he opposed the PLO's acceptance of UN resolution 242.

86. *Al-Fajr*, September 6, 1987.

87. Emile Sahliyeh, *In Search of Leadership: West Bank Politics Since 1967* (Washington, D.C.: Brookings Institution, 1988), p. 154, and also *Al-Shihab*, November 1983, no. 1, p. 7.

88. Fathi Yakin, *Mushkilat al-Da'wa wal-Da'iyya [Problems of the Call and the Caller]* (Beirut: Mu'assasat al-Risala, 1981), p. 233.

89. "Munadhamat al-Tahrir," *al-Muntalaq*, p. 9.

90. *Mithaq Harakat al-Muqawama al-'Islamiyya (Hamas) [Charter of the Islamic Resistance Movement (Hamas)]*, August 18, 1988, pp. 29–30.

91. See, for example, the statement that was issued in Damascus on September 17, 1992, and signed by 10 Palestinian factions, including Hamas, the PFLP, and the DFLP. This same statement was also circulated in the Occupied Territories.

92. *Al-Ra'i* (Jordan) January 31, 1993.

3. The *Intifada*

1. Meron Benvenisti, *The West Bank Data Base Project: 1987 Report* (Jerusalem: Jerusalem Post, 1987).

2. These figures are taken from a speech delivered by Abu-Jihad, the second man in the Fatah movement, to the Arab Lawyers Guild, Cairo, March 30, 1987.

3. A leaflet issued by Fatah and distributed in the Occupied Territories, marking the anniversary of the Balfour Declaration of November 2, 1917. (Arabic)

4. Benvenisti, p. 5.

5. *The Jerusalem Post*, March 4, 1988.

6. Harakat al-Muqawama al-'Islamiyya (Hamas) [The Islamic Resistance Movement (Hamas)], Leaflet no. 36, February 25, 1989.

7. A personal interview with Sheikh Ahmad Yasin, leader of the Muslim Brotherhood Society and founder of the Islamic Center in the Gaza Strip and the Islamic Resistance Movement (Hamas), Gaza, May 2, 1989.

8. Ibid.

9. A personal interview with Sheikh Bassam Jarrar, a prominent Islamic figure in the West Bank, al-Bireh, May 11, 1989.

10. Muhsin Radi, "Hiwar ma' Ibrahim al-Quqa" [Interview with Ibrahim al-Quqa], *Liwa' al-'Islam,* November 11, 1988, no. 8, p. 15.

11. A personal interview with an Islamic source from the Muslim Brotherhood Society, who requested that his name not be given, the West Bank, August 9, 1989.

12. A personal interview with Yusuf al-'Azm, a Muslim Brotherhood leader and member of parliament in Jordan, Amman, May 30, 1989.

13. Jarrar.

14. Radi.

15. Yasin, May 2, 1989.

16. Al-Tayib al-Mahdi, "Muqabala ma' Dr. 'Abd-al-'Aziz al-Rantisi" [Interview with Dr. 'Abd-al-'Aziz al-Rantisi], *Al-Sirat,* February 1988, no. 10, p. 25.

17. Ibid.

18. Radi, pp. 14–15.

19. Hilmi Muhammad Qa'ud, "Al-Tariq al-Sahih li-Tahrir Filastin" [The Correct Path to the Liberation of Palestine], *Al-I'tisam,* December 1988, no. 8, p. 11.

20. Adham al-Qassam, "Al-Intifada al-Mutamayyiza" [The Distinct Intifada] *Filastin al-Muslima,* March 1989, no. 6, p. 37.

21. Ibid., p. 39.

22. Ibid.

23. Radi, p. 15.

24. Al-Qassam, p. 37.

25. A personal interview with Dr. Ibrahim al-Yazuri, the executive director of the Islamic Center in Gaza and a founder of Hamas, Gaza, July 9, 1991. All of these founders, except for Yasin and al-Yazuri, were among the Hamas leaders and activists who were deported by Israel to southern Lebanon in December 1992 in the aftermath of the kidnapping and killing of Israeli border policeman Nessim Toledano by Hamas elements.

26. Ibid.

27. Ze'ev Schiff and Ehud Ya'ari, *Intifada: The Palestinian Uprising— Israel's Third Front* (New York: Simon and Schuster, 1989), p. 227.

28. Ibid.

29. Ibid., p. 222.

30. Ibid.

31. *Mithaq Harakat al-Muqawama al-'Islamiyya (Hamas) [Charter of the Islamic Resistance Movement (Hamas)],* August 18, 1988, p. 5.

32. *Ila Filastin,* no. 30, March 1988.

33. Yasin, May 2, 1989.

34. Al-Qiyada al-Wataniyya al-Muwahhada lil-Intifada [The United National Leadership of the *Intifada*], Leaflet no. 25, September 6, 1988.

35. Ibid.

36. A personal interview with an Islamic source from the Muslim Brotherhood.

37. Yasin, May 2, 1989.

38. Harakat al-Muqawama al-'Islamiyya (Hamas), "Nida' ila al-Dawra al-Tasi'a 'Ashra lil-Majlis al-Watani" [Appeal to the Nineteenth Session of the Palestine National Council], November 10, 1988.

39. Al-Qiyada al-Wataniyya al-Muwahhada, Leaflet no. 28, October 30, 1988.

40. Harakat al-Muqawama al-'Islamiyya (Hamas), [Appeal to the Nineteenth PNC].

41. Al-Qiyada al-Wataniyya al-Muwahhada, Leaflet no. 29, November 20, 1988.

42. Personal interviews with Dr. Muhammad Saqr, president of the Islamic University in Gaza, Amman, May 29, 1989, and with Yusuf al-'Azm.

43. Interview with Sheikh Ahmad Yasin, *Al-'Islam wa Filastin,* December 30, 1988, no. 10, p. 10.

44. *Liwa' al-'Islam,* December 11, 1988, no. 9, p. 17.

45. Harakat al-Muqawama al-'Islamiyya (Hamas), Leaflet no. 36, February 25, 1989.

46. Ibid.; Harakat al-Muqawama al-'Islamiyya (Hamas), Leaflet no. 40, April 17, 1989.

47. Harakat al-Muqawama al-'Islamiyya (Hamas), Leaflet no. 39, April 5, 1989.

48. Harakat al-Muqawama al-'Islamiyya (Hamas), Leaflet no. 34, January 12, 1989.

49. Ziad Abu-Amr, *Emerging Trends in Palestinian Strategic Political Thinking and Practice* (Jerusalem: Palestinian Academic Society for the Study of International Affairs, 1992), pp. 24–26.

50. Yasin, May 2, 1989.

51. Saqr.

52. *Al-Sirat,* June 1988, no. 1, p. 23.

53. *Al-Sha'b,* September 11, 1987.

54. An interview with Sheikh Ahmad Yasin, *Al-Nahar,* April 30, 1989.

55. Yasin, May 2, 1989.

56. Ibid.

57. *Al-Sirat,* June 1988, no. 1, p. 25.

58. The writer was unable to confirm the authenticity of this claim.

59. Harakat al-Muqawama al-'Islamiyya (Hamas), *Bayan bi-Munasabat Dhikra al-Isra' wal-Mi'raj* [Statement on the Anniversary of the Prophet Muhammad's Ascension to Heaven], March 13, 1988.

60. Harakat al-Muqawama al-'Islamiyya (Hamas), statement issued in January 1988.

61. Harakat al-Muqawama al-'Islamiyya (Hamas), statement issued on March 4, 1988.

62. Sheikh Yasin, May 2, 1989.

63. The reply sheet of Ahmad Yasin to the charges of the Israeli Military Court in Gaza, Case no. 115 25/89.

64. Ibid.

65. *Al-Da'wa,* (November/December 1985), p. 14.

66. Ziad Abu-Ghanima, "Filastin al-'Islamiyya hiya Filastin al-Muharrara" [Islamic Palestine Is Liberated Palestine], *Liwa' al-'Islam,* January 19, 1989, no. 10, p. 25.

67. *Mithaq Harakat al-Muqawama al-'Islamiyya (Hamas), [Charter of the Islamic Resistance Movement (Hamas)],* August 18, 1988, p. 5.

68. Ibid., p. 7.
69. Ibid., p. 8.
70. Ibid., p. 9.
71. Ibid., p. 11.
72. Ibid., pp. 14–15.
73. Ibid., p. 15.
74. Ibid., p. 26.
75. Ibid., p. 28.
76. Ibid., p. 29.
77. Ibid., pp. 29–30.
78. Ibid., p. 31.
79. An Islamic source, who asked that his name not be used, West Bank, August 10, 1989.
80. *Al-Quds,* May 11, 1992.
81. Abu-Amr, *Emerging Trends,* pp. 24–25.
82. This information is included in the minutes of a PLO Central Council meeting in 1990.
83. These sources, whom the author met in Amman, Jordan in February 1993, asked that their names not be identified.

4. The Islamic Jihad

1. A personal interview with Sheikh 'Abd-al-'Aziz 'Auda, the spiritual leader of the Islamic Jihad movement in the Occupied Territories, Gaza, April 24, 1987.

2. "Al-Qadiyya al-Filistiniyya min Mandhur 'Islami" [The Palestinian Issue from an Islamic Perspective], a booklet published in the Occupied Territories, originally printed in *al-Mukhtar al-'Islami,* July 1980, no. 13, pp. 28–41.

3. 'Auda.

4. The Atonement and Holy Flight Organization, led by Shukri Mustafa, is the group that in July 1977 kidnapped and murdered the former Egyptian minister of Waqf (religious endowment), Sheikh Muhammad al-Dhahabi, while the Jihad Organization was the group that assassinated Egyptian president Anwar al-Sadat in October 1981. As for Salih Sirriyya, he was a Palestinian by birth who in 1974 led a group of his colleagues in an operation to take over the Military Technical Academy and attempted to overthrow the government in Egypt. This attempt, in which eleven people were killed and twenty-seven wounded, ended in failure. To learn more about these groups, see 'Adil Hammuda, *Qanabil wa-Masahif: Qissat Tandhim al-Jihad [Bombs and Korans: The Story of the Jihad Organization]* (Cairo: Sina' lil-Nashr, 1986), p. 35, and Hasan Hanafi, *Al-Harakat al-Diniyya al-Mu'asira [Contemporary Religious Movements]* (Cairo: Maktabat Madbuli, 1988), p. 334, as well as Sa'd Eddin Ibrahim, "Islamic Militancy as a Social Movement: The Case of Two Groups in Egypt," in Ali E. Hillal Dessouki (ed.), *Islamic Resurgence in the Arab World* (New York: Praeger, 1982), p. 118.

5. Elie Rekhess, "The Rise of the Palestinian Islamic Jihad," *The Jerusalem Post,* October 21, 1987.

6. "Sheikh As'ad al-Tamimi Imam al-Masjid al-Aqsa" [Sheikh As'ad al-Tamimi, Imam of al-Aqsa Mosque], *Al-Mukhtar al-'Islami,* June/July 1987, no. 53, p. 41.

7. Hala Mustafa, "Al-Jihad al-'Islami fil-Ard al-Muhtalla" [The Islamic Jihad in the Occupied Territories], *Qadaya Fikriyya,* April 1988, no. 6, p. 179.

8. Elaine Ruth Fletcher, "The New Moslems," *The Jerusalem Post Magazine,* October 19, 1987. p. 5.

9. 'Auda.

10. "Al-Qadiyya al-Filastiniyya min Mandhur 'Islami," p. 14.

11. Elie Rekhess, "The Iranian Impact on the Islamic Jihad Movement in the Gaza Strip," a paper submitted to a conference entitled "The Iranian Revolution and the Muslim World," held in the Dayan Center, Tel Aviv University, January 4–6, 1988, p. 16.

12. Mikhal Sila', "The Story of Religious Groups in the Gaza Strip," *Kutirut Rashit,* translated article, *Al-Quds,* October 22, 1987.

13. Personal conversation by the author with Muslim Brotherhood Society supporters, the West Bank, May 1989.

14. Ahmad al-Qasim, "Al-Jihad al-'Islami 'ala Abwab al-Quds" [The Islamic Jihad at the Gates of Jerusalem], *Al-Mukhtar al-'Islami,* March/April 1987, no. 51, p. 30. Certain Fatah sources say that of those people who executed the operation, two were members of the Fatah movement, while the rest were from the Islamic Jihad movement. This operation came against a background of early coordination between Fatah and the Islamic Jihad.

15. Radio Israel in Arabic, August 17, 1988.

16. Muhammad Ahmad Khalafalla, "Al-Sahwa al-'Islamiyya fi Misr" [The Islamic Awakening in Egypt], in Isma'il Sabri 'Abdallah et al., *Al-Harakat al-'Islamiyya al-Mu'asira fil-Watan al-'Arabi [Contemporary Islamic Movements in the Arab Homeland]* (Beirut: Markaz Dirasat al-Wahda al-'Arabiyya, 1987), p. 41.

17. Sayyid Qutb, *Ma'alim 'ala al-Tariq [Signs along the Way]* (Beirut: Dar al-Mashriq, 1986), p. 21.

18. Ibid.

19. Ibid.

20. Hasan Hanafi, *Al-'Usuliyya al-'Islamiyya* [Islamic Fundamentalism] (Cairo: Maktabat Madbuli, 1989), p. 50.

21. Muhammad Ahmad Khalafallah, "Al-Sahwa al-'Islamiyya fi Misr," pp. 59–60.

22. Samih Hammuda, *Al-Wa'i wal-Thawra [Consciousness and Revolution]* (Jerusalem: Jam'iyat al-Dirasat al-'Arabiyya, 1986), p. 13.

23. Nels Johnson, *Islam and the Politics of Meaning in Palestinian Nationalism* (London: Kegan Paul, 1982), p. 40.

24. "Al-Qadiyya al-Filastiniyya min Mandhur 'Islami," p. 18.

25. Johnson, p. 41.

26. Ibid., p. 25.

27. Bayan Nuwaihid al-Hout, *Al-Sheikh al-Mujahid 'Izz-al-Din al-Qassam fi Tarikh Filastin [Sheikh 'Izz-al-Din al-Qassam in the History of Palestine]* (Beirut: Dar al-Istiqlal lil-Dirasat wal-Nashr, 1987), p. 12.

28. Johnson, p. 38.

29. "Al-Qadiyya al-Filastiniyya min Mandhur 'Islami," p. 23.

30. Ibid.

31. Fathi 'Abd-al-'Aziz (al Shaqaqi), *Al-Khomeini: al-Hall al-'Islami wal-Badil [Khomeini: The Islamic Solution and the Alternative]* (Cairo: al-Mukhtar al-'Islami, 1979), p. 33.

32. Rekhess, "The Iranian Impact," p. 7.

33. 'Abd-al-'Aziz, p. 37.

34. Hanafi, *Al-'Usuliyya al-'Islamiyya,* p. 123.

35. Ibid., p. 110.

36. 'Adil Hammuda, p. 36.

37. "Qira'a fi Fiqh al-Shihada" [A Reading in the Islamic Law of Martyrdom] (appendix 1), *Al-'Islam wa-Filastin,* June 5, 1988, p. 5.

38. Rekhess, "The Iranian Impact," p. 10.

39. 'Abd-al-'Aziz, p. 47.

40. Mahmud Muru, "Al-'Ilmaniyya: al-Mushkila wal-Hall" [Secularism: The Problem and the Solution], *Al-Mukhtar al-'Islami,* February 1985, no. 33, p. 27.

41. "Al-Qadiyya al-Filastiniyya min Mandhur 'Islami," p. 15.

42. Rekhess, "The Iranian Impact," p. 10.

43. "Qira'a fi Fiqh al-Shihada," p. 14.

44. 'Auda.

45. Ibid.

46. Avinu 'Am Bar Yosef, "Al-Jama'at al'Islamiyya fi Ghazza fil-Kharita al-Siyasiyya" [Islamic Groups in Gaza in the Political Map], *Ma'ariv,* translated article, *Al-Quds,* August 8, 1987.

47. *Financial Times,* November 9, 1987.

48. Elie Rekhess, "The Iranian Impact," p. 11.

49. "Al Qadiyya al-Filastiniyya min Mandhur 'Islami, p. 15.

50. Ibid., p. 6.

51. Ibid., p. 15.

52. Mu'min 'Abd-al-Rahman, *Al-Masira al-'Islamiyya bain al-Madd wal-Jazr [The Rise and Decline of the Islamic March]* (publisher and date of publication not given), pp. 81–82.

53. 'Abd-al-'Aziz, p. 28.

54. Tawfiq al-Tayyib, *Al-Hall al-'Islami ma ba'd al-Nakbatain [The Islamic Solution after Two Disasters]* (Cairo: al-Mukhtar al-'Islami, 1979), p. 10.

55. Ibid., p. 13.

56. Ibid., pp. 36–37.

57. Mustafa, p. 179.

58. *Al-Quds,* November 13, 1987.

59. 'Auda.

60. Radio Monte Carlo, August 4, 1989.

61. Radio Monte Carlo, August 15, 1989.

62. Sila', "Religious Groups in the Gaza Strip."

63. Rekhess, "The Iranian Impact," p. 12.

64. *Al-Ma'sa al-Filastiniyya: Fatah min al-Intilaqa ila al-Biqa' [The Palestinian Tragedy: Fatah from Its Launch to the Biqa']* (author, publisher, date and place of publication not given), p. 7.

65. "Al-Ma'sa al-Filastiniyya 'Akhir al-Lail" [The Palestinian Tragedy at the End of the Night], *Al-Tali'a al-'Islamiyya,* August 1983, no. 8, p. 24.

66. Ibid., p. 25.

67. *Al-Ma'sa al-Filastiniyya: Fatah min al-Intilaqa ila al-Biqa',* p. 5.

68. Ibid., p. 33.

69. "Al-Ma'sa al-Filastinayya 'Akhir al-Lail," p. 37.

70. *Al-Fajr,* August 28, 1987.

71. Al-Qasim, pp. 31–32.

72. A personal interview with a Fatah movement source in Jordan, who asked that his name not be used, Amman, June 28, 1989.

73. *Al-Sabil,* January 27, 1989.

74. *Al-Quds,* August 26, 1987.

75. "Al-Ma'sa al-Filastiniyya 'Akhir al-Lail," p. 41.

76. Ibid.

77. Ibid., p. 41.

78. *Al-Jihad fi Filastin: Farida Shar'iyya wa-Darura Bashariyya [The Jihad in Palestine: A Religious Obligation and Human Necessity]* (author, publisher, date and place of publication not given), p. 33.

79. Ibid., pp. 33–35.

80. Salama Amin, "Al-Ittijahat al-Diniyya wa-Dawruha fil-'Amal al-Watani al-Filastini" [Religious Trends and Their Role in Palestinian National Action], *Tariq al-Intisar,* May 1, 1988, no. 199, p. 27.

81. 'Auda.

82. Fahmi Huwaydi, "Ha'ula al-'Usuliyyun fil-'Aradi al-Muhtalla" [These Fundamentalists in the Occupied Territories], *Al-Ahram,* December 8, 1987, p. 5.

83. *Al-Hadaf,* December 21, 1987, no. 892, p. 26.

84. Ibid.

85. Ibid., p. 27.

86. *Tariq al-Intisar,* ibid., p. 28.

87. *Al-'Islam wa-Filastin,* December 30, 1988, no. 10, p. 16.

88. Ibid.

89. Ibid., p. 3.

90. Ibid.

91. Ibid., February 10, 1989, p. 2.

92. Statement issued by the "Islamic Jihad in Palestine," Jerusalem, March 2, 1989.

93. *Al-'Islam wa-Filastin,* December 30, 1989, p. 3.

94. 'Abd-al-Rahman, pp. 100–101.

95. Fathi Yakin, *Mushkilat al-Da'wa wal-Da'iyya [Problems of the Call and the Caller]* (Beirut: Mu'assasat al-Risala, 1981), p. 215.

96. Ibid., p. 154.

97. Ibid., p. 155.

98. Ibid., pp. 11–12.

99. Ibid., p. 216.

100. *Ma'rakat Beirut: Al-Tajriba al-Filastiniyya min Mandhur 'Islami* *[The Battle of Beirut: The Palestinian Experience from an Islamic Perspective]* (author, publisher, place and date of publication not given), p. 4.

101. Ibid., p. 13.

102. Ibid., p. 18.

103. *Al-Fajr,* August 23, 1987.

104. Elie Rekhess, "The Iranian Impact," p. 7.

105. 'Auda.

106. Yakin, pp. 220–21.

107. 'Izz-al-Din al-Faris and Ahmad Sadiq, "Al-Qadiyya al-Filastiniyya hiya al-Qadiyya al-Markaziyya lil-Haraka al-'Islamiyya [The Palestinian Issue Is the Central Issue for the Islamic Movement], *Al-Mukhtar al-'Islami,* July 1980, no. 13, p. 28.

108. Ibid.

109. Ibid., p. 29.

110. *Ma'rakat Beirut: Al-Tajriba al-Filastiniyya min Mandhur 'Islami,* p. 17.

111. "Al-Ma'sa al-Filastiniyya 'Akhir al-Lail," p. 41.

112. *Al-Jihad fi Filastin,* pp. 27–28.

113. 'Auda.

114. *Al-Fajr,* August 28, 1987.

115. Muhammad 'Abd-al-Salam Faraj, *Al-Jihad: Al-Farida al-Gha'iba [Jihad: The Absent Duty]* (Jerusalem-Palestine: Maktabat al-Batal 'Izz-al-Din al-Qassam," 1982), p. 9.

116. "Al-Ma'sa al-Filastiniyya 'Akhir al-Lail," p. 38.

117. "Al-Haraka Al-Tullabiyya al-'Islamiyya fil-Jami'a al-'Islamiyya" [The Islamic Student Movement in the Islamic University], *Al-Tali'a al-'Islamiyya,* August 1983, no. 8, p. 46.

118. A statement issued by the Islamic Student movement entitled "Hawl Ahdath al-Sabt al-Aswad bil-Jami'a al-'Islamiyya" [About the Events of Black Saturday at the Islamic University], June 4, 1983.

119. A statement issued by the Independent Islamists entitled: "Hadha Bayan lil-Nass" [This Is a Statement for the People], n.d.

120. *Al-Nadhir,* n.d., p. 35.

121. 'Auda.

122. Islam Mahmud, "Al-Shi'a wal-Sunna: Dajja Mufta'ala wa-Mu'sifa" [Shi'ism and the Sunna: A Fabricated and Unfortunate Outcry], *Al-Mukhtar al-'Islami,* n.d., pp. 48–55.

123. A personal interview with Sheikh Ahmad Yasin, Muslim Brotherhood leader and founder of the Islamic Center in the Gaza Strip, Gaza, April 27, 1987.

124. *Al-Fajr,* August 23, 1987, p. 9.

125. Ibid.

126. "Al-Qadiyya al-Filastiniyya min Mandhur 'Islami," p. 17.

127. 'Auda.

128. A personal interview with a member of the Islamic Jihad movement in the West Bank, who asked that his name not be used, Jerusalem, October 1987.

129. A personal interview with Sheikh Bassam Jarrar, a prominent Islamic leader in the West Bank, al-Bireh, May 11, 1989.

130. A personal interview with Ibrahim Ghusha, the official spokesman of Hamas, and with an Islamic Jihad leader who asked for anonymity, Amman, January 1992.

Conclusion

1. A personal interview with Dr. Mahmud al-Zahhar, an Islamic leader in the Gaza Strip, December 4, 1991.

2. A personal interview with Sheikh Bassam Jarrar, an Islamic leader in the West Bank, Ramallah, December 22, 1991.

3. Harakat al-Muqawama al-'Islamiyya (Hamas) [The Islamic Resistance Movement (Hamas)], Leaflet no. 61, August 15, 1990.

4. Harakat al-Muqawama al-'Islamiyya (Hamas) [The Islamic Resistance Movement (Hamas)], Leaflet no. 62, August 22, 1990.

5. Ahmad Bin-Yousef, *Ahmad Yasin: Al-Dhahira al-Mu'jiza wa-'Usturat al-Tahaddi [Ahmad Yasin: The Miraculous Phenomenon and the Myth of Challenge]* (Illinois: The Islamic Center for Research and Studies, n.d.), p. 40.

REFERENCES

Arabic Sources

Books

'Abd-al-'Aziz (al-Shaqaqi), Fathi, *Al-Khomeini: al-Hall al-'Islami wal-Badil [Khomeini: The Islamic Solution and the Alternative]* (Cairo: Al-Mukhtar al-'Islami, 1979).

'Abd-al-Halim, Mahmud, *Al-'Ikhwan al-Muslimun: Ahdath Sana'at al-Tarikh [The Muslim Brotherhood: Events That Made History]* (Alexandria: Dar al-Da'wa, 1985).

'Abd-al-Rahman, Mu'min, *Al-Masira al-'Islamiyya bain al-Madd wal-Jazr [The Rise and Decline of the Islamic March]* (no publisher or date).

'Abdallah, Isma'il Sabri et al., *Al-Harakat al-'Islamiyya al-Mu'asira fil-Watan al-'Arabi [Contemporary Islamic Movements in the Arab Homeland]* (Beirut: Markaz Dirasat al-Wahda al-'Arabiyya, 1987).

Abu-al-Namil, Hussein, *Qita' Ghazza 1948–1967: Tatawwurat Iqtisadiyya wa-Siyasiyya wa-Ijtima'iyya wa-'Askariyya [The Gaza Strip 1948–1967: Economic, Political, Social, and Military Developments]* (Beirut: Markaz al-Abhath, Munadhamat al-Tahrir al-Filastiniyya, 1979).

Abu-Amr, Ziad, *'Usul al-Harakat al-Siyasiyya fi Qita' Ghazza: 1948–1967 [The Origins of Political Movements in the Gaza Strip: 1948–1967]* (Jerusalem: Dar al-Aswar, Acre, 1987).

Abu-Amr, Ziad, *Al-Haraka al-'Islamiyya fil-Daffa al-Gharbiyya wa Qita' Ghazza [The Islamic Movement in the West Bank and the Gaza Strip]* (Jerusalem: Dar al-Aswar, Acre, 1989).

Al-'Arif, 'Arif, *Al-Nakba: Nakbat Beit al-Maqdis wal-Firdaws al-Mafqoud 1947–1955 [The Disaster: The Disaster of Jerusalem and the Lost Paradise: 1947–1955]* (Sidon-Beirut: Al-Maktaba al-'Asriyya, n.d).

Al-Haqiqa al-Gha'iba [The Absent Truth] (no author, publisher, or date).

Al-Hout, Bayan Nuwaihid, *Al-Qiyadat wal-Mu'assasat al-Siyasiyya fi Filistin: 1917–1948 [Political Leaders and Institutions in Palestine: 1917–1948]* (Beirut: Mu'assasat al-Dirasat al-Filastiniyya, 1986).

Al-Hout, Bayan Nuwaihid, *Al-Sheikh al-Mujahid 'Izz-al-Din al-Qassam fi Tarikh Filastin [Sheikh 'Izz-al-Din al-Qassam in the History of Palestine]* (Beirut: Dar al-Istiqlal lil-Dirasat wal-Nashr, 1987), p. 12.

Al-Jihad fi Filastin: Farida Shar'iyya wa-Darura Bashariyya [The Jihad in Palestine: A Religious Obligation and Human Necessity] (no author, publisher, or date).

Al-Mahdawi, Tariq, *Al-'Ikhwan al-Muslimun 'ala madhbah al-Munawara: 1928–1986 [The Muslim Brotherhood on the Altar of Maneuver: 1928–1986]* (Beirut: Dar Azal, 1986).

Al-Ma'sa al-Filastiniyya: Fatah min al-Intilaqa ila al-Biqa' [The Palestinian Tragedy: Fatah from Its Launch to the Biqa'] (no author, publisher, or date).

Al-Tamimi, As'ad Bayoud, *Zawal Isra'il Hatmiyya Qur'aniyya [The Destruction of Israel Is a Koranic Imperative]* (no publisher, 1988).

Al-Tayyib, Tawfiq, *Al-Hall al-'Islami ma ba'd al-Nakbatain [The Islamic Solution after Two Disasters]* (Cairo: Al-Mukhtar al-'Islami, 1979).

Bin Yousef, Ahmad, *Harakat al-Muqawama al-'Islamiyya [The Islamic Resistance Movement]* (Illinois: The Islamic Center for Research and Studies, 1990).

Bin Yousef, Ahmad, *Ahmad Yasin: Al-Dhahira al-Mu'jiza wa-'Usturat al-Tahaddi [Ahmad Yasin: The Miraculous Phenomenon and the Myth of Challenge]* (Illinois: The Islamic Center for Research and Studies, n.d.).

Faraj, Muhammad 'Abd-al-Salam, *Al-Jihad: al-Farida al-Gha'iba [Jihad: The Absent Duty]* (Jerusalem-Palestine: Maktabat al-Batal 'Izz-al-Din al-Qassam, 1982).

Hammuda, 'Adil, *Qanabil wa-Masahif: Qissat Tandhim al-Jihad [Bombs and Korans: The Story of the Jihad Organization]* (Cairo: Sina' lil-Nashr, 1986).

Hammuda, Samih, *Al-Wa'i wal-Thawra [Consciousness and Revolution]* (Jerusalem: Jam'iyat al-Dirasat al-'Arabiyya, 1986).

Hanafi, Hasan, *Al-Harakat al-Diniyya al-Mu'asira [Contemporary Religious Movements]* (Cairo: Maktabat Madbuli, 1988).

Hanafi, Hasan, *Al-'Usuliyya al-'Islamiyya [Islamic Fundamentalism]* (Cairo: Maktabat Madbuli, 1989).

Harakat al-Shabiba al-Tullabiyya, *Al-'Ikhwan al-Muslimun: ma Ashbah al-Yawm bil-Bariha [The Muslim Brotherhood: How Similar Are Today and Yesterday]* (July, 1985).

Isma'il (al-Sharif), Kamil, *Al-'Ikhwan al-Muslimun fi Harb Filastin [The Muslim Brotherhood in the War of Palestine]* (Cairo: Dar al-Kitab al-'Arabi, 1951).

Ma'rakat Beirut: Al-Tajriba al-Filastiniyya min Mandhur 'Islami [The Battle of Beirut: The Palestinian Experience from an Islamic Perspective] (no author, publisher, or date).

Nawfal, Ahmad, *Al-Tariq ila Filastin [The Road to Palestine]* (no publisher or date).

Qa'ud, Ibrahim, *'Umar al-Tilmisani Shahidan 'ala al-'Asr: Al-'Ikhwan al-Muslimun fi Da'irat al-Haqiqa al-Gha'iba [Omar al-Tilmisani, Witness to an Era: The Muslim Brotherhood in the Circle of the Absent Truth]* (Cairo: al-Mukhtar al-'Islami, 1985).

Qutb, Muhammad 'Ali, *Madhabih wa-Jara'im al-Tafteesh fil-Andalus [Massacres and Crimes of the Inquisition in Andalusia]* (Cairo: Maktabat al-Qur'an, 1985).

Qutb, Sayyid, *Ma'alim 'ala al-Tariq [Signs along the Way]* (Beirut: Dar al-Mashriq, 1986), p. 21.

Shubaib, Nabil, *Al-Waqi' al-Qa'im wa-'Iradat al-Taghyeer [The Existing Reality and the Will to Change]* (Bonn: Al-Dar al-'Islamiyya lil-I'lam, 1983).

Yakin, Fathi, *Mushkilat al-Da'wa wal-Da'iyya [Problems of the Call and the Caller]* (Beirut: Mu'assasat al-Risala, 1981).

Articles and Studies

'Abd-al-Maqsud, Salah, "'Ashar Ittihamat Muwajjaha ila al-Jama'a" [Ten Accusations Directed at Society], *Liwa' al-'Islam*, February 7, 1989, no. 11.

Abu-al-Nasr, Muhammad Hamid. "Al-'Ikhwan al-Muslimun wa-I'lan al-Dawla al-Filastiniyya" [The Muslim Brotherhood and the Declaration of the Palestinian State], *Liwa' al-'Islam*, December 11, 1988, no. 9.

Abu-Ghanima, Ziad, "Filastin al-'Islamiyya hiya Filastin al-Muharrara" [Islamic Palestine Is Liberated Palestine], *Liwa' al-'Islam*, January 9, 1989, no. 10.

Abu-Mus'ab, "Filastin fi Fikr al-Imam al-Shahid Hasan al-Banna" [Palestine in the Thought of the Martyred Imam Hasan al-Banna], *Liwa' al-'Islam*, February 7, 1989. no. 11.

Al-Ghazali, Sa'id, "Adwa' 'ala al-Harakat al-'Islamiyya fil-Daffa al-Gharbiyya wal-Qita'" [Lights on the Islamic Movements in the West Bank and the Gaza Strip], *'Abir*, September 1987, no. 14.

"Al-Qadiyya al-Filastiniyya min Mandhur 'Islami" [The Palestinian Question from an Islamic Perspective], *Al-Mukhtar al-'Islami*, July 1980, no. 13.

Al-Qassam, Adham, "Al-Intifada al-Mutamayyiza" [The Distinct Intifada], *Filastin al-Muslima*, March 1989, no. 6.

"Al-Quwa wal-Hai'at al-Wataniyya wal-'Islamiyya al-'Amila Did al-Wujud al-Isra'ili fil-Aradi al-'Arabiyya al-Muhtalla" [Nationalist and Islamic Forces and Institutions Working against the Israeli Presence in the Occupied Arab Territories], *Qadaya Fikriyya*, April 1988, no. 6.

Amin, Salama, "Al-Ittijahat al-Diniyya wa-Dawruha fil-'Amal al-Watani al-Filastini" [The Religious Trends and Their Role in the Palestinian National Action], *Tariq al-Intisar*, May 1, 1988, no. 199.

Bar Yosef, Avinu 'Am, "Al-Jama'at al'Islamiyya fi Ghazza fil-Kharita al-Siyasiyya" [Islamic Groups in Gaza in the Political Map], *Ma'ariv*, translated article, *Al-Quds*, August 8, 1987.

Huwaydi, Fahmi, "Ha'ula' al-'Usuliyyun fil-'Aradi al-Muhtalla" [These Fundamentalists in the Occupied Territories], *Al-Ahram*, Cairo, December 8, 1987.

Huwaydi, Fahmi, "Husn al-Qira'a Qabl al-Kitaba wal-Ittiham" [Good Reading Is Required before Writing and Accusing], *Liwa' al-'Islam,* February 7, 1989, no. 11.

Muhammad, Zakariyya, "Al-Intifada wal-Islah al-Tandhimi fi Munadhamat al-Tahrir al-Filastiniyya" [The *Intifada* and Organizational Reform in the PLO], *Al-Fikr al-Dimuqrati,* Winter 1989, no. 5.

Mahmud, Islam, "Al-Shi'a wal-Sunna: Dajja Mufta'ala wa-Mu'sifa [Shi'ism and Sunna: A Fabricated and Unfortunate Outcry," *Al-Mukhtar al-'Islami,* n.d.

"Munadhamat al-Tahrir al-Filastiniyya: min Mihna ila Mihna" [The PLO: From one Ordeal to Another], *Al-Muntalaq,* November 1968, no. 16.

Mustafa, Hala, "Al-Jihad, al-'Islami fil-Ard al-Muhtalla" [The Islamic Jihad in the Occupied Territories], *Qadaya Fikriyya,* April 1988, no. 6.

Mustafa, Hala, "Al-Tayyar al-'Islami fil-Ard al-Muhtalla" [The Islamic Trend in the Occupied Territories], *Al-Mustaqbal al-'Arabi,* July 1988, no. 113.

"Nash'at wa-Tatawwur al-Ahzab wal-Quwa al-Siyasiyya fil-'Urdun: al-Quwa al-Salafiyya" [Emergence and Development of Political Parties and Forces in Jordan: The Salafi Forces], *Al-Nashra,* April 4, 1987, no. 92.

Qa'ud, Hilmi Muhammad, "Al-Tariq al-Sahih li-Tahrir Filastin" [The Correct Path to the Liberation of Palestine], *Al-I'tisam,* December 1988, no. 8.

Periodicals

Al-Da'wa
Al-Fikr al-Dimuqrati
Al-Hadaf
Al-'Islam wa-Filastin
Al-I'tisam
Al-Mukhtar al-'Islami
Al-Muntalaq
Al-Mustaqbal al-'Arabi
Al-Nadhir
Al-Nashra
Al-Sabil
Al-Sahwa
Al-Shihab
Al-Sirat
Al-Tali'a al-'Islamiyya
Filastin al-Muslima
Liwa' al-'Islam
Qadaya Fikriyya
Shu'un Filastiniyya
Tariq al-Intisar

Newspapers

Al-Ahram (Cairo)
Al-Fajr (Jerusalem)
Al-Nahar (Jerusalem)
Al-Quds (Jerusalem)
Al-Ra'i (Jordan)
Al-Sha'b (Jerusalem)

Bulletins and Leaflets

A statement issued by the Islamic Bloc at Birzeit University, January 21, 1983.

A statement issued by the Islamic Student Movement entitled "Hawla Ahdath al-Sabt al-Aswad bil-Jami'a al-'Islamiyya" [About the Events of Black Saturday at the Islamic University], June 4, 1983.

A statement issued by the Islamic Bloc at Birzeit University entitled "Bayan Hawla al-I'tida' al-'Athim 'ala al-Shabab al-'Islami fi Jami'at Birzeit" [a Statement concerning the Criminal Attack on the Islamic Youth at Birzeit University], June 6, 1983.

Leaflet no. 3 issued by the Central Leadership of the United Palestinian National Front, Gaza, June 8, 1983.

A statement issued by the National Movement in the Occupied Territory, June 1983.

"Limadha la Ya'tarif al-'Ikhwan al-Muslimun bi-Munadhamat al-Tahrir al-Filastiniyya?" [Why Does the Muslim Brotherhood Not Recognize the PLO?], a statement issued by the Progressive Student Action Front—Birzeit University Branch, September 1987.

A statement issued by the Islamic Bloc at Birzeit University entitled "Difa'an 'an al-Kutla al-'Islamiyya" [In Defense of the Islamic Bloc], 1987.

Harakat al-Muqawama al-'Islamiyya (Hamas) [The Islamic Resistance Movement (Hamas)], a leaflet issued in January 1988.

A leaflet issued by the Islamic Jihad movement in Occupied Palestine, Jerusalem, February 3, 1988.

Harakat al-Muqawama al-'Islamiyya (Hamas) [The Islamic Resistance Movement (Hamas)], a leaflet issued on March 4, 1988.

Harakat al-Muqawama al-'Islamiyya (Hamas) [The Islamic Resistance Movement (Hamas)], a leaflet issued on March 13, 1988.

Harakat al-Muqawama al-'Islamiyya (Hamas), *Bayan bi-Munasabat Dhikra al-Isra' wal-Mi'raj* [Statement on the Anniversary of the Prophet Muhammad's Ascension to Heaven], March 13, 1988.

Harakat al-Muqawama al-'Islamiyya (Hamas) [The Islamic Resistance Movement (Hamas)], an irregular Islamic bulletin, March 1988.

Mithaq Harakat al-Muqawama al-'Islamiyya (Hamas) [Charter of the Islamic Resistance Movement (Hamas)], August 18, 1988.

Al-Qiyada al-Wataniyya al-Muwahhada lil-Intifada [The Unified National Leadership of the *Intifada*], Leaflet no. 25, September 6, 1988.

Al-Qiyada al-Wataniyya al-Muwahhad lil-Intifada [The Unified National Leadership of the *Intifada*], Leaflet no. 28, October 30, 1988.

Harakat al-Muqawama al-'Islamiyya (Hamas) [The Islamic Resistance Movement (Hamas)], "Nida' ila al-Dawra al-Tasi'a 'Ashra lil-Majlis al-Watani" [Appeal to the Nineteenth Session of the Palestine National Council], November 10, 1988.

Al-Qiyada al-Wataniyya al-Muwahhad lil-Intifada [The Unified National Leadership of the *Intifada*], Leaflet no. 29, November 20, 1988.

Harakat al-Muqawama al-'Islamiyya (Hamas) [The Islamic Resistance Movement (Hamas)], Leaflet no. 34, January 12, 1989.

Harakat al-Muqawama al-'Islamiyya (Hamas) [The Islamic Resistance Movement (Hamas)], Leaflet no. 26, February 25, 1989.

A leaflet issued by the Islamic Jihad in Palestine, Jerusalem, March 2, 1989.

Harakat al-Muqawama al-'Islamiyya (Hamas) [The Islamic Resistance Movement (Hamas)], Leaflet no. 40, April 17, 1989.

Harakat al-Muqawama al-'Islamiyya (Hamas) [The Islamic Resistance Movement (Hamas)], Leaflet no. 39, May 25, 1989.

Harakat al-Muqawama al-'Islamiyya (Hamas) [The Islamic Resistance Movement (Hamas)], Leaflet no. 61, August 15, 1990.

Harakat al-Muqawama al-'Islamiyya (Hamas) [The Islamic Resistance Movement (Hamas)], Leaflet no. 62, August 22, 1990.

A statement issued by the student council in the Islamic University entitled "Al-Tahaluf al-Shuyu'i al-Shi'i ila 'ayn?" [The Communist Shi'ite Alliance: Where To?] (n.d.).

A statement issued by the Independent Islamists entitled "Hadha Bayan lil-Nass" [This Is a Statement for the People] (n.d.).

A statement entitled "Hawla Muhawalat al-'Ightiyal al-Fashila lil-Ustadh l-Da'iyya 'Abd-al-'Aziz 'Auda" [About the Abortive Assassination Attempt of the Teacher and Islamic Advocate 'Abd-al-'Aziz 'Auda] (n.d.).

A statement issued by the Islamic Center entitled "Suqut al-Aqni'a al-Shuyu'iyya" [The Collapse of the Communist Masks], Gaza (n.d.).

A statement issued by the Islamic Center, Gaza (n.d.).

Personal Interviews

A former Muslim Brotherhood leader in the Gaza Strip who asked that his name not be identified, Gaza, October 1986.

Sheikh 'Abd-al-'Aziz 'Auda, the spiritual leader of the Islamic Jihad movement in the Occupied Territories, Gaza, April 24, 1987, and May 2, 1989.

Sheikh Ahmad Yasin, the spiritual leader of the Muslim Brotherhood Society in the Gaza Strip and the founder of the Islamic Center and the Islamic Resistance Movement (Hamas), Gaza, April 27, 1987, and May 2, 1989.

An Islamic Jihad supporter in the West Bank who asked that his name not be mentioned, Jerusalem, October 1987.

A number of the supporters of the Muslim Brotherhood Society and the Islamic Jihad movement in the West Bank and the Gaza Strip, who asked that their names not be mentioned, the West Bank and Gaza, December 1987–August 1989.

Sheikh Bassam Jarrar, a prominent Islamic figure in the West Bank, al-Bireh, May 11, 1989, and December 22, 1991.

Muhammad Saqr, the president of the Islamic University in Gaza, Amman, May 29, 1989.

Yusuf al-'Azm, Muslim Brotherhood leader and member of parliament in Jordan, Amman, May 30, 1989.

Marwan al-Barghuthi, the deported president of the student council at Birzeit University, Amman, June 28, 1989.

Ibrahim Ghusha, the official spokesman of the Islamic Resistance Movement (Hamas), Amman, January 1992.

An Islamic Jihad leader who asked that his name not be identified, Amman, January 1992.

Other Sources

Books

Abu-Amr, Ziad, *Emerging Trends in Palestinian Strategic Political Thinking and Practice* (Jerusalem: Palestinian Academic Society for the Study of International Affairs, 1992).

Benvenisti, Meron, *The West Bank Data Base Project: 1987 Report* (Jerusalem: Jerusalem Post, 1987).

Burns, E. L. M., *Between Arab and Israeli* (London: George G. Harrap, 1962).

Cohen, Amnon, *Political Parties in the West Bank under the Jordanian Regime, 1949–1967* (Ithaca: Cornell University Press, 1982).

Dessouki, Ali E. (ed.), *Islamic Resurgence in the Arab World* (New York: Praeger, 1982).

Esposito, John L. (ed.), *Islam and Development: Religion and Socio-Political Change* (New York: Syracuse University Press, 1980).

Johnson, Nels, *Islam and the Politics of Meaning in Palestinian Nationalism* (London: Kegan Paul, 1982).

Legum, Colin, ed., *Middle East Contemporary Survey* (New York: Holmes and Meier, 1984), vol. 6.

Mitchell, Richard P., *The Society of the Muslim Brothers* (London: Oxford University Press, 1969).

Sahliyeh, Emile, *In Search of Leadership: West Bank Politics since 1967* (Washington, D.C.: Brookings Institution, 1988).

Schiff, Ze'ev, and Ehud Ya'ari, *Intifada, The Palestinian Uprising—Israel's Third Front* (New York: Simon and Schuster, 1989).

Shipler, David, *Arab and Jew: Wounded Spirits in a Promised Land* (New York: Penguin, 1987).

Articles and Studies

Fletcher, Elaine Ruth, "The New Moslems," *The Jerusalem Post Magazine* (October 19, 1987).

Ibrahim, Sa'd Eddin, "Islamic Militancy as a Social Movement: The Case of Two Groups in Egypt," in Ali E. Hillal Dessouki (ed.), *Islamic Resurgence in the Arab World* (New York: Praeger, 1982), p. 118.

Legrain, Jean François, "Islamistes et lutte nationale Palestinienne dans les territoires occupés par Israel," *Revue Française de Science Politique,* vol. 26, no. 2. (April 1986).

Mayer, Thomas, "The Military Force of Islam: The Society of the Muslim Brethren and the Palestine Question, 1945–1948," in Elie Kedourie and Sylvia G. Haim (eds.), *Zionism and Arabism in Palestine and Israel* (London: Frank Cass, 1982).

Rekhess, Elie, "The Iranian Impact on the Islamic Jihad Movement in the Gaza Strip," a paper submitted to a conference entitled "The Iranian Revolution and the Muslim World," held in the Dayan Center, Tel-Aviv University (January 4–6, 1988).

"The Rise of the Palestinian Islamic Jihad," *The Jerusalem Post* (October 21, 1987).

Shadid, Mohammed K., "The Muslim Brotherhood Movement in the West Bank and Gaza, *Third World Quarterly* (April 1988), vol. 10, no. 2.

Newspapers

Al-Fajr, English (Jerusalem)
The Jerusalem Post (Jerusalem)

INDEX

al-Abasiri, Sheikh Muhammad, 7
'Abbas, Hussein, 143n.57
'Abd-al-'Al, 'Abd-al-Hai, 16
'Abd-al-'Al, 'Abd-al-Hamid, 143n.57
'Abd-al-'Al, Mustafa, 16
'Abd-al-'Al, 'Umar, 16
'Abd-al-'Aziz, Ahmad, 2
'Abd-al-Nasir, Jamal, 4, 5, 7–8,
    139n.24
'Abdu, Mahmud, 2
'Abdu, Sheikh Muhammad, 98
Abu-al-'Awf, Isma'il, 16
Abu-'Azza, Dr. 'Abdalla, 145n.85
Abu-Ghanima, Ziad, 40–41, 80
Abu-Jihad, 111
Abu-al-Kas, Ahmad, 16
Abu-Kuwayk, Ya'qub, 16
Abu-Marzuq, Dr. Musa, 65
Abu-Mu'ammar, Fayez, 95
Abu-al-Nasr, Muhammad Hamid, 30
Abu-Qura, 'Abd-al-Latif, 2
Abu-Ruqayyiq, Salih, 143n.57
Abu-Seidu, Muhammad, 7
Abu-Seidu, 'Uthman, 7
Abu-Sha'ban, Zuhdi, 8
Abu-Silmiyya, Jawad, 37, 143n.53
Abu-Tayr, Muhammad, 91–92
al-Agha, Dr. Riad, 42, 48
al-Agha, Dr. Salim Amin, 145n.85
al-'Alami, Emad, 65
al-'Alami, Sheikh Sa'd-al-Din, 49
*Al-Farida al-Gha'iba [The Absent
    Duty]* (Faraj), 101
'Ali (cousin of prophet Muhammad),
    125
'Amira, 'Ayish, 7
Amman Summit Conference (Novem-
    ber 1987), 56
'Ammar, Jabr, 94–95
'Aqabat Jabr refugee camp, 6

Arab-Israeli War of 1967, 11, 90–91,
    105–106
Arab-Israeli War of 1973, 11, 13
Arab Medical Association, 21
Arab Nationalist Movement, 9
Arafat, Yasir: and Muslim Brotherhood
    in Gaza Strip prior to 1967, 8; Mus-
    lim Brotherhood criticism of, 31, 49;
    PLO conflicts with Muslim Brother-
    hood, 39, 72; Fatah movement and
    religious references in speeches of,
    47; appointment of Saqr as president
    of Islamic University, 48; recognition
    of Israel, 73; PLO and financial sup-
    port of Islamic Resistance movement,
    88
al-Asad, Hafiz, 27, 38, 48, 123
al-Astal, Zari', 144n.84
al-Aswad, Fayez, 95
Atonement and Holy Flight movement,
    xiv, 12, 91, 148n.4
al-'Attar, 'Issam, 124
'Auda, Sheikh 'Abd-al-'Aziz: founding
    of Islamic Jihad, 93, 94; Islamic Ji-
    had control of mosques in Gaza
    Strip, 96; Islamic Jihad policy on
    Palestine, 105; on Fatah movement,
    110; Islamic Jihad interpretation of
    Islam, 119–20; on Islamic Jihad rela-
    tionship with Iran, 124–25
'Auda, Suleiman, 95
al-Azhar, 124
al-'Azm, Yusuf, 5, 34, 41, 60
'Azzam, Nayef, 95

Bahais, Muhammad, 111
Balfour Declaration, 25, 55
al-Banna, 'Abd-al-Rahman, 1
al-Banna, Hasan: as leader of Islamic
    thought, xv; and founding of Muslim

Ziad Abu-Amr
is
Associate
Professor
of
Political
Science
at Birzeit
University
in the
West Bank.

Middle East Studies

Political Science

As the Palestinian Liberation Organization engages in negotiations with Israel toward an interim period of limited Palestinian self-rule, this timely book provides an insider's view of how the growing hold of Islamic fundamentalism in the West Bank and Gaza challenges the peace process. Working from interviews with leaders of the movement and from primary documents, Ziad Abu-Amr traces the origin and evolution of the fundamentalist organizations Muslim Brotherhood (Hamas) and Islamic Jihad and analyzes their ideologies, their political programs, their sources of support, and their impact on Palestinian society. With a solid grasp of the dynamics of these movements, Abu-Amr charts the struggle between the fundamentalists and the PLO to define the identity of Palestinian society, its direction, and its leadership.

ZIAD ABU-AMR is Associate Professor of Political Science at Birzeit University and has published several books in Arabic on Palestinian politics and society.

Indiana Series in Arab and Islamic Studies
  —*Salih J. Altoma, Iliya Harik, and Mark Tessler, general editors*

Indiana University Press

BLOOMINGTON AND INDIANAPOLIS

ISBN 0-253-20866-1

90000

9 780253 208668